RANDOM HOUSE PUZZLEMAKER'S HANDBOOK

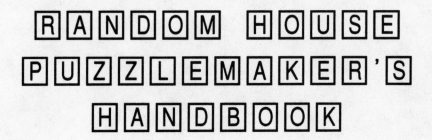

RANDOM HOUSE PUZZLEMAKER'S HANDBOOK

Mel Rosen & Stan Kurzban

An earlier edition of this work was originally published in 1981 by Van Nostrand Reinhold Company.

Grateful acknowledgment is made to the following for permission to reprint previously published material:

The New York Times: "Diagramless, 22x23" by Stanley A. Kurzban (9/20/81) and "Solution to Diagramless, 22x23" (9/20/81). Copyright © 1981 by The New York Times Company. Reprinted by permission.

Saturday Review Publication, Ltd.: "Double-Crostic #1" from the March 1934 issue of Saturday Review. Copyright © 1934 by Saturday Review. Reprinted by permission of Saturday Review Publication, Ltd.

ISBN 0-8129-2544-0

Manufactured in the United States of America

9 8 7 6 5 4 3 2
First Times Books Edition

To my mother, Ruth, who introduced me to words, and my wife, Peggy, who encouraged me to play with them

—Mel Rosen

To my father, Alexander M. Kurzban, who introduced me to word puzzles

—Stan Kurzban

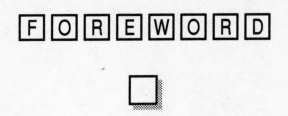

FOREWORD

Almost thirty years ago I sold my first puzzle to a national magazine for a whopping $5, and I'll never forget the thrill of receiving that first check!

These days the crossword field is a bit more remunerative—a good Sunday puzzle, for example, can fetch up to $350. So while crossword constructing is by no means a get-rich-quick scheme, someone who's prolific and skilled can make a fair amount of money from it.

There are many other reasons, of course, to make crosswords: the joy of seeing your name in print, the fun of playing with words, the pleasure of entertaining your friends and family, the opportunity to expand your vocabulary and knowledge, and the practical benefit of sharpening your mental skills. Psychologists say that crossword solving is one of the best mental exercises in the world, and from my experience constructing crosswords is even better.

This book, by two old hands in the puzzle business, will tell you everything you need to know about crossword making, from how to get started (if you're a beginner) to polishing your puzzles for the best-paying markets (if you're an expert). It has been completely revised and updated from its first edition, published fourteen years ago. Much of the information and advice here has never, to my knowledge, appeared in print before.

Have a pencil and some ruled paper handy as you read, and may you, too, experience the joys of gridlock!

Will Shortz
Crossword Editor,
The New York Times

ACKNOWLEDGMENTS

Regarding *The Random House Puzzlemaker's Handbook*:

Marilynn Huret, for helping convert the text of *The Compleat Cruciverbalist* to computer files. Masato Ihara, Robert Malinow, and Henri Picciotto, for providing information about crossword puzzles in foreign languages. Ravin Korothy, for valuable comments. Crossword editors in many venues, for permission to print their guideline sheets.

Regarding *The Compleat Cruciverbalist*:

Will Weng, for inspiration, encouragement, and constructive criticism. Nina Kurzban, Peggy Rosen, and Robert Malstrom, for additional valuable comments.

We also thank *The St. Louis Post-Dispatch* for permission to reprint Arthur Wynne's original "word-cross" puzzle, which was first published December 21, 1913, in the *New York World*.

C O N T E N T S

P R E F A C E

Perhaps more often than people in any other profession, crossword writers find themselves in casual conversation answering the question, "How do you do that?"

Everyone knows that dentists go to school for many years and that professional athletes combine natural ability with physical conditioning and endless practice. We may ask a chef or a sculptor to explain a particular technique in some detail, but we understand the overall nature of the work and the professional's development. For some reason, though, people outside the business have little grasp of the puzzlemaker's craft.

We wrote *The Compleat Cruciverbalist, or How to Solve and Compose Crossword Puzzles for Fun and Profit* to answer the question "How do you do that?" in 1980, when the puzzle world was very different from what it is today.

- Most puzzle editors accepted without question puzzles that contained a lot of *crosswordese*, that curious collection of words ordinary people never encounter except in puzzles. Composers (or *puzzlemakers* or *constructors* in this book) toughened crosswords by adding obscure words, old names, and little-known facts. Definitions stressed primary and secondary dictionary meanings with little humor.

- Puzzlemakers used the same tools as puzzle solvers: paper, pencil, eraser, and some well-thumbed reference books.

- With only a few exceptions, puzzlemakers earned very little for their efforts.

It's all changed.

- Puzzle editors in today's premium markets frown on obscurity, crosswordese, and plain definitions. Instead, they urge constructors to reflect current culture (or, at least, to be timeless), to stick to words most well-rounded people know, and to write lively definitions with humor and nondictionary information.

Sniglets, by Rich Hall & Friends (Collier Books, Macmillan Publishing Company, New York, 1984), defines *zyxnoid* as "Any word that a crossword puzzler makes up to complete the last blank, accompanied by the rationalization that there probably is an ancient god named Ubbbu, or German river named Wfor, and besides, who's going to check?" *Zyxnoid* has appeal, but we'll stick with *crosswordese*.

- New tools make puzzle writing easier and more fun than before. Niche reference books abound. Handheld gizmos that quickly search lexicons of 250,000 words cost less than $50. Anyone with $1,500 to spend can have a desktop computer, with an on-line encyclopedia and dictionary only a keystroke away.
- With only a few exceptions, puzzle markets pay fairly, and sometimes handsomely.

Even for constructors who use the latest of everything, though, the basics of puzzle writing are the same as they've always been: The words have to fit together, and they must provide solvers an entertaining challenge.

So, whether you're seriously seeking an opportunity to earn some money by combining a love of words with the desire to learn a craft, or just casually asking the question "How do you do that?" this updated and expanded version of the book originally titled *The Compleat Cruciverbalist* has the answers.

Mel Rosen and Stan Kurzban
November 1994

PREFACE TO THE COMPLEAT CRUCIVERBALIST

Crossword puzzles and related diversions provide countless hours of entertainment for people all over the world at relatively little cost. Many books contain definitions and lists of words arranged for the convenience of solvers. Curiously, however, few books have any advice on how to solve crossword puzzles, and almost none tell you how to compose them. The main topics of our book are the solving and composing of crosswords.

You don't have to be an Oxford scholar to solve or compose puzzles. Obviously, a large vocabulary and familiarity with languages help—wit is also a tool of the trade. But these are not prerequisites; they are easily and speedily developed with practice.

Our book focuses on the conventional American crossword puzzle as found in magazines and most daily and Sunday newspapers. We also discuss other forms of crossword puzzles, such as the typical British cryptic crossword, with its initially indecipherable definitions; the diagramless puzzle, a very satisfying type for the solver, and not nearly so difficult as it appears at first; and the acrostic puzzle.

We have divided our book into three independent sections. The first part is about the history of crossword puzzles and the people who were prominent in that history. The next part tells you how to solve crossword puzzles, but as a *solver,* you should also read the following part, on composition. An insight into the composer's thoughts can help you solve puzzles.

We hope that the chapters on composition will persuade you to try your own hand at our emotionally most rewarding hobby. Therefore, we have included a chapter devoted to considerations of marketing puzzles.

To spice our *chef d'oeuvre,* we have included an appendix on non-English puzzles. Finally, although we define the words that make up our puzzler's jargon as they are introduced, we have included a glossary.

Titles of puzzles appear in the text capitalized and in quotation marks ("WIRE SER-VICE"). Examples of definitions appear in quotation marks ("Three-toed sloths"). Words or phrases used as examples of answers are capitalized and not in quotation marks (CURRENT EVENTS). Terms found in the glossary are *italicized* when they first appear in the text.

When we are not apuzzling, we work as computer scientists. We are often asked what role the computer will play in composing tomorrow's crosswords. A program[*] has been written which, its author claims, produces German crossword puzzles as good as those that people create, within the constraints of a small (10,000-word) vocabulary and small puzzle size. Projects based on puzzles in English have not been so ambitious. [*By 1994, several computer programs with lexicons exceeding 50,000 words were producing acceptable crosswords. And we're no longer working as computer professionals.—M.R., 1995*] In practice, phrases, abbreviations, foreign words, proper nouns, etc., enlarge a human composer's vocabulary far beyond the largest computer's ability to cope with the resulting possibilities for compositions. When computers can make puzzle composers obsolete, they will already have wrought far more interesting changes to our world.

A final point: the Italian word for crossword puzzle is *cruciverba,* whence the title of our

 1. Volume

Stan Kurzban and Mel Rosen, 1980

BOOK, OPUS, TOME, WORK

---

[*] O. Feger, "Program for Constructing Crossword Puzzles," *(Ein Programm zur Konstruktion von Kreuzworträtseln), Angewandte Informatik 5,* 1975, pages 189–195.

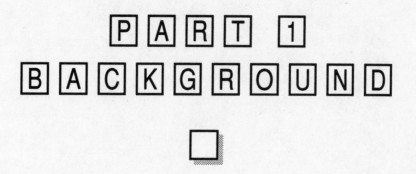

PART 1
BACKGROUND

If we simply wrote down our "rules" for composing contemporary crosswords and related word puzzles, you would probably get by. However, history provides a necessary context for all knowledge. Today's crosswords descend from a long tradition of linguistic diversions pursued by *Homo ludens*, man at play.

Like Newton, we see as far as we do only from our perch on the "shoulders of Giants." The giants of cruciverbalism are the innovators, the women and men who devised and refined the diverse forms we discuss in the later chapters of this book.

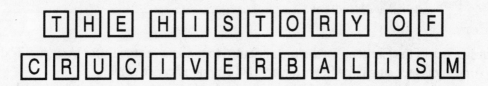

THE HISTORY OF CRUCIVERBALISM

1

In the beginning was the Word.
—John 1:1

EARLY PUZZLE FORMS

Games, puzzles, and geometric arrangements involving letters and words have amused people ever since the beginnings of written language. Ancestral forms of the crossword puzzles we enjoy today existed more than two thousand years ago.

Magic squares and other shapes in which numbers are arranged in special ways—to produce a constant sum when rows or columns are added, for instance—were well known in ancient times. The oldest known word square, a derivative of the magic square using letters instead of numbers, dates from the first century A.D.:

ROTAS
OPERA
TENET
AREPO
SATOR

You can read this square row by row, column by column, forward or backward. The Latin words translate as "Arepo, the sower, watches over his works," which may have meant something like "God watches over the universe."

The Sator Square, as this arrangement is known, was first discovered in England in 1868, in a church built by the Romans about A.D. 300. Theologians debated its religious significance for years. In the 1930s, though, it surfaced among the ruins at Pompeii. As that particular inscription must have predated the eruption of Vesuvius in A.D. 79, all the religious theories lost credibility, because Christianity was not common in that region then, and because much of the Christian symbolism attributed to the square arose after Vesuvius. Today, no one knows for sure if the Sator Square had any significance at all.

Another old arrangement of letters is the "stele of Moschion," an engraving in alabaster created about A.D. 300. This artistic curiosity is a square grid with thirty-nine small squares on each side. Each small square contains a single Greek letter. Beginning at the center of the grid and progressing outward in many ways, an inscription reads "Moschion to Osiris, for the treatment that cured his foot."

In the mid-1800s, one form of entertainment—the arrangement of letters into word squares and other pleasing shapes—merged with another entertainment, the riddle or conundrum. Magazines began publishing "clues" that, if solved, led to word squares. Through most of the Victorian age puzzles involving crossing words were of this form, although in 1875 *St. Nicholas* magazine ran a small grid in which the Across answers were different from the Down answers.

CROSSWORD PUZZLES

Late in 1913, Arthur Wynne, who composed a page of puzzles every week for the Sunday *New York World*'s FUN section, decided to create something different from his usual fare of *rebuses* (picture puzzles), anagrams, word squares, and riddles. Appearing for the first time on December 21, 1913, his new "word-cross" puzzle was an instant sensation. See Figure 1.1.*

Wynne constructed another "word-cross" puzzle for the following Sunday's paper, and, to the irritation of the paper's typesetters, fans clamored for more—even writing angry letters if the weekly FUN section happened not to contain a word-cross. Readers' original compositions began arriving at the newspaper at the rate of about one a day.

The *World* was the only publisher of crossword puzzles for about ten years. The paper downplayed the feature by setting it in a very small typeface, clearly ignoring its popularity. The puzzle's shape gradually settled into the square or rectangle form we all know today and some general "rules" concerning definitions were adopted, but Wynne's awkward numbering scheme, using two numbers for each definition, remained in effect until 1923, when a puzzler calling himself "Radical" suggested that solvers could reasonably be trusted to write answers either horizontally or vertically in the grid provided both the starting square and direction were known.

---

* Answers to puzzles appear at the back of their respective chapters.

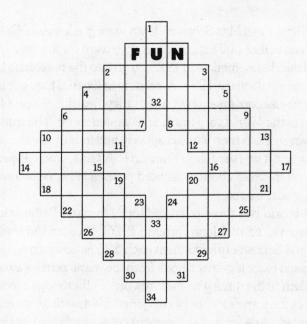

2-3. What bargain hunters enjoy.
4-5. A written acknowledgement.
18-19. What this puzzle is.
22-23. An animal of prey.
26-27. The close of a day.
28-29. To elude.
30-31. The plural of is.
8-9. To cultivate.
12-13. A bar of wood or iron.
16-17. What artists learn to do.

20-21. Fastened.
24-25. Found on the seashore.
10-18. The fiber of the gomuti palm.
6-22. What we all should be.
6-7. Such and nothing more.
10-11. A bird.
14-15. Opposed to less.
4-26. A day dream.
2-11. A talon.
19-29. A pigeon.

F-7. Part of your head.
23-30. A river in Russia.
1-32. To govern.
33-34. An aromatic plant.
N-8. A fist.
24-31. To agree with.
3-12. Part of a ship.
20-29. One.
5-27. Exchanging.
9-25. To sink in mud.
13-21. A boy.

Figure 1.1. _Arthur Wynne's first "word-cross" puzzle_

In 1921, Dick Simon met Max Schuster. Both were graduates of Columbia University, but had not known each other while at college as they were three years apart in class. They became friends and decided, sometime in 1923, to go into the publishing business together. Their (ad)venture began in January, 1924. According to legend, they got the idea to publish crosswords from a casual conversation in which they heard that one of Simon's cousins enjoyed the puzzles in the *World* very much and wanted more. The truth was not quite so serendipitous, however: Both men worked actively and in businesslike fashion to develop potential book ideas, and it was very likely Franklin P. Adams, who happened to be a friend of Simon and who often wrote about crossword puzzles in his *New York World* column, who first proposed a puzzle book.

By 1924, the *World* had three puzzle editors: Margaret Petherbridge (who became Margaret Farrar when she married John Farrar in 1926), Prosper Buranelli, and F. Gregory Hartswick. Simon and Schuster offered them each $25 as advance against royalties to do a little moonlighting and piece together a book from the many puzzles awaiting appearance in the newspaper. Each of the three wrote a foreword. Petherbridge credited F.P.A.'s complaints about errors as the inspiration for her diligence. Hartswick wrote an essay on solving, in which he commented, "As a form of amusement cross words are very instructive [and] as a form of instruction they are very amusing." Buranelli wrote of ancient riddles, puzzles, palindromes, and other word amusements. Hartswick composed the first puzzle in the book, using the pseudonym Gregorian to disguise his authorship.

Simon and Schuster were concerned that they might be hooted out of the publishing business after only a few months in it, and so, when the book was published on April 10, 1924, it carried the name Plaza Publishing Company on the title page. "Plaza" was the telephone exchange at Simon and Schuster's offices.

The first printing (3,600 copies) of *The Cross Word Puzzle Book* sold out quickly. Simon and Schuster emerged from the "Plaza" façade, and by the end of 1924 they had four books on the bestseller list. For good luck, and for sentimental reasons, the name Plaza remained on the title page of the puzzle books for several years. Simon and Schuster, success assured, expanded into other publishing avenues. The three coeditors continued to compile puzzle books—to the delight of millions of eager buyers.

On May 18, 1924, six weeks after the first book's publication, some three hundred people met in New York City and founded the Cross Word Puzzle Association of America. Joseph E. Austrian was elected president. At that meeting William A. Stern II solved a puzzle of eleven rows and columns (now commonly written "11x11") in a little over ten minutes, thereby winning the "Cross Word Puzzle Championship of the World."

The *Sunday Express* published England's first crossword puzzle in early November 1924. Curiously, the coauthor of that puzzle was none other than Arthur Wynne! (Well, maybe it's not so curious. Nearly all we know of Wynne's life is that he was a Liverpudlian who emigrated to America as a journalist.) Wynne had shown some of his puzzles to a syndicator, C. W. Shepherd, who persuaded the *Sunday Express* to run a few. The first one chosen had an American spelling, so Shepherd set out to make what he thought would be a trivial change. By the time he was finished he had revised several words and clues, firmly establishing, if not inaugurating, the continuing tradition of unlimited editorial privilege to tinker with intention to improve.

Crossword puzzles quickly became one of the most popular amusements of the time, both in America and in Europe. Never before had a fad received such extensive news coverage. Between November 17 and December 23, 1924, *The New York Times* published more than twenty articles and editorials related to crossword puzzles. The paper continued to run articles and editorial comments from time to time for the next five years. The material in the remainder of this section is drawn primarily from items that appeared in the *Times*. (Dates cited refer to publication and not necessarily to the actual events.)

On November 17, 1924, *The New York Times* editorialized that crossword puzzles were "scarcely removed from the form of temporary madness that made so many people pay enormous sums for mah jong sets." Another editorial less than a week later continued the ridicule.

November 24: Scholars at Johns Hopkins University in Baltimore speculated that an artifact called the "Phaestus Disk" could have been a forerunner of modern word puzzles. This terra-cotta disk, apparently of Cretan origin and perhaps dating from 2000 B.C., was on display in the Johns Hopkins Archeological Museum. It had a spiral design of then-untranslated symbols, which may have made sense when read working outward from the center, or inward from the rim.

A week later, two Princeton University professors issued challenges to their respective classes. Robert Root, a professor of English, made the still-excellent suggestion that establishing an English vocabulary course using crossword puzzles as text material would be very useful. Warner Fite, a professor of logic, offered a prize for a successfully compiled crossword puzzle in which a single set of definitions would lead to two completely different yet equally correct sets of answers for a single diagram. No one claimed the prize.[*]

---

[*] A remarkable partial attempt at *double entendre* occurred in 1980. Someone sent a puzzle to *The New York Times* with instructions to "print this on Election Day." 1 Across was a six-letter word defined as "Winner of today's election," and the top-left corner of the puzzle could have been completed with either CARTER or

December 1: George McElveen, a Baptist preacher in Pittsburgh, stayed up all night "working out his combinations" for a crossword puzzle, the solution to which was the text for his next sermon. The church overflowed with puzzle fans the following Sunday. The congregation solved the puzzle, which was set up on a large blackboard at the front of the church, before Reverend McElveen delivered the sermon.

While Reverend McElveen was hard at work using his crossword puzzle to entice people to church, another man came to regret his encounter with a puzzle. W. Nathan became engrossed in a puzzle book while dining at a New York restaurant. Armed with a dictionary, and with kibitzers looking over his shoulder, he refused to leave his table at closing time. He was finally arrested for disturbing the peace.

December 2: The *Times* profiled Fanny Goldner, whom they called the city's oldest puzzle fan. The 103-year-old woman became interested in puzzles when an attendant at her nursing home compiled one in Yiddish. The *Times* did not report whether the puzzle used English or Hebrew letters.

December 11: A woman in Cleveland was granted a divorce from a puzzle addict. In court she testified, "Morning, noon, and night, it is crossword puzzles."

December 12: The United States Department of Agriculture, bowing under the weight of many requests from puzzle solvers, released an announcement revealing the name of the Roman goddess of agriculture: Ops. The announcement went on to say that the department was in no way setting a precedent, either for itself or for any other governmental body, by giving out such information.

The Baltimore and Ohio Railroad announced that it would supply dictionaries in its club cars for passenger convenience, initially on the main rail lines, and probably eventually on the branch lines as well.

December 20: Two inmates in a Pittsburgh jail got into a fight. They were using a crossword puzzle book to pass the time while they did time. When they came to a four-letter

---

REAGAN. It wasn't published. We don't know all the details, but we can speculate that a major factor was the logistical problem of inserting the right answer grid with no lead time.

Several compilers of cryptic crossword puzzles have achieved double entendre, thanks in part to the wordiness of cryptic clues. One concise clue leading to two answers was "Note in Latin (2)." Both LA and TI are hidden in "Latin." More typical was "If you tip me just a little, I'll give you a glare—something bitter to swallow (6)." The answers were ALEGAR and PORTER, both of which are "bitter to swallow." ALEGAR is an anagram of "a glare," and its clue uses ten words to establish that there's an anagram at work. For PORTER, the first twelve words represent a baggage carrier speaking. (If this seems cryptic to you, see our explanation of cryptic clues in chapter 4, "Solving Cryptic Crossword Puzzles.")

word defined as "Place of punishment," with the letters "_ELL" filled in, they could not resolve the choice, CELL or HELL, without resorting to fisticuffs.

Articles in *The New York Times* over the next several days commented on increased dictionary sales. The Los Angeles Public Library established a five-minute limit on the use of a dictionary. In an editorial *The New York Times* commented, "The only comfort of non-puzzlers is that the paper on which the sacred documents are printed cannot endure through the ages . . . no one has yet seen fit to engrave his favorite puzzle on his headstone."

Late in the year, a "wild-eyed mob" besieged the Carnegie Library in Pittsburgh, demanding the curator tell them a word of seven letters meaning "a bird of the suborder of *Eleutherodactyli oscines*." After some reflection, the curator responded "Sparrow"— hardly the extinct relative of the pterodactyl the crowd thought it was seeking.

The first few days of 1925 made it clear that the fad was not dying out. In Paris, it was reported, American women were infatuated with hosiery imprinted with black and white squares in random patterns. The Parisian women, needless to say, pronounced the fashion "hideous." At the same time, an American designer produced a line of clothes made from material depicting puzzle fragments.* A book given away with each purchase contained the complete set of puzzles and definitions. Anyone answering all the puzzles in the book was entitled to a discount on other dresses in the line. (No one ever reported any difficulties trying to solve a puzzle while a dress was occupied.)

January 4, 1925: The Carnegie Library in Pittsburgh announced that it had no books of puzzles in the library and, furthermore, that it had no intention of acquiring any, as "they're not literature." Yale beat Wellesley the next day in a crossword-puzzle-solving contest arranged as a benefit for Bryn Mawr.

January 6: *The New York Times* reported that a group of puzzle enthusiasts had to be reprimanded in a New York City courtroom because they had become so involved with their collective efforts that they had failed to notice the arrival of the judge. It turned out that one of the puzzle-doers was a defendant who was in court for the second time because he'd ignored a fine imposed the week before. His excuse? He had been sidetracked by a puzzle.

January 13: An article reported that Queen Mary and some of her companions had taken time out from other activities to try solving crossword puzzles. In an editorial the next day *The New York Times* commented, "Royalty in ages past has been worse employed

---

* Crossword puzzles have provided a novelty clothing motif through the years. In 1993, newspapers nationwide ran stories about Abraham Hirschfeld, who was negotiating to buy *The New York Post* at the time. The stories invariably mentioned Hirschfeld's trademark crossword necktie, which he wore to make light of his not-very-intellectual image, and his giving identical ties to *Post* staffers, friendly or otherwise, and many other New Yorkers.

more than once." The paper went on to say that Queen Mary's participation in puzzling, and similar popular activities by other rulers, "humanizes royalty."

January 21: The *Times* reported that a newspaper called the *Daily Graphic,* which offered prizes for successful puzzle solving, was seeking an injunction barring another paper, the *Bronx Home News,* from publishing the answers. The *Home News* claimed during its defense that while the puzzles might have been copyrighted, the answers were not. (Once a puzzle has been published, the answers are merely publicly ascertainable facts, so no copyright protects them as such.)

Crossword puzzles really "arrived" on January 29, 1925, with an item on page 1 of *The New York Times.* W. R. Baker, president of the British Optical Association, warned of headaches due to eyestrain caused by the combination of the small type used for puzzles and the need to shift the eyes and refocus rapidly when solving puzzles.

February 1: *The New York Times* conceded, "the almost universal hobby of the moment is the crossword puzzle." However, the editorial went on to observe that such activity serves "no useful purpose whatever."[*]

The following week, the *Times Sunday Magazine* featured a biography of Roget, calling him "the patron saint of crossworders."

On February 15, the Associated Press reported that Paris—and, indeed, all of mainland Europe—had taken to crosswords. Newspapers awarded prizes to successful solvers, but ran afoul of lottery laws and police seized six thousand submitted solutions.

The next day brought news that a library in Dulwich, England, was blotting out the daily puzzles because crossword addicts were keeping the papers from other readers. Two days later, the Wimbledon Library removed all "volumes of lexicography" from the shelves due to damage.

February 22: A report profiled the Foreign Language Information Service, an organization whose purpose was to help immigrants learn English. One tool was crossword puzzles, with definitions in sixteen different languages and answers in English. A list of some four thousand "most needed" words, augmented by names of historically important Americans, supplied the answers.

On the same day, *The New York Times* reported that the Prime Minister of Britain, Stanley Baldwin, had relaxed by solving a puzzle with the help of M. Panileve, the Premier of France, and M. Briand, the French Foreign Minister.[†]

---

[*] But recent studies indicate, to the contrary, that solving crosswords can slow mental decline due to aging.

[†] Bill Clinton is known to be an excellent crossword solver. One television newscast showed him working on a puzzle with British Prime Minister John Major looking over his shoulder.

March 9: The Chicago Department of Health got into the act with an announcement that made page 1 of the *Times*. In their view, "crossworditis" was beneficial to health and happiness. (They undoubtedly meant "crosswordosis.")

In March, the *New Republic* concluded that crosswords were not educational, being but "bad exercise for writers and speakers." A March 10 editorial in *The New York Times* commented that "the craze is evidently dying out fast" and that crosswords were "going the way of mah jong." A Mr. Brockelbank rebutted the *Times* in a letter published a week later, arguing that mah jong was "doomed from the start," being too much based on luck.

In June, a trade paper for undertakers carried a crossword puzzle featuring scientific and technical terms dealing with funeral directing and embalming.

On Broadway, the show *Tell Me More!* contained this snapper: "I hope you're stranded on a desert isle with a crossword puzzle and without a dictionary." *Puzzles of 1925* went even further, with a skit depicting puzzle addicts as patients in a sanitorium. Songs of the era included "Crossword Mama, You Puzzle Me (But Papa's Gonna Figure You Out)" and "Cross Words (Between Sweetie and Me)."

The phrase "Long live Otto," supporting nationalistic calls to put Archduke Otto on the Hungarian throne, cropped up in a puzzle in a Hungarian paper in October 1925. The dictatorial government of Admiral Horthy immediately began censoring the puzzles.

The year 1925 ended on an unhappy note, as far as news about crossword puzzles is concerned. Theodore Koerner, a twenty-seven-year-old employee of the New York Telephone Company, shot and wounded his wife because she refused to help him solve a crossword puzzle. He then killed himself.

The next year brought more unhappy news about puzzle enthusiasts. A Budapest waiter named Julius Antar committed suicide. He explained why in a crossword puzzle which, alas, the police were unable to solve.

At a National Puzzlers' League convention in February 1927, Secretary Lewis Trent said that crossword puzzles had no place in the life of a "true puzzler." According to Trent, pastimes such as anagrams, enigmas, and rebuses deserved more attention. At that convention, incidentally, William Grossman presented what some people still call "the perfect anagram" (appositeness being the primary criterion). The conventioneers sat enthralled as the words THEY SEE were written on a blackboard, then rearranged to form THE EYES. In his introduction to *The Cross Word Puzzle Book*, Buranelli had reprinted several word forms (squares, diamond, and triangle shapes) written by NPL members. He called the NPLers "skillful adepts," and wrote that, for them, "Any word that has ever been printed in an English book is allowable."

February 23: Picking up on Trent's remarks, the *Times* printed an editorial declaring the "crossword epidemic" to be over. The paper noted the popularity of new amusements—cryptograms and anagrams.

Ultimately, *The New York Times* climbed on the bandwagon. The paper hired Margaret Farrar to be puzzle editor, and on February 15, 1942 the Sunday Magazine carried a 23x23 crossword puzzle of "topical interest." A 15x15 humorous puzzle titled "Riddle Me This," contributed by one Anna Gram, accompanied the large puzzle.* An announcement on the same page invited freelance contributions.

The *Times* began offering a daily crossword puzzle in 1950. On about the third day, however, the printers somehow omitted it. When they discovered the error partway through the press run, there was a big to-do and the presses were stopped to insert the puzzle for the rest of the edition.

REVIVAL OF SOLVING TOURNAMENTS

In 1977, a sales manager hoped a crossword-solving tournament would lure people to his Stamford (Connecticut) Marriott Hotel over a lightly booked 1978 winter weekend. Puzzle expert Will Shortz, co-organizer of a group of puzzle enthusiasts and composers (and a Stamford resident at the time), commissioned new crosswords for a contest, devised word games to entertain the contestants in the evening, and prevailed on five friends to judge. More than 150 entrants showed up, posing a severe challenge to the judges' endurance and ability to score accurately without sleep.

The American Crossword Puzzle Tournament is now an annual event. More than 230 people entered in 1995, divided into skill divisions based on past results. Secondary prizes were awarded to winners in different age groups and geographic regions. More than twenty people helped judge, and a computer kept track of the leaders. Scoring placed a premium on accuracy, with a large bonus for an error-free solution. Speed bonuses for each minute saved against a benchmark time separated the good from the amazing. For the last round, each skill division's three leaders competed head-to-head on giant diagrams at the front of the room while the rest of the contestants watched and silently cheered for their favorite.

Many other venues have held solving contests and related activities, with varied success. Grossinger's, that venerable Catskills resort, hosted tournaments for several years. Solvers have competed in Cleveland, Baltimore, Tampa, Los Angeles, New Jersey, and Long Island.

---

* The pseudonym, or *nom de puzzle*, Anna Gram has concealed the identities of several puzzle constructors, including Margaret Farrar herself.

The Cleveland tournament was unique: Sponsored by a bookstore, the contest was run as a twenty-four-hour marathon. Solvers could use any reference material in the store, which stayed open all night until winners were declared. Nobody solved the puzzle completely in the alloted time. Two surviving annual contests are conducted as fund-raisers for libraries in Connecticut and Massachusetts.

GAMES sponsored a national solving contest for several years, with a puzzle in the magazine serving as the entry form and preliminary challenge. To encourage participants who could not afford to travel to New York City to compete in person at the actual tournament, the magazine awarded a cash prize to one lucky entrant whose correct puzzle was drawn at random. At least four cruises have featured a crossword theme, with lectures, games, puzzles to solve, and prizes.

CONTEMPORARY CROSSWORD PUZZLES

Only one puzzle in the first two *Cross Word Puzzle Book* collections had no two-letter words and had every letter in both an Across and a Down word (that is, "fully checked"). Every definition provided a dictionary meaning: There were no puns or other tricky clues, no fill-in-the-blank definitions, and no literary or cultural references except as required by straightforward dictionary information. The editors apologized because one of the grids demanded a two-word answer!

Even so, the editors sensed that they could, and should, demand more of the composers. Hartswick's essay in the first book remarked that some words ("old favorites") had a way of "recurring ceaselessly" in the puzzles. He clucked over the two-letter words and abbreviations and noted many repeaters among the three-letter words. In addition, the editors took mild slaps at some puzzles for having many black squares and praised those with few unchecked letters.

Unchecked letters disappeared completely, two-letter words vanished from high-quality publications, and topical puzzles emerged during the 1940s. Multiword answers became staples during the next decade, with short phrases and parts of quotations occasionally filling even three- and four-letter spaces. The 1960s brought novelties like Eugene T. Maleska's *Stepquote* invention, Frances Hansen's original verses, Will Weng's outrageous puns, and gimmicks involving word substitutions.

Still, as recently as the middle 1970s crosswords remained vocabulary challenges with dollops of crosswordese. A Sunday puzzle in *The New York Times* satirized the practice: "FULLER EXPLANATIONS" had typical repeater answers as thematic definitions, and the trite definitions that normally served as their clues were the puzzle's long entries. (For example, "Adits" defined MINE ENTRANCES.)

The most recent transformation began in the late 1970s. Several things happened over a period of about five years:

- Will Shortz brought his editorial viewpoint to the crosswords accepted by *GAMES*, drastically reducing crosswordese and obscurity in favor of references to current culture. *GAMES* offered premium pay for the few puzzles it published each issue, and it became (and remains) a highly competitive market. As more composers sent puzzles calculated to gain Shortz's favor, he was able to eliminate nearly all crosswordese and obscurity born of desperation.

- Several younger composers broke into the business. Led, perhaps, by Henry Hook, Merl Reagle, and Mike Shenk, they got past nasty places in grids with product brand names and inventive but well-clued letter combinations rather than variant spellings and obsolete words. Moreover, they stressed cleverness and currentness in the definitions. Hook, for example, entertained contestants at one Stamford tournament with his "Cook book" clue for COMA. Judges positioned around the room's perimeter reported being able to gauge who had progressed how far through the puzzle by the chuckles and groans.*

     One of Reagle's weekly *San Francisco Examiner* crossword puzzles earned national publicity in 1991. A man and woman had become friends on learning they both solved the puzzles avidly. The man arranged with Reagle to conceal a marriage proposal in a puzzle, and to incorporate several answers that would appear normal to most solvers, but would have significance for the woman so she could not attribute anything to coincidence. Their story appeared on CNN and *The Today Show*, in *People*, and in *USA Today*. Reagle attended their wedding the following year.

- Dell Puzzle Publications started a second editorial department with an entirely independent line of issues. Magazines published under the Dell Champion logo took up the *GAMES*-style philosophy while providing a much larger market for composers than *GAMES*. Unlike Dell's original puzzle department, which deprecates brand names as "free advertising," the crosswords in the Dell Champion collections use product names in moderation, and figurative and punny clues in abundance.

- Stanley Newman, winner of many crossword-solving tournaments, began the *Cross-worder's Own Newsletter*—a self-published, subscription-only publication. Each issue

---

* Robin Cook wrote the novel *Coma*.

contained articles, book reviews, and industry gossip, along with a dozen or so puzzles rated for difficulty. In *CON*, which he renamed *Tough Puzzles* when he dropped the easy puzzles and added more hard ones, Newman articulated the approach taken by Shortz and the Dell Champion staff, perhaps more clearly than they themselves had thought it through. He claimed modernization was necessary to vie with MTV, video games, and so on for young people's time, lest aging demographics make crosswords extinct. He wrote vigorous editorials espousing the viewpoint and exhorting his subscribers to complain to their local newspapers about "tired" crosswords, and he challenged those papers to run a "contemporary crossword" alongside their existing Sunday puzzle and poll solvers' preferences. No less than *The Wall Street Journal* (the last major daily newspaper without a crossword) reported the controversy.

Newman backed up his stance with the puzzles he published. They were difficult despite a complete absence of crosswordese and the like, and entertaining because the clues used a lot of wordplay and featured many references to current culture.

To be sure, some solvers still prefer the older style, with its predominantly literal definitions, occasional odd words, comfortable crosswordese, and almost no mention of current popular culture. *The New York Times* acknowledged and endorsed the continuing crossword evolution, however, by naming Will Shortz their puzzle editor in 1993. Shortz, by the way, was commissioned to write the riddles for the 1995 film *Batman Forever*.

TECHNOLOGY

Simon and Schuster's original *Cross Word Puzzle Book*s were hardbound publications approximately 6x8" in size, with definitions and diagrams on facing pages. The pages' dimensions increased along the way to today's familiar 8½x11" size, and nearly all publishers' bookstore collections now use a spiral binding so pages can lie flat. Puzzle magazines are available in both digest and large-size formats, and many publishers provide collections especially to satisfy people who find extra-large print a convenience or necessity.

Mail-order puzzles came into existence because devoted fans of Will Weng's editorial style did not want to lose their regular "fix" when he retired from *The New York Times* in 1977. The Crosswords Club was the result. Thousands of subscribers receive monthly packages of Sunday-size, premium-quality puzzles. Mel Rosen succeeded Weng in 1993. Other, similar clubs today include The Crossword Puzzles of the Month Club (edited by Henry Hook) and The Uptown Puzzle Club (edited by Stanley Newman and published by the same company as The Crosswords Club).

You should not be surprised to learn that crosswords are available on computers. Several programs exist, all operating essentially the same way: First, you select a puzzle from the stock supplied with the program. Then, using a mouse or similar pointing device, you select a slot in the grid and the program shows you the corresponding clues. (Because the computer can figure out where you're pointing, the grids don't need any numbers.) You type in an answer, select another slot, and repeat. Most of the programs offer a "competition mode" by keeping track of how much time you take to solve the puzzle, how many mistakes you make, and so on.

Puzzlemaker and computer user Trip Payne reviewed some of these programs for *GAMES*. He had specific comments about how they stacked up against each other, but his overall reaction was more interesting. The programs worked as advertised, he said, but unless you really like playing computer games, the activity wasn't as satisfying as holding a book and pencil. Besides, he added, you wouldn't take a computer to the beach.

Another puzzle-related computer activity involves on-line discussions in various electronic bulletin boards linked together by Internet, the worldwide connection of computers and computer networks. Most of the discussions focus on clues in cryptic crosswords, often with a British point of view, but other topics exist. At this writing no regular paying market exists solely for on-line puzzle subscription or distribution, but more than a few newspapers and magazines offer computer access to their crosswords.

CRYPTIC AND HUMOROUS CROSSWORD PUZZLES

England's first published crossword puzzle appeared in late 1924, as we have noted. The *Sunday Times* first offered a crossword early in 1925, the *Daily Telegraph* added a puzzle in July of the same year, and the *Observer*'s puzzle began in March 1926. The London *Times* introduced a weekly crossword puzzle on January 23, 1930. The *Daily Telegraph* ran an advertisement in the *Times* the very next day, featuring a crossword puzzle and telling *Times* readers to buy the *Daily Telegraph* if they wanted a puzzle every day. The *Times* received many letters asking for a daily puzzle feature, and one began less than two weeks later. *The New York Times* editorialized that crossword puzzling was "plainly past its prime in the U.S." and wondered why the London *Times* had bothered to start a crossword puzzle feature.

At first, British puzzle diagrams looked very much like ours, and composers used literal definitions. By 1930, however, tricky clues were popular. In a February 15, 1930, editorial titled "It presupposes a University education," *The New York Times* wrote that the London

Times had erred by allowing humor and whimsy into the puzzle definitions, and cited the clue "Sounds like a curious song." The answer was ODDITY, which sounds like ODD DITTY, a "curious song." This "may be imagination or anagrams or Badminton or something, but it's not crossword puzzling," said *The New York Times*.

Crosswords featuring humorous definitions also found a following in America. Ted Shane, Albert Morehead, and Jack Luzzatto were among the first American constructors to create crossword puzzles that, as *Judge* magazine once said, were "not edited in conformity with any rules whatever," as long as the definitions were "ambidextrous and witty."

The American magazine *The Nation* has carried a humorous puzzle since 1943. Upon the death of the its first composer, readers chose Frank Lewis to carry on over another aspirant, Jack Luzzatto, based on twelve puzzles published anonymously. Lewis's puzzles combine cryptic clues, puns, other wordplay, literary allusions, and many cross-references, along with figurative and conventional definitions in a cryptic-style diagram.

The New York Times has carried humorous puzzles on the Sunday puzzle page since the beginning. *Puns and Anagrams* crosswords feature anagrams, puns, and other wordplay in an otherwise conventional, fully-checked, low-word-count 15x15 diagram.

Newman's *Tough Puzzles* publication offered another variety of humorous crossword. The *Something Different* puzzles allowed as answers any conjured phrases and letter combinations that could be fairly clued. For example, the clue "Grizzly gulch, e.g." might lead to the nonsense answer A BEAR AREA. Mike Shenk and Merl Reagle were two of the pioneers of this theater-of-the-absurd genre, and Trip Payne eventually became the sole provider. Because entries needed to be only semiplausible at best ("Phrase from a first-grader's dance manual" was the clue for SEE SPOT BOOGIE), the 21x21 grids were astonishingly wide open. Tallies of only 28 black squares and 96 entries were not unusual, even against a typical 21x21's 75 and 142, respectively.

The cryptic puzzles published in England went beyond *Judge*'s "ambidextrous and witty." By the early 1940s, British puzzle writers, especially disciples of A. F. Ritchie, had developed a "square-dealing" style of definitions, about which we'll have a lot to say later. Ritchie's apt pseudonym was Afrit, a demon of Arabian myth and an incorporation of his initials and part of his surname.

Because of the deviousness of the puzzles, and because people are naturally drawn to competition, British puzzle fans took to writing letters to the newspapers congratulating themselves on the speed with which they could solve the puzzles. According to the *Guinness Book of World Records,* Roy Dean solved a puzzle in less than four minutes. His achievement was remarkable in that it occurred under extreme pressure—a London *Times* contest conducted in the BBC studios on December 19, 1970. A woman in Fiji established a perverse record when she notified the London *Times* in May 1966 that she had just completed puzzle number 673, published in April 1932.

British puzzle fans tried to deduce the identity of the compilers (their term for puzzlemakers) based on recurring clues, themes, and technical or literary references. The first puzzle compiler for the London *Times* was a Suffolk farmer named Adrian Bell. A relative recommended him to the paper. He had never even solved a puzzle before being hired.

The *Daily Telegraph* became the target of a spy investigation because several puzzles published in the spring of 1944 contained answers that happend to match code names used to designate military operations. On June 2, for example, OVERLORD appeared; it was the code name of the D day invasion. The puzzles' author, who lived in the south of England, where training was going on, convinced investigators that he had heard the words in conversation in town (evidently a case of loose lips) and found them interesting just as words, but that he had not known their significance when he used them in crosswords. In the end, no charges were filed.

The first American puzzle composer to popularize cryptic crosswords for an American audience was probably Stephen Sondheim, in *New York* magazine in the late 1960s. When Broadway opportunities and demands usurped his time, he turned the feature over to Richard Maltby, a Broadway friend and occasional guest writer of cryptic puzzles.

Today, ardent American fans of cryptic crosswords can find them in such publications as *GAMES*, *Dell Champion Crosswords*, *Atlantic Monthly* (where Emily Cox and Henry Rathvon have a large following), *The New York Times*, *New York* (reprints of the London *Times* puzzles—they discontinued Maltby's feature in the mid-1970s), and *Harper's* (where Maltby resurfaced, and where he and Ed Galli have an avid audience).

ACROSTIC PUZZLES

Acrostic puzzles have two ancestors, the acrostic and the anagram.

ACROSTICS

The word *acrostic* comes from the Greek roots *akros*, "extreme," and *stikhos*, "line of verse." Thus, an acrostic is a verse or set of lines in which the first letters, in order, spell something significant.

It is likely that the early bards and balladeers used acrostic devices as memory aids for recalling verses of epic poems and songs. Several specimens of acrostics occur in the original

Hebrew scriptures. The best known is Psalm 119: In Hebrew, the first verse begins with *aleph,* the second with *beth,* and so on through the Hebrew alphabet. The acrostic is lost in translation, but many modern Bibles use Hebrew letters to mark off the verses.

The fish as a symbol for Christ remains as a vestige of a Greek acrostic. The Greek word for "fish" is ιχθυς, and the acrostic runs as follows:

ιησους	—	Jesus
χριστος	—	Christ
θεου	—	of God
υιος	—	Son
ςωτηρ	—	Savior

According to Cicero, the Sibyls, ten women inspired with prophetic power by the god Apollo, often wrote their oracles in acrostic form. Other mystical claims and writings through the years were based on acrostics. Nevertheless, acrostics never took hold as a general form of amusement, perhaps because they represent no puzzle. They are, after all, simply an arrangement of letters.

As an art form, acrostics came into some favor toward the end of the seventeenth century. An 1875 book titled *Gleanings for the Curious from the Harvest-Fields of Literature, a Mélange of Excerptia,* collected (or "collated," as the title page puts it) by C.C. Bombaugh, contains this uncredited acrostic poem on the poet Wordsworth:

> **W**andering, through many a year, 'mongst Cumbria's hills,
> **O**'er her wild fells, sweet vales, and sunny lakes,
> **R**ich stores of thought thy musing mind distils,
> **D**ay-dreams of poesy thy soul awakes:—
> **S**uch was thy life—a poet's life, I ween;
> **W**orshipper thou of Nature! *every scene*
> **O**f beauty stirred by thy fancy's deeper mood,
> **R**eflection calmed the current of thy blood:
> **T**hus in the wide "excursion" of thy mind,
> **H**igh thought in *words of worth* we still may find.

Of course, many writers used the acrostic and related devices to excess. Here, from the same book, is part of a title page "for a book of extracts from many authors":

Astonishing Anthology from Attractive Authors.
Broken Bits from Bulky Brains.
Choice Chunks from Chaucer to Channing.

•

•

•

Xcellent Xtracts Xactly Xpressed.
Yawnings and Yearnings for Youthful Yankees.
Zeal and Zest from Zoroaster to Zimmerman.

This is an example of a *pangram* (containing all letters) or an alphabetic alliteration. Like most forays into this arena, it becomes more than a little strained at the letter X.

Various people over the years have claimed to have found in Shakespeare's plays acrostics and cryptograms "proving" that someone else actually wrote them. Other evidence exists as well, but Elizabeth Friedman, an expert cryptanalyst during World War II, showed that the acrostics and cryptograms could plausibly be attributed to statistical probability or coincidence.[*]

Today the acrostic appears in decline as an art form. Except for acrostic puzzles as described in this book, its most common appearances are on political billboards, where the letters in a candidate's name are used as the initial letters of words in a list of praiseworthy attributes, and on banners at sporting events.

ANAGRAMS

The second ancestor of the acrostic puzzle, the anagram, also arose in antiquity. The word comes from the Greek roots *ana*, "back or reversed" and *gramma*, "letter" (or *grammos*, "line"). An anagram is a rearrangement of the letters in a word or phrase to produce a new word or phrase. For example, "astronomers" can be rearranged to form "moon starers" or "no more stars."

A Greek writer named Lycophron, who lived during the fourth century before Christ, may have originated the oldest surviving anagrams. His poem "Alexandra," in which Cassandra prophesied the fall of Troy, contained flattering anagrams on the names of the reigning Egyptian king and queen.

---

[*] In a *Scientific American* article on probability and coincidence, Martin Gardner wrote that if there were no coincidences, that would indeed be a coincidence.

Soothsayers, oracles, and prophets used anagrams as one source for their advice. They labored to rearrange the letters in names, trying to produce apt phrases. Both supporters of Martin Luther and those opposing his doctrines composed anagrams on his name in German and in Latin to make their points. Martin Luther became *lehrt in Armut* (He teaches in poverty). *Martinus Luterus* became both *vir multa struens* (the man who builds up much) and *ter matris vulnus* (He wounded the mother [church] three times). In 1605 Pompeu Salvi published in Genoa some five hundred anagrams on the Ave Maria.

In the 1800s the phrase "Govern, clever lad" honored Grover Cleveland. More recently, the descriptive phrase "now has a wide, ever-delighted grin" emerged from the letters in "General Dwight David Eisenhower."

The anagram remains a popular entertainment, much more so than the acrostic. This is undoubtedly because more skill is needed to create an anagram, especially an apt one. Indeed, much of the significance attributed to the Sator Square came from the many anagrams composed from its letters. In 1925, for instance, a Reverend Hicks noted that SATOR OPERA TENET was an anagram of PATER NOSTER A ET O. A ET O was taken to mean "Alpha and Omega," or, "the Beginning and the End" (referring to the Greek alphabet and Revelation 1:8).

Anagrams play a large part in the clues for cryptic crossword puzzles and humorous puzzles such as *Puns and Anagrams*. Occasionally some outstanding ones crop up in conventional crossword puzzles. "Tut" of the National Puzzlers' League produced "It's now seen live" from TELEVISION NEWS, and Will Shortz brought it prominence in a nationally published crossword.

INVENTION OF THE MODERN ACROSTIC PUZZLE

Unlike the seemingly accidental invention of the crossword puzzle, the acrostic puzzle was a quite deliberate creation. In the early 1930s a woman named Elizabeth Kingsley returned to her alma mater, Wellesley College, for a class reunion. While visiting the campus, Kingsley perceived the current undergraduates' taste in literature as substandard, and set out to devise a puzzle specifically to heighten their literary appreciation by, as she later noted, "reviewing classical English and American poet and prose masters." The first Double-Crostic was published by *The Saturday Review of Literature* on March 31, 1934. (See Figure 1.2 on pages 22 and 23.) The magazine invited solvers to make suggestions to improve the puzzle—for example, by making the clues harder or easier—and published letters concerning the puzzle for some weeks.

NOTICE

This is the first of a series of ingenious literary puzzles invented by Elizabeth S. Kingsley for *The Saturday Review*. A new puzzle will be published each week, and the answer to the previous puzzle will appear regularly in this space. Let us know if the DIRECTIONS are clear. And after you have solved several of the puzzles we should like to know whether you think them too hard or too easy—our DEFINITIONS will be governed accordingly! Write to THE PUZZLE EDITOR, THE SATURDAY REVIEW, 25 WEST 45TH STREET, NEW YORK CITY.

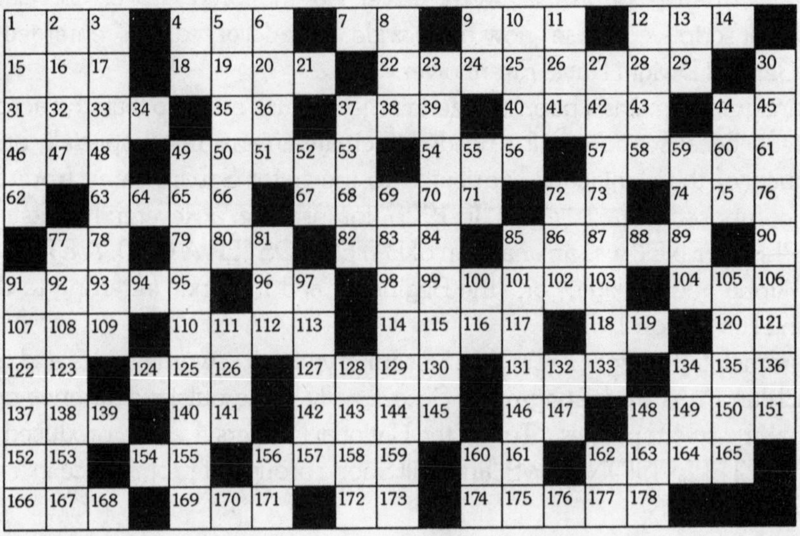

DIRECTIONS

To solve this puzzle, you must guess twenty-five words, the definitions of which are given in the column headed DEFINITIONS. The letters in each word to be guessed are numbered (these numbers appear at the beginning of each definition) and you are thereby able to tell how many letters are in the required word. When you have guessed a word each letter is to be written in the correspondingly numbered square on the puzzle diagram. When the squares are all filled in you will find (by reading from left to right) a quotation from a famous author. Reading up and down, the letters mean nothing! The black squares indicate ends of words; therefore words do not necessarily end at the right side of the diagram.

Either before (preferably) or after placing the letters in their squares you should write the words you have guessed on the blank lines which appear to the right in the column headed WORDS. The initial letters of this list of words spell the name of the author and the title of the piece from which the quotation has been taken.

Figure 1.2. *Double-Crostic #1*

DEFINITIONS

WORDS

I. 1-14-23-50-95. A perfume of roses.

I. _____

II. 145-6-28-90-137. Child's game played with cards and numbers.

II. _____

III. 97-8-79-146-98-61-75-77-76-32-27-19-133. Light as a feather.

III. _____

IV. 80-85-60-113-51-58-48. Held in high esteem; worshipped.

IV. _____

V. 81-172-31-84-24-176-65-89. Insubstantial.

V. _____

VI. 112-45-114-164-149-173-142-36. The business section of a city.

VI. _____

VII. 144-102-2-63. Material for bandages.

VII. _____

VIII. 37-4-66-82-110-116-62. Upholstered backless seat.

VIII. _____

IX. 100-106-33-5-122-41-138-69-83-13-162-127. A Russian pianist.

IX. _____

X. 40-59-52-25. A drupe with a single seed.

X. _____

XI. 135-175-3-73. Movement of the ocean.

XI. _____

XII. 130-43-129-107-111-55-139-47. To alienate.

XII. _____

XIII. 15-121-92-136-101-39. A mighty hunter.

XIII. _____

XIV. 167-9-140-46-105. Artless; simple.

XIV. _____

XV. 119-54-104-17-153-34. Hebrew God.

XV. _____

XVI. 134-63-128-168-16-30. Flat, dark image.

XVI. _____

XVII. 155-125-78-148-143-165-158-56. Prejudiced (compound).

XVII. _____

XVIII. 12-96-120-11-7-170-150-21-68-174. Significant, unusual.

XVIII. _____

XIX. 97-141-171-161-67-20-10-126. Not propitious.

XIX. _____

XX. 177-99-152-163-108-115. Member of the tribe of Levi.

XX. _____

XXI. 42-88-26-159-49-91. Doodle dandy.

XXI. _____

XXII. 22-71-151-118-131-147-38-94-160-29. Watchword (Bibl.).

XXII. _____

XXIII. 109-86-132-124-72-117-123-178. Uttered a harsh sound.

XXIII. _____

XXIV. 157-44-93-53-166-18-35-103. Forceful.

XXIV. _____

XXV. 156-154-74-169-70-57. To stop the flow.

XXV. _____

Acrostic puzzles combine acrostics, anagrams, and definitions. The writer of an acrostic puzzle rearranges the letters in an excerpt from some published work to form a series of words. The solver must deduce the words from definitions. The series of words forms an acrostic: The first letters of the words, taken in order, spell something—usually the name of the author of the passage and the title of the work from which the passage was taken. (Sometimes the acrostic spells the name of a person or place that is the subject of the quotation.)

Today millions of solvers enjoy the special challenge of acrostic puzzles.

OTHER FORMS

Just as crosswords and acrostic puzzles descended from earlier amusements, new puzzle forms have arisen from crosswords and acrostic puzzles. The names for the types of puzzles differ from publisher to publisher, of course, but some of the popular ones are skeletons, in which solvers fit words from a list into a loosely interlocking pattern; fill-ins, in which solvers fit words from a list into a conventional crossword puzzle pattern; and cross-numbers, in which solvers enter digits into a crossword-style pattern to add to specific sums (the definitions).

The Reporter, an American magazine published from 1949 to 1968, carried what may be the ultimate form of crossword puzzle. The Acrostickler, composed by Henry Allen, had diagrams and clues similar to cryptic crossword puzzles. The unchecked letters in the diagram recombined to form words in an acrostic yielding the name of some prominent person. A few answers in the diagram pertained to that person in some way, perhaps consisting of the person's birthplace, profession, or the like.

Harper's Monthly picked up the Acrostickler when *The Reporter* ceased publication, but dropped it at the end of 1969. It may simply have been too exotic to survive.

ANSWERS TO PUZZLES

ARTHUR WYNNE'S FIRST WORD CROSS PUZZLE

If you solved this puzzle, you may have noticed a few flaws. First, the answer DOVE appears twice—on the sixth row and in the fifth column. Had HARD (in the eighth row) been changed to HARM, the crossing word would have been MOVE. Next, the definition for 9 Down appears to be in error; "To sink in mud" uses a simple present-tense infinitive, but the answer (MIRED) is past tense. Finally, TANE (in the ninth column) is a word from Scotland and northern England appearing to mean "the one" (not "one"). It could have been VANE without difficulty.*

```
                      R
                   F  U  N
                S  A  L  E  S
             R  E  C  E  I  P  T
          M  E  R  E     F  A  R  M
       D  O  V  E           R  A  I  L
    M  O  R  E                 D  R  A  W
       H  A  R  D           T  I  E  D
          L  I  O  N     S  A  N  D
             E  V  E  N  I  N  G
                E  V  A  D  E
                   A  R  E
                      D
```

DOUBLE-CROSTIC #1

Publishers of acrostic puzzles usually present the answers as ordinary prose or as set poetry, rather than in a grid format, probably so solvers can read the material as the original author intended.

In this first Double-Crostic, FEATHERWEIGHT's definition was "Light as a feather." Similarly, the definition for LEVITE was "Member of the tribe of Levi." We would expect not to see significant parts of answers in their own definitions today. Also, two letters from

* Then again, TANE may have been part of Wynne's working vocabulary, bearing in mind his origin.

FEATHERWEIGHT fell into the same word in the quotation . . . something today's editors don't allow. At any rate, here is the passage quoted in the first Double-Crostic, followed by the word list with bold letters emphasizing the acrostic formed by the author's name and the title of the poem.

> And 'tho
> We are not now that strength which in old days
> Moved earth and heaven; that which we are, we are;
> One equal temper of heroic hearts,
> Made weak by time and fate, but strong in will
> To strive, to seek, to find, and not to yield.
> —Alfred Lord Tennyson, "Ulysses"

WORD LIST:

Attar
Lotto
Featherweight
Revered
Ethereal
Downtown

Lint
Ottoman
Rachmaninoff
Date

Tide
Estrange
Nimrod
Naive
Yahweh
Shadow

One-sided
Noteworthy

Untoward
Levite
Yankee
Shibboleth
Squawked
Emphatic
Stanch

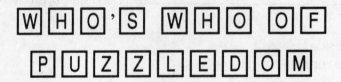

*These were honored in their generations, and were
the glory of the times.*
—Ecclesiasticus

THE INVENTORS

ELIZABETH KINGSLEY

Elizabeth Kingsley, inventor of the acrostic puzzle, had two careers. A Wellesley College graduate, Kingsley taught English at Girls High School in Brooklyn for many years. When she first encountered crossword puzzles in 1926, her reaction was "It's fun, but what's the good?" As noted earlier, her disapproval of reading habits among undergraduates at Wellesley in the early 1930s caused her to seek out a new form of puzzle. Always adept at anagrams and other scrambled-word recreations, she constructed the first acrostic puzzle, which she called a "Double-Crostic," at the age of sixty-one! In six months she had made one hundred of these puzzles.

A friend suggested that *The Saturday Review of Literature* would be an appropriate outlet. The magazine agreed. Kingsley constructed puzzles for the magazine at the rate of one a week from 1934 until her retirement in 1952. She also found time to compose and publish collections of Double-Crostics for Simon and Schuster, and to carry on a lively correspondence with fans. Her correspondence eventually formed the basis for a column in *The Saturday Review* called "The Acrostics Club."

Kingsley was constantly looking for new words, especially ones that disposed of *h* (which always seemed to crop up far too often), *j*, and *q*. Helpful fans continually supplied her with potentially useful words.

Doris Nash Wortman, one of Kingsley's successors at *The Saturday Review* and Simon and Schuster, introduced a variation called *telestich*, in which the last letters of the defined words, not the first, constitute the acrostic feature. Thomas H. Middleton, the last Double-Crostics writer at *The Saturday Review* (which is now defunct), writes acrostic puzzles for *The New York Times* and produces Double-Crostic collections for Simon and Schuster. His books occasionally offer the telestich variation, and once in a while a puzzle has cryptic clues rather than straight definitions.

EDWARD POWYS MATHERS

Edward Powys Mathers was born in Forest Hill, England, and was educated at Trinity College, Oxford. He was a successful literary critic and was well known as a poet. When he first encountered crossword puzzles, he was unimpressed by the tame definitions and developed a cryptic style of clue that required more of the solvers than mere general knowledge. By 1926, his puzzles were featured regularly in the London *Observer.* The initial reaction to his clues was that solving them took too much time, but his style caught on, and in a few years he was under pressure to extend himself, and his fans, further.

Mathers took up the *nom de puzzle* Torquemada, an excruciatingly apt choice, as Tomás de Torquemada was the first and most infamous Grand Inquisitor of the Spanish Inquisition. The twentieth-century Torquemada compiled some 670 puzzles for the *Observer,* the solving of which constituted weekly ordeals for British cryptic fans.

Torquemada's method of creating a puzzle was to select a theme, frequently a bit of verse or some other quotation, and then to generate a list of pertinent words. While he pondered clues, his wife had the mundane chore of fitting the words into a diagram that she devised.

Torquemada popularized two crossword variations. The first, called the *bar crossword*, uses heavy bars between squares, instead of black squares, to mark the ends of the words. In a well-constructed bar crossword, just as in a conventional crossword or black-square cryptic crossword, the pattern is symmetrical. Figure 4.1 on page 50 is an example.

The second variation is seldom seen here. It also uses a bar diagram, but dispenses with clues altogether. Instead, a narrative with some omitted words confronts the solver. The solver is told where in the diagram the missing words belong, and the words must be deduced from context.

Derrick Macnutt and Jonathan Crowther, successors to Mathers at the *Observer,* took up the names Ximenes and Azed, respectively. Ximenes immediately followed Torquemada as Grand Inquisitor. Azed, a nice span of the alphabet (*z* being called "zed" in England), is a reversal of Deza, referring to Don Diego de Deza, who was Grand Inquisitor from 1498 to 1507.

British crossword puzzle composers (or setters, as they're called there) regularly use pseudonyms. Among the well-known ones are Apex, meaning "to copy, or ape, *X* [that is, Ximenes]" and Virgilius, the name of an eighth-century Irish monk with a penchant for composing acrostics. In the early days of puzzling in the United States, fanciful pen names such as Gregorian, Persephone, and Neophyte appeared frequently, but the use of *noms de puzzle* has gone out of fashion here. A current puzzle constructor, Mel Taub, has been accused of using a pen name, which he does not. What a lovely coincidence, however, that the name most often seen in recent years above the "Puns and Anagrams" puzzle in *The New York Times* is an anagram of the word *mutable*! Taub insists that he had not noticed the rearrangement before someone pointed it out to him.

LEWIS CARROLL

Charles L. Dodgson, better known as Lewis Carroll, composed puzzles in many forms, including short quizzes in which the answers formed an acrostic. He also wrote acrostic verses for friends and neighbors.

Carroll invented a form of puzzle he called "Doublets," involving two words of the same length. The solver's task is to get from one word to the other by changing one letter at a time, forming an intermediate chain of words. The magazine *Vanity Fair* ran a Doublets competition from March 29 to July 26, 1879. Each week's issue contained three Doublets; the competition was to find the shortest chain. The shortest Doublet in the entire competition, clued "CARESS PARENT," needed only two links, CAREST and PAREST. (Both intermediate words are now obsolete. The first is a past participle of CARESS; the second seems related to PARE.) The longest Doublet, "Put ROUGE on CHEEK," required sixteen links. You may enjoy working out this one for yourself before checking the answer at the end of this chapter. Doublets remain popular today, appearing under several names, including "Laddergrams" and "Word Ladders."

Carroll's preface to the Doublets competition included the admonition "It is, perhaps, needless to state that it is *de rigueur* that the links should be English words, such as might be used in good society." Thus, we may credit him with formulating the traditional rule that crossword writers and editors still follow—namely, that words used in puzzles should be in good taste.

THE EDITORS

MARGARET PETHERBRIDGE FARRAR

In the first *Cross Word Puzzle Book* Margaret Petherbridge called herself the "unwilling" puzzle editor of the *New York World.* The *World* had assigned Miss Petherbridge, a Smith College graduate, to select the puzzle that would appear in the Sunday paper. Her method was to pick a "good-looking" one and send it off to be set in type. When Franklin P. Adams carped, in his popular "Conning Tower" column, about typographical errors, missing definitions, and other mistakes in the puzzles, she decided to treat the puzzles more seriously.

Simon and Schuster's success firmly established Margaret Farrar as America's preeminent puzzle editor. *The New York Times* hired her when it began offering a puzzle feature in 1942. After Farrar retired from the *Times* in 1969, she edited collections of new puzzles for Simon and Schuster and for Pocket Books, and kept an eye on reprints of *Times* puzzles. She died in 1984.

Farrar held one rule inviolable throughout her long career: The solver must enjoy working the puzzle. To this end, she honored Carroll's counsel, banning anything that might be considered in poor taste. She once demanded revision of a puzzle because BLOOD TESTS appeared among several thematic answers related to weddings and marriage.

Farrar particularly remembered several crosswords. One was "YKCOWREBBAJ" by Frances Hansen. The puzzle proved, she said, that "some people managed to grow up without knowledge of *Alice in Wonderland.*" (The title of the puzzle is the word *Jabberwocky* in reverse.)

Another favorite, by Jules Arensberg and Herbert Ettenson, "FIGURES OF SPEECH" contained outrageous examples of different figures of speech and their technical names.

Puzzlemakers and editors from all over the country came to New York City in 1974 to celebrate Farrar's fiftieth anniversary as Simon and Schuster's crossword editor. To encourage continued camaraderie among the attenders, Reverend Edward J. O'Brien, an adept composer who enjoyed working amusing puns into his puzzles, later compiled and distributed "A Compendium of Cruciverbalists." That directory probably marks the first general print appearance of the word *cruciverbalist.*

Counting the people who owe thanks to Farrar for hours of entertainment is impossible. Counting the constructors she helped and encouraged is almost impossible. She truly was the Queen of Puzzledom.

WILL WENG

Will Weng, who succeeded Farrar at *The New York Times,* was born in Terre Haute, Indiana. He planned to become an educator, but his father pushed him into journalism. He graduated from the Columbia University School of Journalism having learned how to "report fires and write editorials," and joined the *Times* as a reporter.

Weng eventually became head of the city desk, in charge of editing other reporters' stories and writing headlines. In his spare time, he contributed some puzzles to the *Times* Sunday Magazine. For that reason, and because he "happened to be handy," the *Times* selected him to be puzzle editor when Farrar retired.

During his reign at the *Times* Weng brought a different style of puzzle into vogue. He had always enjoyed puns, and he accepted puzzles with them in greater numbers than they had ever been accepted before. In one of his own compositions the definition "Is your doctor influential?" led to the answer NO, BUT MY DENTIST HAS PULL.

Weng was occasionally forced to explain the puzzle gimmicks to bewildered solvers. William Lutwiniak once supplied a puzzle with the definition "AVI." The answer turned out to be THE CENTER OF GRAVITY. (Notice the letters in the middle of the word *gravity*.) The same puzzle had "EL," the BOTTOM OF THE BARREL, and "OA," the MIDDLE OF THE ROAD. The puzzle's apt title was "SPOT ANNOUNCEMENTS."

Another remarkable construction Weng published was "SQUARELY FIGURED," by A. J. Santora. This puzzle's gimmick was that solvers had to write digits in the diagram, and sometimes two or three digits in a single square—but what a puzzle! Each occurrence of digits coincided with a square that already contained those digits as a natural result of numbering the diagram. At 76 Down, for instance, the answer was 76 TROMBONES. Both digits fit in a single square. The crossing answer referred to Philadelphia's basketball team, the 76ERS.

Weng allowed other experiments, including ideas taken from rebus puzzles. He accepted Sunday puzzles in which symbols had to be drawn in the squares to substitute for letter combinations or sounds. In one puzzle, for example, the composer used the cent sign (¢) instead of the word *cent*. In another, the solver had to leave some squares completely empty to represent the word *blank*.

Weng tried to reshape the Sunday subsidiary puzzles. He eliminated the occasional cryptic puzzle that Farrar had published. He also tried to do away with the diagramless puzzles that appeared once a month, but an avalanche of letters (twelve, he said, is an avalanche) forced him to reconsider. To add spice to the Sunday puzzle page, he accepted puzzles featuring made-up "should-be words." (Sample definition: "Main boxing events." The answer, LIMINARIES, makes sense when you realize that *preliminaries* come before the main bouts.) He also permitted April Fool's Day pranks (in which, for example, horizontal answers were to be written right-to-left) and puzzles that were entirely normal except that the solvers were told not to bother entering any vowels in the diagram—no room had been left for them anyway.

Weng liberalized the format of the humorous puzzle, introducing a rectangular shape called "Puns and Twists." The 17x13 diagram allowed the puzzlemaker more opportunity for long phrases than the 15x15 "Puns and Anagrams" shape. One definition was "Sleat or drizzel or hurrycane." The answer was BAD SPELL OF WEATHER.

After retiring from the *Times* in 1977, Weng remained active in puzzling. He edited new crosswords for Times Books and shepherded collections of reprints of puzzles from his *Times* editorship. Weng also helped launch the Crosswords Club, the first of the gift subscription services, for which he edited puzzles until shortly before his death in 1993.

EUGENE T. MALESKA

Eugene Maleska became the *Times* crosswords editor when Weng retired. He was born in New Jersey and was graduated from Montclair State College. He was an English and Latin teacher, and later a New York City Assistant Superintendent of Schools.

Maleska's second career, crossword puzzling, spanned sixty years. He invented several very successful puzzle forms revolving around the use of quotations. Four of them (*Stepquote*, *Boxquote*, *Slidequote*, and *Circles-in-the-Square*) are described in the glossary. His first Stepquote puzzle received a favorable reaction from *Times* solvers, and the paper reprinted the solution two weeks after it originally appeared, with a heavy line drawn through the diagram to highlight the innovative idea.

As editor at the *Times,* he reintroduced the cryptic puzzle and continued the other humorous puzzle forms. His classical knowledge (including opera and historical facts) influenced his editorial style. Away from the *Times*, he edited collections of puzzles for Simon and Schuster, often focusing on puzzles that incorporated quotations, and wrote several books about words in general and crosswords in particular.

WILL SHORTZ

When Maleska died in 1993, Mel Taub, a longtime composer of humorous puzzles, became interim *New York Times* crosswords editor while the paper sought a permanent successor.

Will Shortz, former *GAMES* editor-in-chief, and conductor of a weekly word game feature on National Public Radio's *Weekend Edition*, was their choice.

Shortz's background in puzzles of all types is unmatched. He created a crossword puzzle at age nine, and wrote a puzzle feature for Dell Publishing Company for several years starting when he was just sixteen. At Indiana University he devised an independent program leading to a degree in enigmatology—the study of puzzles. (He also has a law degree, by the way, from the University of Virginia.) His extensive private collection of puzzle-related books, magazines, and ephemera includes many first editions and other historically important items. As the best-known American "puzzle person" in Europe, Shortz regularly attends competitions and conventions there, and was interviewed on Radio Free Europe.

A recurring theme in Shortz's puzzle activities is inviting others to share the fun. He was instrumental in reviving the National Puzzlers' League by reinstituting annual conventions in 1976, after a gap of eighteen years. He organized a group of New England enthusiasts to play word games and talk about crosswords. In response to an idea by a hotel sales manager, he organized the first modern-day crossword-solving tournament. Finally, his National Public Radio feature reaches many thousands of listeners; hundreds vie each week for a chance to go one-on-one with him on the air.

Shortz's philosophy of what makes a good crossword puzzle is easy to sum up: A good puzzle is fun to solve . . . it stresses today's world and words, relying on wordplay and brain-stretching clues rather than bits of arcane knowledge. The first Sunday puzzle under his editorship announced his approach with a flourish. It was created by Peter Gordon, and the answers included none of the puzzle repeaters or obscurities that make otherwise well-educated people say "I can't do those things." The puzzle's theme was phrases involving colors. To spice things up, the diagram provided only a single square wherever a name of a color should appear; an elegant way to solve the puzzle was with crayons of appropriate hues. When completed by this technique, the middle row contained the ROY G. BIV rainbow sequence (red, orange, yellow, green, blue, indigo, violet).

Like Maleska when he succeeded Weng (and like Weng when he succeeded Farrar before that), Shortz had to accommodate solvers' reactions to the change in style and had to adjust clues and puzzle content to achieve the difficulty level solvers wanted, consistent with his overall philosophy. Over the years, for instance, a pattern had evolved at the *Times* regarding the daily crossword, and the solvers knew and expected it: Monday's puzzle was of medium difficulty, and the puzzles got harder each day, with Saturday's being a real challenger. Shortz figured he had about got things right when some people said the Wednesday puzzle was still too easy while others said it was too difficult.

ANSWER TO PUZZLE

Put ROUGE on CHEEK (Doublet by Lewis Carroll)

ROUGE, ROUGH, SOUGH, SOUTH, SOOTH, BOOTH, BOOTS, BOATS, BRATS, BRASS, CRASS, CRESS, CREST, CHEST, CHEAT, CHEAP, CHEEP, CHEEK.

(*Sough* is a verb meaning "to make a murmuring or moaning sound, as the wind." It is in the current dictionaries.)

PART 2
SOLVING

Galileo observed, "You cannot teach a man anything; you can only help him to find it within himself." And so, the discovery procedures we present here are strategies to help you think of words you can't recall immediately and to help you arrive at words that are not in your everyday working vocabulary.

Many educators believe that people can learn a rational approach to thinking. Experiments have demonstrated that people can improve their ability to solve problems by adopting a disciplined strategy.

You may say: "Solving crossword puzzles is no big deal. Either I can think of the right word or I can't." You are probably correct in large measure. However, there are certain principles that you apply, perhaps subconsciously, when you solve a puzzle. We believe that increased awareness of these techniques on your part will accomplish two things:

1. It will make you a better solver.
2. It will start you thinking along lines that will prove helpful when you start composing puzzles. A composer who is ignorant of (or who ignores) the solver's perspective is merely exercising self-indulgence. You will do solvers the greatest service by understanding their thinking process and seeking to make your creations as rewarding for them as possible.

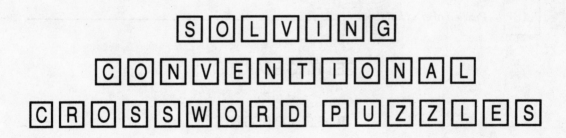

SOLVING CONVENTIONAL CROSSWORD PUZZLES

3

How long a time lies in one little word.
—Shakespeare, *King Richard II*

By "conventional crossword puzzles" we mean the ones like those printed in your daily newspaper. These puzzles differ from cryptic puzzles (the ones printed in British newspapers, for instance) in two respects:

- Except for quick puns and misleading but sanctioned senses of words, the definitions in conventional crossword puzzles are generally straightforward vocabulary tests or factual quizzes. In cryptic crosswords, though, the definitions (which we call *clues* to stress the distinction) challenge the solver in diverse ways and are not limited to the information in dictionaries or other standard reference books.
- The answers in conventional crossword puzzles interlock completely. That is, every letter is part of a word reading across and an intersecting word reading down. In contrast, cryptic crossword puzzles have some letters that appear in only one word, either across or down.*

---

* Will Rogers once remarked that the best thing crossword puzzles ever did was teach the general public the difference between "Horizontal" and "Vertical," the original designations for "Across" and "Down."

GETTING STARTED

WHERE TO BEGIN?

To anyone about to tackle a puzzle of sufficient difficulty to present a challenge, we recommend three methods for finding a starting point.

- Glance over the definitions, looking for one that involves a phrase with a missing word; such definitions use underscores or long dashes to represent the word that completes the phrase, such as "Hollywood and ___." These fill-in-the-blank definitions are usually giveaways. When you spot one you can complete, write the answer (VINE, in our example) in the diagram.
- Start at the definitions for 1 Across. Read each definition in order, quickly, and look at the place in the diagram where the corresponding answer is to be written. The first time you think of an answer of the right number of letters, stop and write that answer in the diagram. The surer you are, the more heavily you write.
- Like the previous approach, but start from the last Down definition and work backward. The last few Down answers are likely to be short words, and shorter words are easier to think of than longer ones.

You should not have to spend a great deal of time finding a place to start. If you can't find one quickly, you should suspect that you may not finish this particular puzzle.

Once you have found a starting point you should work systematically. In particular, you should not enter answers scattered all over the diagram, but should try to use answers you already have as bases for other answers. It is easier to think of a "good word" when you know one or more of the letters in that word. Furthermore, the more uncommon the letters you have filled in and the shorter the unknown crossing word, the fewer the options for that unknown word and, therefore, the more likely you are to figure it out.

TESTING A HYPOTHESIS

Every answer you write in the diagram is, in some sense, a hypothesis that subsequent answers will test and either verify or call into question. There are two ways of testing.

The obvious test involves filling in one or more of the intersecting answers. The more intersecting words you can fill in, the surer you can be that your original guess was correct.

If you are unable to complete any of the crossing answers, your first try may have been wrong and you may have to come up with another one.

A related test involves partially completed words. Suppose that the letter at the point of intersection is *s* and it is the last letter of a crossing word (as in Figure 3.1 at 3 Down). Is it reasonable from the definition to suppose that the crossing word ends in *s*, perhaps because it is a plural noun or a verb in the third person singular?

You can make similar guesses and draw conclusions for the letters *ing* at the end of a participle or gerund, and for *d* at the end of a verb in the past tense. You should use partially completed words to question newly proposed answers. Some letter combinations are improbable in English: *mk*, for example, or *q* not followed by *u*. On the other hand, if a new answer puts vowels next to consonants, and vice versa, in crossing words, that's a pretty good sign.

Applying these tests will help your solving efforts a great deal.

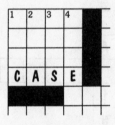

Figure 3.1. *Verifying one word by reasoning about a crossing word*

RUNNING THE GAMUT

A most effective way of recalling a word you already know, given a few letters in a diagram, is to plug each letter of the alphabet in turn into one of the gaps and attempt to pronounce the result, to see if the combination suggests anything useful. Often this "alphabet scan" triggers the memory. (But be sure you pronounce the combination correctly. AISLES rhymes with LISLES, but MISLED is not even close. And, of course, the combination OUGH is TOUGH and requires careful THOUGHT.)

When you run through the alphabet in this way, you naturally rule out some combinations that you "know" cannot be part of the language. However, you may fall into a trap because you know too much! Consider "Endeavor with extravagance," and the incomplete word S_L_ _ _ _. Suppose you decide to scan the alphabet for inspiration. SAL_ _ _ _ leads to SALLIED, which might do if *endeavor were endeavored*. You can reject SBL_ _ _ _ without stopping to think about it. SCL _ _ _ _ leads only to words like *sclerosis* that have nothing to do with the definition. None of the other plausible combinations—SEL _ _ _ _, SIL_ _ _ _, SOL _ _ _ _, SUL _ _ _ _, or SYL _ _ _ _—evokes anything useful, and you're stymied. In fact, you have fallen into a trap. You have unconsciously adopted a false hypothesis: The missing letter is a vowel. To deal fully with the situation, you must look at the crossing word.

Suppose that your dilemma involves the word at 15 Across in Figure 3.2, and that 7 Down is as shown. Common sense should lead you to refocus on the likelihood that the third letter of 7 Down is a consonant. You must reject your false notion and double-check the alphabet to find SPL _ _ _ _, which could lead to many words, one of which is the required answer, SPLURGE. Of course, if the answer were something like ST. LOUIS, even pronouncing each combination would not be helpful.

Figure 3.2. *Using information about one word to direct thinking about another word*

REJECTING A HYPOTHESIS

The most difficult thing to do when solving a crossword puzzle is to put irrevocably out of your mind a word that is of the right length but is definitely wrong because it provides no help with crossing answers or leads to implausible intersections. Be resolute: If you think a word is wrong, erase it from your memory or paper. Otherwise, you will only waste your time and frustrate yourself.

USING ALL THE INFORMATION

SUBTLETIES IN DEFINITIONS

Definitions have come a long way over the years. Composers have developed ways of giving you information yet concealing it from you in some way. With practice you can learn to recognize the disguises.

- *Definition by Model.* If a definition contains an abbreviated word, chances are the answer is also an abbreviation, especially if it is a short word. Given the definition "Spring mo." (in which *month* is shortened to "mo."), you should favor APR (for April) over MAY. Similarly, "NCO" (for "noncommissioned officer") usually leads to the answer SGT (*sergeant*) or CPL (*corporal*).
- *Definition by Class.* A definition by class consists of a word or two representing a category of things, such as "Tree." Your task as solver is to think of an item in that category, say OAK or MAPLE.
- *Definition by Example.* This type of definition is similar to definition by class except that the roles are reversed. In other words, the definition "Oak or maple" should lead you to TREE. "Mark or Thomas" is a definition by example for SAINT.
- *Implied Fill-in-the-Blank.* Ordinary fill-in-the-blank definitions (like "Little ___ Annie") are usually giveaways. Puzzlemakers often try to conceal such common phrases. For instance, instead of handing you "Little ___ Annie," the composer may write "Annie, for one." "Word with pone" is another way of saying "___ pone," for which the answer is CORN.

   Though this form is now losing favor among some editors, you may see the questioning variation "Sort of pone?" (still CORN) and, if the composer and editor are conspiring in a bit of wordplay, "Type of ship?" may turn out to be FRIEND.

   Another form of the same disguise involves two seemingly unrelated words separated by the word *or*, as in "Word before bag or cuff." This may be the same as "___ bag or ___ cuff," which is not a well-formed definition since it shows two missing words. (The answer is HAND.) If the conjunction is *and* instead of *or*, the answer is plural.

   When the sought word follows the presented word, the definition ordinarily reads something like "Corn chaser, for one." If you mentally substitute "Corn ___," you'll come up with PONE.

Yet another form of the same disguise involves two words that ordinarily go together with the word *and* between them, as in "cap and gown." The constructor may prepare a definition such as "Gown's partner." When you spot a definition like this one, you must try both possibilities, here "___ and gown" and "Gown and ___" to come up with the intended answer (CAP).

Proper names lend themselves to this disguise because so many names can stand alone as words. "Wood" can be part of a definition for actor PEGGY, and "Carpenter" can be part of the definition for pop singer KAREN. In other words, be on your toes.

- *Ambiguous Words.* A clever constructor will take advantage of ambiguous words in definitions. "Put" may be present or past tense. "Close" may lead to SHUT or NEAR. "Craft" may indicate one ship or a whole fleet.

- *Combinations.* Definitions may combine several techniques. Consider "Jeanne d'Arc, et al." The name is French, not English, which could indicate use of definition by model. The phrase "et al." implies a definition by example was used. Furthermore, "et al.," being itself an abbreviation, implies the answer is an abbreviation. If you put all of this information together, you'll conclude that the definition really is a shorthand way of writing "the abbreviation for the word meaning 'female saints' in French." The answer is STES.

WHAT'S IN A NAME?

The New York Times Sunday Magazine puzzle, the *Washington Post* Sunday puzzle, a few syndicated puzzles, and crosswords in many newsstand magazines and book collections have titles. Unless the title is something like "WORDS, WORDS, WORDS," it provides extra information for you. In "NATIONAL LEAGUE," for instance, each thematic answer included the name of a country. A puzzle called "WIRE SERVICE" dealt with electricity.

IMPASSES

HOPSCOTCH

Sometimes you reach a point where, because of a cluster of long words or some obscure crossings, you can't seem to continue building on your growing set of letters. If that should be the case, you need to find another starting place. The ideal place to look is alongside of, or very near to, the area of the diagram that has stumped you. Existing letters frequently suggest that certain letters of nearby words are vowels or consonants. Often the addition of one more word is an icebreaker.

Of course, you may choose to find any other starting place and begin over again. Eventually the separate sections of answers will approach one another and merge.

HALFTIME

Another perfectly acceptable way to deal with an apparent impasse is to take a break. Do something else for a while (but preferably not another puzzle, or any other intellectual activity), then return. A break will frequently refresh your ability to concentrate.

LOOK IT UP

Some people think it isn't enough for puzzles to amuse, they must also educate. If you can't come up with an answer because you don't understand the definition, or if you need to find an obscure geographical name, educate yourself through the use of a reference book. After all, how do you think the constructor did it? Of course, if you overdo the use of dictionaries and atlases you can take some of the pride out of solving puzzles, but we see nothing objectionable in occasional consultation.

When a definition has you stumped, the most obvious way to use the dictionary is to look up that definition. That gives you the best chance to remember a word that just won't come to mind. Don't skim through the dictionary looking for words that "just might fill the bill." And, anyway, you *can't* find a word meaning "absquatulate" by thumbing through Webster's for all possible three-letter words that begin HI_. If you look up *absquatulate*, though, you'll (be amused to) learn that it means "to move off hastily; to depart quickly and secretively," to HIE. You'll also learn that the word has a bogus Latin etymology along the lines of "go off and squat someplace else." (It doesn't come up often in ordinary conversation, but what the heck. . . .)

Using an atlas can be educational and entertaining. While you peruse a map to find that "Austrian river," you might learn a bit about the geography of Austria, and your mind might wander, however briefly, to Alps, ornate architecture, and Viennese waltzes.

Crossword puzzle dictionaries are also useful. They contain lists of definitions with possible answers. You might find five Austrian rivers to choose from, arranged in alphabetical order or in order by number of letters and alphabetically within lengths. If your primary concern is to finish the puzzle, a crossword puzzle dictionary is by far the easiest way to find obscure words.

TRIVIA

As you solve more and more puzzles, you will gradually acquire a store of *crosswordese*, words that exist, so it seems, for the sole purpose of allowing crossword puzzle constructors to finish. After a while, such words might as well be part of your everyday vocabulary because you recall them so automatically. (Fortunately, as crossword puzzles continue to evolve, those words are disappearing in favor of words you might actually use from time to time in normal conversation.)

THERE MUST BE A CATCH TO IT!

Sometimes you have to reject a likely answer because the diagram simply won't accommodate it properly; there are too few or too many squares. When this happens and you're stuck on a long, apparently thematic answer, you may have encountered a puzzle with a gimmick (particularly if you're working on a puzzle in *The New York Times* or in a book collection). There are two gimmicks in common use today:

- *Substitutions.* One word in the "natural" answer has been replaced by another word, where the switched words have some connection. In a puzzle titled "MALE-FACTORS," masculine nouns replaced feminine ones—producing answers such as MISTER O'LEARY'S BULL. In "INFLATION," the thematic answers involved numbers . . . inflated, as in SIX AND ELEVEN CENT STORE.

- *Rebuses.* A word or group of letters in the "natural" answer has been replaced by a shape or drawing. In a puzzle called "WINNING A GOLD ONE," the letters *star* were to be squeezed into a single square and represented by a drawn star, even in answers such as NO ★CH IN MY COLLAR PLEASE. One of the funniest puzzles of this type featured SECURITY BLANKET and similar answers. The solver had to represent the word *blank* by leaving an empty square in the diagram!

Once you suspect that you are dealing with a puzzle with a gimmick, you have to gather your wits. The composer of the puzzle is trying to rattle you. Think about the title of the puzzle: What relationship might it have to the gimmick? What about the timing of the puzzle? Newspapers like *The New York Times* and the Sunday *Washington Post* commemorate many events and holidays throughout the year with apt thematic puzzles. Do your hypothetical answers seem proper for some occasion or national holiday? Is there some part of the answer that lends itself to a rebus or substitution? A title such as "BY THE NUMBERS" should 4WARN you.

A good gimmicky puzzle contains short answers as well as long ones using the trick, so keep alert—and enjoy yourself. Solving crossword puzzles that feature a gimmick is especially satisfying.

THE ULTIMATE IMPASSE

If you're down to the last couple of empty squares and you have exhausted all the guidelines in this chapter (and yourself in the process), you can take the extreme step thought up by someone we know to finish the puzzle: Decide which letters would look *pretty* in the empty squares. Under no circumstances refer to the definitions again. Write a letter *j* here and an *r* there, then put down your pencil and say "Another job well done."

GAMES EXPERTS PLAY

No discussion of the process and techniques for solving crossword puzzles would be complete without some mention of the restrictions experts place on themselves. (Actually, an expert puzzle solver is merely anyone who is working on too easy a puzzle.)

- Use pen, not pencil. There's no room for error. You can impress people around you with this stunt. (We have heard of two ways of cheating, believe it or not. One person simply wrote random letters in the diagram and was careful to crumple and discard the puzzle before anyone else on the commuter train had a chance to look too closely. Another bought the evening edition of the paper, spent hours solving the puzzle, then bought *another copy of the paper* the next morning and swiftly wrote in the correct answers for the benefit of amazed kibitzers on the subway.)

- Work only from the Down definitions. If you can't complete the whole puzzle in this fashion, try to guess the Across answers from letters in the diagram. If you have to, use the Across definitions to verify your guesses.

- Write in only the *e*'s in the answers. In this way you can work the whole puzzle and save both energy and your pencil.

- Don't use pencil *or* pen. Mentally work through the definitions until you deduce one of the thematic answers. Then say "That's obvious" and give the puzzle to someone who still feels the need to see the answers on paper.

If these games don't challenge you sufficiently, try competition. Contests for puzzle solvers offer pressure, pleasure, prizes, and the chance to meet constructors, editors, and other avid crossworders.

COMPETITION SECRETS

People who win puzzle-solving contests develop mechanical and mental techniques for writing faster without sacrificing accuracy. A simple mechanical trick is to enter the letter *e* always in lower case with a continuous stroke; it's faster than printing the capital letter. Another one is to figure out where to position your writing arm so it doesn't hide the definitions; you can learn to write a few letters without looking at them while your eyes find the next definition you want to tackle. (One contest offered pages typeset especially for left-handed entrants. The annual Stamford tournament provides left-handers two copies of each puzzle.)

Frequent winner David Rosen developed the skill of entering letters from bottom to top or right to left about as fast as he can enter them in the normal directions. It saves time as he moves his pencil to his next answer.

Another frequent winner, Douglas Hoylman, reads and memorizes several definitions so he can write three or four answers without having to change focus back and forth.

Experts develop a great sense for thematic entries. Once they catch on to a puzzle's gimmick or other theme, whether pun, rebus, or collection of related words, they seem to have a knack for solving long entries quickly, thereby making the shorter, crossing answers duck soup.

A correctly solved puzzle earns a bonus score for each full minute shaved from the announced time limit. So, instead of turning in their solutions as soon as they enter the last letter, experienced contestants use nearly all the time remaining until the next tick of the minute hand to double-check their work. In this regard, we recommend you try to sit in the center of the room so you can see the clock's sweep-second hand.

And a final thought: If you doubt you'll earn a prize for speed and accuracy, try for the handwriting award!

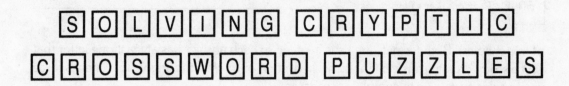

SOLVING CRYPTIC CROSSWORD PUZZLES

4

*The question is . . . whether you can make words mean
so many different things.*
—Lewis Carroll, *Through the Looking Glass*

Cryptic puzzles written for Americans appear in *GAMES*, Dell Champion publications, *Atlantic Monthly*, *Harper's*, a few book collections, and, occasionally, *The New York Times*, to the delight of an enthusiastic and growing audience.

Many of the statements made about solving conventional crossword puzzles apply equally to solving cryptic crosswords. You must be just as aware of endings and patterns of vowels and consonants, for example, and you are just as likely to benefit from guessing at single letters or letter groups, or from taking a break. In fact, the essential difference between conventional and cryptic puzzles is just the difference between a straightforward definition and a cryptic puzzle's less direct *clue*. But that difference is great.

This chapter focuses on the *square-dealing* clue, which has both a more-or-less straightforward definition of the answer and a *hint*, or bit of wordplay, leading to that same answer by another route. Both definition and hint are contained in a grammatically correct phrase or sentence. (Some venues relax the "squareness" rule, but we believe it's important to know how the strictest clues work because they have become the norm and, besides, they are more predictable.)

DIAGRAMS

Cryptic grids come in two main styles: the black-square, or lattice, diagram, and the bar diagram. Figure 4.1 shows a typical black-square diagram and a bar diagram design (smaller but similar to those often used for *variety cryptic puzzles*, which we discuss toward the end of this chapter). Both formats are usually made so each answer has at least one letter that isn't also in a crossing answer (an unchecked letter, or *unch* in the lingo). The unches force you to solve *every* clue to complete the puzzle.

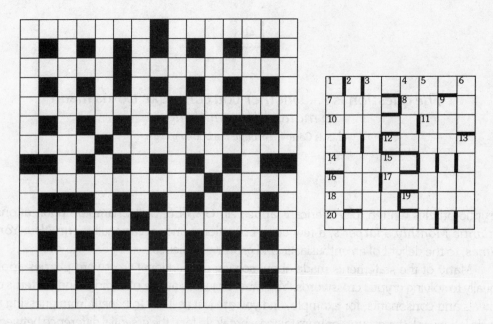

Figure 4.1. *A typical black-square puzzle diagram and a small bar diagram*

CLUES

If you're new to cryptic puzzles, you'll immediately notice two differences between definitions and clues. The first (and easier to explain) is that a clue ends with one or more numbers in parentheses, such as "(3,7)." The numerical information in parentheses indicates the length(s) of the word(s) in the answer. The clue for QUITE A SET-TO would end with "(5,1,3-2)," for example, with the hyphen of SET-TO being indicated by the hyphen in "3-2." In some variety cryptics what you must write in the grid differs from the answer because of some gimmick. In that case, what goes in the grid is properly termed a *light*. In such puzzles, instructions explain the distinction between answer and light, and tell you whether the numbers pertain to answers or to lights.

The second difference is a clue's relative wordiness. This comes about because a clue leads you to the answer in two ways. One part of the clue is a definition, as in a conventional crossword puzzle. That is, IVY might be defined by "Wall climber" or "It climbs walls" or "Plant," for example. But there's more to it than that.

TWO MEANINGS

Paradoxically, the shortest clues usually give you twice as much ordinary information. That is, there may be two conventional definitions. "Personal enlistee (7)" contains two definitions of PRIVATE, for instance.

Where's the challenge, you ask? There's considerable challenge when a definition is figurative, uncommon, or alludes to something the clue writer wrongly assumes you know, or when the clue's language mimics one of the other kinds of cryptic clues. An experienced solver of these puzzles may be temporarily fooled by "Brace for a terrible age (3)" because the word *terrible* often means that there's an anagram lurking about (more soon on what we mean by that). The answer, though, is TWO, and the second definition refers to "the terrible twos," that period when toddlers are often difficult to manage.

On seeing "Gift mailed in advance (7)," you may readily think of PRESENT as a "gift" but not mentally consider it as PRE-SENT.

Try this one: "Feel sorrow for crawling like a snake (6)." (Look up REPENT.) Here's a quick one by Canadian puzzlemaker Rosalie Moscovitch: "Fat goat? (6)" (A goat may sometimes be a BUTTER.) And here's a short one by Frank Lewis of *The Nation*: "Animal attack? (4)." (To attack is "to go at," hence, GOAT.)

Many conventional crossword puzzles feature near-miss homophones for their themes, but puns rarely constitute answers in cryptic puzzles. Their use in cryptic clues is rare, also, because clue writers often find enough to do just by tinkering with the letters. Still, consider: "Estate reduction caused by the high cost of leaving? (11,3)" (The answer is INHERITANCE TAX. The last five words are supposed to make you think of "the high cost of living.")

Here's a final double-definition clue: "Use will power as one way to get one's wind? (7)" (The answer is INHERIT. The first three words play on *willpower* as one definition. The rest of the clue refers to the classic play and film *Inherit the Wind*.)

HINTS

If a clue has only one definition, what's the rest of it? Some form of wordplay instead—a hint, if you will, to the answer. In square-dealing clues containing a hint and a definition:

- Punctuation and capitalization may be used deceptively.
- The most natural sense of the clue as you are likely to read it almost certainly has nothing to do with the answer, but there is a grammatical interpretation of the words that undeniably produces the intended answer.
- Either the definition or the hint may come first, but they do not overlap (with a single exception that we'll discuss later).
- Many hints need *signals* describing the type of wordplay. "Step off rumpled cape (4)" contains the signal "rumpled" to indicate an anagram. In this case, "step off" is the definition, "rumpled [that is, rearranged] cape" is the hint, and the answer is PACE.
- There may be, in addition to the signal and the wordplay, a *linking word* that plays no real role in the clue except to tie the hint to the definition. In a sense, a cryptic clue is like an equation, matching hint to definition, and you may view the linking word as the equals sign.

The hint's wordplay may involve

- The whole answer at once—as with PACE, above.
- The answer's parts taken in order, at either a natural or a surprising break point. A clue writer might see FORESTALL as FORE + STALL or as FOREST + ALL, for example.
- The answer's parts taken out of order. A clue writer might look at FORESTALL and see *ores* and the letter *t* inside *fall*.

In the rest of this chapter we use small capital letters for the straight definition and show the signal in italics. For example: "STEP OFF *rumpled* cape (4)."

KINDS OF WORDPLAY AND SIGNALS

Composers of cryptic puzzles use different classification schemes to describe the various kinds of hints, and there are probably enough different signals to make a book by themselves. Our classification includes hidden words, anagrams, reversals, charades, containers, homophones, homographs, additions and deletions and changes, abbreviations and selections, and "and literally so."

HIDDEN WORDS

Hidden-word clues are perhaps the easiest of the wordplay clues to solve, because the answer's letters are right there in front of you, in correct order, without interruption. For example: "MALE *among* Comanches (3)." You see the answer, MAN, inside "Comanches," of course.

Most clues of this sort do a little better at hiding the answer by splitting it across two or more words, and clever surface reading may distract you for a time, but the letters are right there, and all you need to do is copy them to the grid. A slightly sneakier way of hiding MAN in plain sight is: "FELLOW mama needs, *essentially* (3)."

Signals for hidden-word clues include words and phrases implying containership, display, or carrying: *in*, *contains*, *spanning*, *some*, *part of*, *within*, *shows*.

Consider: "Limo chauffeur *carries* COFFEE (5)." (MOCHA spans the first two words of the clue.)

ANAGRAMS

An anagram is a simple transposition of letters that appear together in the clue as one or more whole words. Our clue for PACE, above, typified the anagram clue.

Any word or phrase implying rearrangement, falling, destruction, newness, intricacy, sickness, being out of control, and so on could be the signal for an anagram. Here are a few: *bad(ly)*, *poor(ly)*, *broken*, *ravished*, *damaged*, *ill*, *exercised*, *sick(ly)*, *awkward(ly)*, *clumsy*, *destroyed*, *wild(ly)*, *confused*, *edited*, *possibly*, *perhaps*, *changing*, *new*, *off*, *snarled*, *Byzantine*, *wrong(ly)*, *upset*, *reformed*, *doctored*.

Try this one: "*Butcher* takes BEEF FOR DINNER (5)." (*Butcher* doesn't mean "a meat seller" here; it's a direct order telling you to scramble the word *takes* to get STEAK.) And here's one by Mel Taub: "NOT MOVING ABOUT in *rickety* attics (6)" (Scramble *attics* to get the answer STATIC.)

REVERSALS

Offhand, a reversal seems to be a particular kind of anagram—namely, one running the letters backward. An important difference, however, is this: The letters that participate in an anagram appear literally in the clue, while a synonym may substitute for the letters in a reversal. Indeed, *except for hidden-word clues and anagrams*, any hint may include synonyms for one or more parts.

Here's an example of a reversal clue: "BEST place *seen from the other side* (4)." (A synonym for *place* is *spot*. Seen from the other side—reversed—it spells TOPS.) And look at this smooth one by Emily Cox and Henry Rathvon: "HOT singer *makes a comeback* (4)." (A *diva* is a kind of singer. Making a comeback—reversed, again—it spells AVID [hot].)

Any word or phrase implying reversal may serve as a signal: *turnabout, setback, returning, going the opposite way,* and so on. And clue writers often use signals matching the answer's horizontal or vertical direction in the grid: *up, left, going north, westward.*

Consider this one, for an Across answer: "Sailboat *heading west* to SMALL BODIES OF WATER (5)." (One kind of sailboat is a *sloop.* Spelling it backward produces POOLS. And notice that this clue contains a linking word: *to.*) Here's a clue for a Down answer: "A fanatic *goes up* for FISH (4)." (Reversing "a nut" produces TUNA.)

CHARADES

Hints that build up answers one piece at a time in order are called *charades,* just like the parlor game.[*] For example: "Mother *and* children become STONEWORKERS (6)" leads to the answer MASONS (MA + SONS). This example uses synonyms for both parts of the charade, and *become* is another linking word.

Consider this one, which is more complicated than the other examples we've shown you so far, even though it's only four words: "STOP, stop! Ahead, *ahead!* (9)." (A synonym of *stop* with a synonym of *ahead* ahead of it is FORE + STALL.)

Charade signals include words and phrases implying adjacency: *and, gets, at, by, to, follows, leads,* and *goes before.* Then again, a charade clue may simply present answer pieces side by side with no signal at all. Here's one by another Canadian, Fraser Simpson: "Gold sun god's HALOS (5)" (Au [gold's chemical symbol] + Ra's = AURAS.)

Charade clues need not build the answer along normal word boundaries. One could argue that the more successful charade clues—or, at any rate, the more amusing ones—do just the opposite, in fact. Try this Henry Hook clue: "MEET lame horse (4,4)." (A synonym for *lame* is *bum.* One kind of horse is a *pinto.* Put those words side by side and you get the answer BUMP INTO.)

CONTAINERS

Containers are like charades, except that the pieces don't lie side by side. Rather, one is inside another. For example: "Ben *eats*—way to BECOME FULLER (7)." (One *way* is *road.* Hence, B-ROAD-EN.)

---

[*] Margaret Farrar once failed to notice that MAKE A GO OF could also be read as MAKE A GOOF, and a conventional crossword puzzle with that intended answer defined by "Succeed" earned a fair amount of correspondence from solvers who saw it only the other way.

Container clues may describe the relationship from the outside in or from the inside out. Signals include words pertaining to swallowing, holding, residency, entry, and taking.

Try this one by David Ellis Dickerson: "Excommunication *has* to STICK (5)" (A word meaning *excommunication* containing the letters *to* is BA-TO-N, which is a stick.)

HOMOPHONES

Homophones (also called *puns*) are words that sound exactly like other words, regardless of spelling. For example: "STORY's end *read aloud* (4)." (A synonym for *end* is *tail*, which sounds like TALE.)

Homophone signals include anything pertaining to listening or speaking: *hear, say, sounds like,* and so on.

Try this: "CHAIR tossed *to the audience* (6)." (A synonym for *tossed* is *thrown*, which sounds—"to the audience"—like THRONE.)

HOMOGRAPHS

Homographs are words or phrases in clues that are spelled like other words or phrases, regardless of pronunciation or meaning. (The term *heteronym* identifies a homographic pair whose pronunciations and derivations both differ.) For instance: "LIGHT, wicked thing (6)." (This is really a double definition for the answer CANDLE. What makes it tricky is the word *wicked,* here meaning "having a wick," not "evil.")

Purely homographic clues usually lack recognizable signals because they offer double definitions. Considerate clue writers will often supply a question mark to indicate the presence of some sort of pun, though, and you should be alert for words that have two or more meanings from different origins: *flower* ("river"), *number* ("less sensitive"), and so on. The parenthetical number after the clue may not be applicable to both readings because one may involve a phrase.

This one incorporates a different visual trick: "WASHINGTON POST (7,7)." (*Post* means *mail,* the whole clue is in uppercase, and Washington is the capital—so the answer must be CAPITAL LETTERS.) A minimalist clue for the same answer is: "D.C. (7,7)."

ADDITIONS, DELETIONS, AND CHANGES

Some words are "nearly" other words except for a letter here or there. Clues relying on additions, deletions, and changes play on the similarity. For example: "JUDGE babbles *endlessly* (6)." (If you drop both ends from *prates,* you get RATE, a synonym for *judge.*)

Signals for additions and deletions include these appropriate words and phrases: *decapitate, cut short, curtail, endless(ly), interminably, after the beginning, minus, plus,* and the like, as well as many of those used in container clues.

Try this Ed Galli clue: "IT'S TERRIBLE but legal *when losing head* (5)." (Dropping the first letter of *lawful* [legal] leaves the answer AWFUL. Note that this clue uses a short sentence as a definition. In other words, "It's terrible" could be a straight crossword clue for AWFUL.)

Here's another: "*Refinished* ugly DEN (7)." (Changing the last letter of *hideous* [ugly] from *s* to *t* produces HIDEOUT.)

When more than one letter participates in an addition clue it's essentially a container or charade clue. More than one letter may also participate in a deletion clue, producing something like: "Reverie's *about gone*, leaving BLOCKAGES (4)." (The answer is DREAMS, *about* being a synonym for the RE.) Try this one: "PAD *that would make Ron a woman* (3)." (This is an implied charade, of sorts. The answer is MAT, which, when *ron* is added, makes *matron*.)

ABBREVIATIONS AND SELECTIONS

Even the specification of one or two letters may involve trickery. The simplest uses abbreviations. "Short time" may be the letter *t*, for example—but clues in difficult puzzles may not have an abbreviation indicator.

More common (and more interesting) is a cryptic approach, which we call *selection*: "Endless joy" is JO, and "boundless joy" is just O. "Head of state" is S, and "The heart of Texas" is X. "Beethoven's fifth" is H, and "A bit of trouble" is T. "Dimethyl 2-6-4" is IHE (the second, sixth, and fourth letters).

Try this one: "COMMUNIST LEADER in meadow, *oddly* (3)." (The odd letters of *meadow* spell MAO.)

Abbreviations (signaled by *little* or *small*) and other short forms (such as Roman numerals, compass points, and articles in foreign languages) appear frequently, especially in charades. Consider: "CURRENT EVENTS from all points (4)." ("All points" here refers to the compass. Arranged properly, the main compass points' letters spell the answer NEWS.)

AND LITERALLY SO (& LIT)

We said there is an exception to the rule about definitions and hints not overlapping. Here it is. The *and literally so* clue (so termed by Ximenes, abbreviated "& lit" and pronounced "and lit") exhibits the phenomenon that both the definition and the hint occupy the whole thing. In other words, if you read the clue one way, you get the definition; if you read it in another sense, you get the hint. Some people call this clue type *read it again*.

Here's an & lit by Azed: "These adorn many Scotsmen's heads! (4)." (The whole clue is a definition for the answer TAMS. Now read it again, interpreting *heads* as meaning "initial letters," and you'll see **T**hese **a**dorn **m**any **S**cotsmen's heads—TAMS, again.)

Here's another by Azed: "What's tea passed around in? (5)." (You will probably think of CHINA the first time you read this clue, and that's the straightforward answer. Now read it again as a container clue in which you need a specific kind of tea, namely *cha*, and you have *cha* "passed around" *in*, that is, CH-IN-A.)

Many editors provide an exclamation point to show you there's something remarkable afoot. The answer hidden in Will Shortz's "Insane Roman at heart! (4)" is NERO.

Consider this: "Beverage served up in late afternoon! (3)" (On the one hand, TEA is the stereotypical late-afternoon beverage. On the other, it's a beverage hidden in—that is, "served up in"—laTE Afternoon.)

SOLVING CLUES

Remember: The surface sense of a clue probably has little to do with the final answer. Conversely (except for & lit clues), it has at one end a proper definition of the answer, correct as to part of speech, number, tense, etc., and forms a phrase, clause, or sentence with grammatically precise instructions. For example, if a clue uses "I" as the letter *i*, it is not followed by "am." (The instruction "the letter 'I' am . . ." is ungrammatical.) "I will be," on the other hand, is grammatically sound whether "I" is the pronoun or the letter. On the other hand, a pronoun with no antecedent might refer to the answer (first or third person, I or it), the solver (second person, you), or the composer (first person). A number in a clue often refers to the answer at the corresponding number in the puzzle. (The long clue in the footnote on page 8 uses personal pronouns. See Figure 4.3 for a number in a clue.)

To decipher a clue, look first for a word or group of words at the beginning or end of the clue that might be a dictionary definition. Then try to find a signal in the remainder to find out what type of wordplay is involved. A signal like *in* is ambiguous, so be prepared to give up a line of attack that seems fruitless. If there is no signal at all, think in terms of multiple definitions (especially for short clues) or charades.

If you have trouble finding the words used in the wordplay, they may be only defined in the clue rather than provided directly. It is then time to return to what you think is the definition. Try to think of words of the proper length that fit the definition. You may find unobvious meanings for the words in the definitions, such as "that which flows, a river" for *flower*, "more numb" for *number*, or even "one who sews" for *sewer*.

SAMPLE PUZZLE

Figure 4.2 presents a sample puzzle with eight clues. One offers two conventional definitions, one is an & lit, and each of the others uses a different kind of hint. Following the sample is an analysis of the mental process you might go through to solve it.

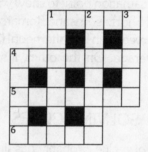

ACROSS

1. Thus taking prosecutor to front of saloon for drinks (5)
4. Indict a terrorist concealing order (7)
5. Lithographer who wants to gain favor? (7)
6. Stores having quite a lot, we hear (5)

DOWN

1. Rescued, in a way! (7)
2. Little darlings' attention is absorbed by molds (7)
3. Some air loses Oxygen and I spread (5)
4. Tied up with transfer (5)

Figure 4.2. *Small cryptic exercise*

ANALYSIS OF SAMPLE CRYPTIC'S SOLUTION

We'll probably have better luck starting with the five-letter words. They're shorter and easier to think of. So, let's examine 1 Across, 6 Across, 3 Down, and 4 Down first.

We'll start with 1 Across just because we come to it first. Look for a definition at the beginning or end. "Thus" doesn't look like the definition of a five-letter word or even the start of such a definition, so we'll try the other end. "Drinks" looks more promising; for example, COLAS or BEERS could be answers. Let's work on the wordplay, which is all the rest of the clue. There are a lot of words here, especially for a five-letter answer. From this observation, we conclude that each part of the wordplay leads to only a few letters in the answer, which probably means this clue rests on a charade. The shortest word defined by "thus" is *so*. Let's see if that leads us anywhere.

Next comes "prosecutor." That could be DA ("district attorney"). This looks promising: SODA_ for "drinks." We're almost satisfied, but we still have "front of saloon" to deal with. Okay, *s* is the letter at the front of "saloon." That does it; the answer must be SODAS. This clue's wordplay is indeed a charade, a sequential building of the answer from its component letters, in this case by two definitions and a selection of the first letter of a word.

We now have the first letters of the answers at 1, 2, and 3 Down. The latter has only five letters, so let's try 3 Down next. Can "spread" be the definition? It looks a lot better than "Some" or "Some air," so let's assume that's it. Then the rest must be the wordplay. What kind? "Loses" could signal a deletion, but of what? Well, the chemical symbol for "Oxygen" is O; "I" is explicit enough, and both letters appear in "Some air." If we remove them we're left with SMEAR, which matches "spread."

We now have a letter for each long answer. Let's try 2 Down next, just because the others start with *s* or end with *e* or *r* (all common to many words). "Little" could be a definition, but so could "Little darlings" (note that we ignore the apostrophe, because punctuation is often used for deception in the surface reading of a cryptic clue and may have no bearing on the solution). What's more, "darlings" does not look like it will be helpful in wordplay because it does not define any short word. But "attention" does: *ear*. If *ear* is in the answer, it follows somewhere after that initial *d* we already have. Um, DEAR looks good; "darling" defines it. Next comes "is absorbed by." That could signal a container; absorption resembles containment. If we're right, "molds" must define a four-letter word beginning with *d*. *Dies* works. That would give us D(EAR)IES. Why not? "Little darlings" is a satisfactory definition of *dearies*.

Now we have two letters in 4 Across and 5 Across. Many seven-letter words probably end in "_A_E"; perhaps slightly fewer in "_I_R." For that reason, try 5 Across next. "Lithographer" cannot be the definition of many words. Actually, the only lithographers we've ever heard of are Currier and Ives, the creators of those famous winter scenes, among other things. What's left? Well, "who wants to gain favor" could refer to a person who . . . what? Curries favor! Looks like a winner: CURRIER defined twice, once as a lithographer and once by a sly pun, signaled by that question mark. Good enough.

Now we have a *c* in the middle of 4 Down. "Up" in a clue for a Down word often signals a reversal. If that's so here, we need a five-letter word meaning "tied" and "(with) transfer" when reversed. *Laced* fulfills that first condition very nicely, but what about the reversal:

decal? Great! A decal is, in fact, a transfer (of an image onto a surface). DECAL it is, and *with* is just a linking word.

Now we have a good start on 6 Across. The words "we hear" on the end often signal a homophone or pun. If they do so here, the definition's up front. "Stores" will do. Too many possibilities; how about that pun? The meaning we need must be "quite a lot." *Scads*? No. How about *loads*? It sounds like *lodes*, and that means "stores." LODES must be right.

Let's try 1 Down, with three letters filled. The exclamation point could signal an & lit. The clue is short, so we need to find something simple. The first word, *rescued*, has the right number of letters, and "in a way" could signal an anagram. What can we do with S_ _ _R_D and the letters *e, c, u,* and *e*? Just plugging those in with no rearrangement gives us SECURED, which can mean "Rescued in a way." Bingo!

Only 4 Across remains, and we already have the letters D_C_A_E. The definition could be either "indict" or "order." If we look at the letters in the grid we can see that *dictate* fits, and it looks good as a word that means "order," but what does that have to do with a terrorist? Oh, we see; the letters of the answer, DICTATE, are being concealed by "inDICT A TErrorist"! Finished. Nothing to it!

ANNOTATING CRYPTIC CROSSWORD ANSWERS

This is a good time to mention that the solution pages for cryptic crosswords may not show completed grids. Instead, they will explain the clues—but with a set of abbreviations and symbols, not full sentences.

The common symbols include "2 defs." or "2" for double definitions; "hid." for hidden words; "*" or "anag." for anagrams; "+" or "char." for charades; "rev." for reversals; lower-case or struck-out letters or "dele" for deletions; parentheses or "cont." for containers; "hom." for homophones; "pun" for homographs; and "& lit."

For example, the solution to our small sample puzzle might appear as: ACROSS: 1. SO+DA+S (char.); 4. DICTATE (hid.); 5. CURRIER (2 defs.); 6. LODES (LOADS homoph.); DOWN: 1. SECURED (anag., & lit.); 2. D(EAR)IES (cont.); 3. SoMEAiR (dele.); 4. DECAL (LACED rev.)

COMPOUND WORDPLAY

If deciphering the hint were all there is to it, cryptic crosswords would be a snap. Many clues combine two or more hints, however, becoming miniature brainteasers in their own right.

You might need to scramble the letters in a short anagram, place them inside a synonym for another word, and add a letter to get the final answer. Complicated? Yes, but the other side of the coin is that you can often solve cryptic crosswords in ink, because you know when you've gotten the answer to each clue.

Here's an example of compound wordplay: "PREVENT store*'s being ransacked in* autumn (9)." (The clue tells you that "store is being ransacked"—that is, scrambled—and the result is inside [a synonym for] "autumn." In other words, F-OREST-ALL, for which "prevent" is the straight definition.) Note that the clue's surface reading uses "'s" as a possessive, but the cryptic intent uses it as the contraction for "it is."

A much harder example is: "AT ANY RATE, the *French can be found surrounding* a wit's *comedy between* two points (9)." ("Surrounding" implies a container clue, and so does "between." A comedy is something "written in a funny style," which implies an anagram. So, the whole clue describes "a wit's" anagrammed between two compass points (here, east and south, or E and S) , all surrounded by *the* in French. The whole structure is L-E-ASTWI-S-E, which means "at any rate.")

The last two examples demonstrate three uses of "'s": (1) as a possessive, (2) as the contraction for "it is," and (3) as the letter *s* in an anagram. Watch for them and similarly misleading punctuation.

And here's one by Rebecca Kornbluh and Henri Picciotto: "Notes fever, *not* a STATE OF EXHAUSTION (7)." (Two of the solmization notes are *fa* and *ti*. The fever every crossword solver knows is *ague*. Deleting that word's *a*—as instructed—and setting the three elements side by side builds the answer FATIGUE.)

SUMMARY OF CRYPTIC CLUING

Every clue in a square-dealing cryptic crossword leads to its answer in two ways. Except in variety forms of cryptic crosswords, that answer is also what you write in the puzzle's grid. The clue may express a direct order to you as written by the constructor, or self-description as though the answer were speaking for itself.

One way the clue leads to the answer is a definition, like any that might appear in a conventional crossword puzzle. That definition begins at the clue's beginning or ends at its end (except in & lit clues, when it occupies the entire clue).

The second way a clue leads to its answer is either another definition occupying the rest of the clue or some form of wordplay, which also occupies the rest of the clue (except in & lit clues, when, like the definition, it constitutes the entire clue).

Clue writers have many methods of wordplay at their disposal. Harder clues often incorporate two or more types of wordplay.

If the answer's letters aren't "hidden in plain sight" you'll have to manipulate strings of letters, often relying on signals to recognize the nature of the manipulation. If strings go together side by side that's called a *charade*; it's a *container* if some letters surround others. Subtracting one or more letters from a set that contains the answer is a *deletion*, and it may involve leading, interior, or trailing letters. The deletion of leading letters is a *beheadment*, of trailing letters a *curtailment*.

You might need to put a string of letters in back-to-front order (*reversal*) or more thoroughly rearrange them (*anagram*) to form the answer.

Except for hidden words and anagrams, the strings of letters you use to build the answer might not appear directly in the clue. Instead, the letters may be defined or collected by *selection* from words in the clue.

SOLVING ADVICE

Don't spend more than about half a minute with each clue the first time you try. If you are ever going to solve the puzzle, at least one or two of its clues will yield fairly quickly.

As with conventional crosswords, the answers you obtain will help you discover the crossing ones. The more letters you know in an answer, and the fewer you lack, the longer you should persist in trying to solve that clue.

Be particularly alert for a signal indicating an anagram. The answer's length will almost always help you figure out quickly what letters are in the anagram (unless the anagram is merely part of a charade).

Be particularly suspicious of odd words, numbers, and proper nouns. Why would a composer use *umbra* instead of *shadow*? Probably as part of an anagram. Convert numbers to Roman numerals or spelled-out words (VI or SIX for 6). Be aware, however, that a number may also refer to a corresponding clue elsewhere in the puzzle. When you think you've assembled all of the anagram's letters, write them down or use tiles or cubes from a word game. Look among the letters for common particles—prefixes, suffixes, or roots—and separate these. Look among the ones remaining for additional letter groups until you form whole words, presumably including the right one.

Guess at long phrase answers from the enumeration. A three-letter word may be *and*, *for*, or *the*. Short initial words are often prepositions like *in*, *to*, *of*, or *by*.

If you don't appear to be getting anywhere, work on the longest unsolved clues. The weight of many words makes misdirection harder.

As you complete more of the puzzle, start doing some wild guessing based on the letters you have. The clues may be of no help, but if the answer is something like "_N_Q_ _," the answer may well be unique. (Get it? uNiQue.) Even if you can narrow the choice only to a dozen words, the list may shrink to one abruptly as you match the words against the clue.

Another fruitful avenue of attack when about half of the puzzle is solved, especially after a break, is to have another crack at the clues for the longest answers. These are susceptible to sudden inspiration. Putting letter groups or short words together might just work and give you quite a leg up on the rest of the puzzle.

GADGETS AND BOOKS

As last resorts, use solving aids, including electronic gadgets and books. For example, several companies make small, hand-held electronic gadgets meant as spell-checking tools. Most of these gadgets offer anagrams and partial-word searches, which makes them useful as crossword-solving aids. If you have a computer, resources include your word processor's spell-checker and electronic dictionaries.

Several publishers once offered books containing lists of words organized in various ways. These books are now out of print or unobtainable in the United States, but if you stumble across one you may want to consider it.

Funk and Wagnalls Crossword Word Finder (Schwartz and Landovitz) and *Cassell's Crossword Finisher* (Griffiths, published in England) listed words by pairs of nonconsecutive letters. *The Anagram Dictionary* (by Edwards) listed words by length according to the alphabetic order of their letters as an anagram solver. (For example, the listing of six-letter words included the entry EILNST with subentries ENLIST, LISTEN, SILENT, and TINSEL.)

W & R Chambers Ltd., publishers of *Chambers 20th Century Dictionary*, a popular British reference book for crossword composers and solvers, applied computer technology to produce several books: *Chambers Words* was a raw listing arranged alphabetically in sections divided by length; *Chambers Back Words* listed the words in the same way, except that alphabetizing was done from the back of the words; *Chambers Anagrams* was similar to *The Anagram Dictionary*; *Chambers Crossword Completer* listed words alphabetized according to every other letter, once using the odd letters and again using the even letters. All the Chambers books, we should note, excluded simple plurals, past tenses, and gerunds, so even if you should be fortunate enough to acquire one you'll need to use your wits even as you browse.

Let your conscience be your guide.

A FULL CRYPTIC EXERCISE

Now that you've had the course, so to speak, Figure 4.3 is a full-fledged 15x15 cryptic to try. Every clue is square-dealing, using one or more of the notions discussed in this chapter.

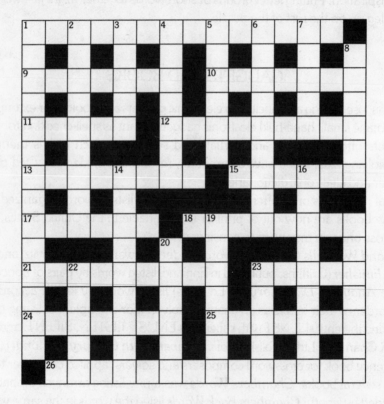

Figure 4.3. *A cryptic challenge*

ACROSS

1. Paid player spilled nog. It's back to bad actor, a seer (14)
9. English church reader is choosy one (7)
10. Home with small bed and broken gate (7)
11. Spot of tea and hasty wreak (5)
12. One for support on slack net (9)
13. Endlessly put off Conservative before Kennedy went over to the other side (8)
15. How Arabs greet orally before I will bring meat (6)
17. Taking all I could, exposing French (6)
18. Loose chord near Peg Giovanni's housing (8)
21. South African region may be seen across flowing lava . . . (9)
23. . . . but an agitated African tribesman is there (5)
24. Reduced red tape? Just the opposite! (7)
25. Morsels I'd bit into took strong beginnings (7)
26. Short Marylanders, I, and, say, 5 natives become dancers (14)

DOWN

1. Make magic before putting one finger in state (14)
2. It sounds like it's more than impressive . . . too bad! (9)
3. Pass score (5)
4. Spruce chopped around line using restraint (7)
5. Chosen port in pinch, once (6)
6. Spanish article caught in a disco light at the Star Clock (9)
7. Speak up with zero speed? (5)
8. No dummies, they, excitedly delivering silver to quints (14)
14. Two half-inch parts—parts flipped in helmet fastener (9)
16. Southern country with antique silver in center of clasp (9)
19. Close gate again after prosecutor leaves cathedral in a dither (7)
20. Leader of Gujarat and leader of Hyderabad—I! (6)
22. Enough maple cut up (5)
23. One waiting for bemused bride (5)

VARIETY PUZZLES

As if the little mysteries posed by cryptic clues weren't enough by themselves, composers of these orthographic exercises constantly seek new ways to challenge you. The challenges may involve clues, answers, the diagram, or all three. The good news is, you never have to deduce the nature of a gimmick because variety puzzles always have instructions.

NONSTANDARD CLUES

Some cryptic puzzles have clues of the types discussed above. Some have more difficult and less standardized clues; others have clues that lead to answers in somewhat different ways. Here are two types of nonstandard clues:

- Printer's devilry: In fact, the clues in printer's devilry puzzles are nothing like those clues we've described so far in this chapter. Instead, each answer was originally a hidden word in a reasonably logical sentence. It was deleted from its place of concealment and the remaining material was closed up (and, probably, respaced) to form new words without any rearrangement of the letters. The resulting sentence usually makes less sense than before, and the answer word probably has little in common with the context of either the original or altered sentence.

  An example is: "I'm too heavy for thesis cover, as it gives way (5)." The answer, TEPID, belongs after the first *s* in *thesis*, yielding the original sentence "I'm too heavy for the step, I discover, as it gives way." ("Andreas" and "Atlantic," in *The Enigma* #1087, October 1994, p. 17.)

  In dealing with printer's devilry, look for incongruous words or proper nouns to find where to split the clue or where words in the original sentence were respaced. When you've found the most likely place from which the answer word was removed, try to imagine what letters could go on either side of the break to form sensible words in context. And think hard.

- Misprints: A single substitution of one letter for another is made in a word in the definition part of each clue. An example is: "The beginning of another free day (4)." The answer is ARID, built up by A ("the beginning of another") + RID ("free"). "Day" is a misprint for "dry." (Apex, *Games and Puzzles* 44, January 1976, p. 39.)

  To cope with misprints, look near one end of each clue (that's where you find definitions) for a word spelled with fairly common letters; it is the one most likely to be transformed into another valid word by a single substitution.

NONSTANDARD ANSWERS

You may have to modify an answer before you write it into the diagram. The tinkering is called a *transformation*, and many cryptic puzzle fans and composers use the term *light* to refer to the diagram entry after the transformation, as distinct from the clue's answer. (Some people use *light* to refer to every cryptic answer.) Examples of transformations include:

- Ciphers. For example, "Change every letter in the Across answers to the one after it in the alphabet, and every letter in the Down answers to the preceding one."
- Jumbling. "Scramble every Across answer. The result may not be a word."
- Omission of letters. "Remove one letter from each answer before entry in the grid. The removed letters, in order, spell a sentence providing further explanation."

- Switching. Just as in conventional American crosswords, you may have to change an incidentally spelled word in the answer to a related word in the light. For instance, BILLBOARD might become WILLIAMBOARD.

NONSTANDARD GRIDS

Still other variety puzzles incorporate gimmicks involving the grid itself. Diagrams for variety puzzles may look quite different from the standard ones. Letter cells may be diamonds, circles, hexagons, or other shapes. Answers may go in L-shaped patterns or in diamonds, or as chessmen move. Variation is unlimited because the rules for solving these puzzles are created by the composer. For example:

- "EIGHTSOME REELS" puzzles feature normal clues leading to answers of exactly eight letters. Each answer goes into the grid in a circular fashion around a central square, but you must decide whether it runs clockwise or counterclockwise based on the adjacent words. A similar idea, using six-letter words instead of eight-letter words, may be called "HONEYCOMB" (because the six-sided letter cells resemble cells in beehives).
- Some puzzles feature a number of unclued slots that have some relationship for you to discover. You fill the slots by combining leftover letters—perhaps.

    One particular type of puzzle with unclued slots is called "THEME AND VARIATIONS." In this puzzle, some unclued lights share a common bond, called the theme. Each of those words has a subsidiary set of related, unclued lights, called the variations. For example, a theme featuring classical composers might unite BACH, BEETHOVEN, and MOZART. The variations for BACH might be types of music: ORATORIO, CANTATA, and CHORALE; for BEETHOVEN, named piano sonatas: MOONLIGHT, PATHETIQUE, and PASTORALE; for MOZART, operas: DON GIOVANNI, COSI FAN TUTTE, and THE MAGIC FLUTE. Other THEME AND VARIATIONS ideas may involve anagrams or other wordplay.
- Some puzzles have normal-looking grids and clues, but the clues are unnumbered and you must fit the answers into the grid much as you'd work a jigsaw puzzle.

A VARIETY CRYPTIC EXERCISE

To conclude this chapter, Figure 4.4 has a small variety cryptic to demonstrate the genre.

Directions: Each Across clue, or a synonym used in building the clue's answer, has an extra letter which you must ignore. The Across answers are normal. The Down clues are normal, but you must scramble their answers to make different, ordinary words—the Down lights.

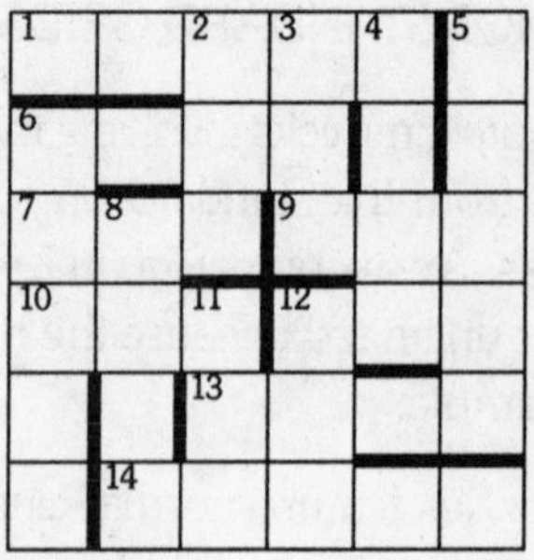

ACROSS

1. GOP: slow way to cross the water (5)
6. Feign rough form of punishment (4)
7. Instrument played backward—it's fate (3)
9. Poet Pound's age (3)
10. Troublemaker is grim spirit, at heart (3)
12. Permit broken tile (3)
13. Chaps' headwear (4)
14. Things may change when it's dark (5)

DOWN

2. Color to suit a nude, essentially (3)
3. We will be returning east for sheep (3)
4. Rabbi takes cheer in movie part (4)
5. Companions' beverages (5)
6. Ransack toy with no top (5)
8. You can see the *Nautilus* captain in one moment (4)
11. Having awareness of roof angle (3)
12. Woman that would make the French acceptable in court (3)

Figure 4.4. *A small variety cryptic challenge*

ANSWERS TO PUZZLES

CRYPTIC EXERCISE

ACROSS: 1. PRO + GNO (*nog**) + STI (*its rev.*) + CATOR (*actor**); 9. E + LECTOR; 10. COT + TAGE (*gate**); 11. Tea + RASH ("hasty"); 12. PROP + ON + ENT (*net**); 13. DEFER + C + TED; 15. SALAM (homophone of *salaam*) + I; 17. GALLIC (hidden); 18.

ARPEGGIO (hidden); 21. TRANS ("across") + VAAL (*lava**); 23. BANTU (*but an**); 24. TAPERED (*red tape* rev.); 25. T + I'D BIT + S (T and S = "took strong" beginnings); 26. TERPS (short Marylanders) + I + CHOREANS (*Koreans* homophone referencing the clue at 5 Down). DOWN: 1. PRE + ST + I + DIGIT + ATE; 2. OVERAWFUL (*overaweful* homophone); 3. NOTCH (2 defs.); 4. SCRUPLE (*spruce** around Line); 5. INCHON (hidden; Chosen = Korea); 6. A + STRO + LA + BE; 7. O + RATE; 8. VENTRILOQUISTS (*silver to quints**); 14. CHIN ("two half-inch parts") + STRAP (*parts* rev.); 16. ARGENT ("antique silver") + IN + A (clasp); 19. RELATCH (*cathedral* – DA,*); 20. GANDHI ("leader of **G**ujarat" + AND + "leader of **H**yderabad" + I; & lit.); 22. AMPLE (*maple**); 23. BIDER (*bride**)

VARIETY CRYPTIC

ACROSS: 1. CRAWL (2 defs., ignore *p* in "GOP"); 6. FINE (*feign**, ignore *g*); 7. LOT (*tool* rev., ignore one *o*); 9. ERA (ignore *z* in "Ezra Pound"); 10. IMP (hid., ignore *s*); 12. LET (*tile**, ignore *i*); 13. HATS (2 defs., ignore *h* in "chaps"); 14. NIGHT (*things**, ignore *s*). DOWN: 2. ANT (*tan*, hidden); 3. WEE (*ew* "we returning" + *e*); 4. LORE (**R**abbi + *ole*); 5. MEATS (*mates*, 2 defs.); 6. FLIER (*trifle*); 8. OMEN (*Nemo*, hidden); 11. HIP (2 defs.); 12. LAG (*legal* [*le* = "the" in French + *gal*]).

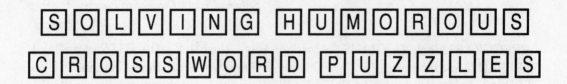

SOLVING HUMOROUS CROSSWORD PUZZLES

5

A good pun may be admitted among the smaller excellencies . . .
—James Boswell, *Life of Samuel Johnson*

Humorous puzzles, which are known by different names in different publications ("Puns and Anagrams" in *The New York Times,* for instance), have diagrams that look just like those of conventional crossword puzzles. However, humorous puzzles are close in spirit to cryptic puzzles. Their clues incorporate many of the devices found in cryptic crossword puzzles, including anagrams, visual (homographic) and auditory (homophonic) ambiguity, reversals, abbreviations, and miscellaneous signals.

In chapter 4, "Solving Cryptic Crossword Puzzles," we discussed methods of deciphering cryptic clues. We also described square dealing, which means that clues follow rules of grammar and that cryptic clues provide two avenues of approach to the desired answers. Humorous puzzles frequently dispense with square dealing and the double approach to answers, and there may be at least this much explanation: A typical 15x15 cryptic puzzle has about thirty-two answers, compared to about seventy in a good humorous puzzle. Now, if the two puzzles are allotted the same space in a publication, there is much less room available for each clue in a humorous puzzle than there is for each one in a cryptic puzzle. The constructor of a humorous puzzle is therefore restricted with respect to the wordiness of clues.

A Briton who is experienced at solving the puzzles in the London *Observer* would, no doubt, consider our humorous puzzles trivial and probably unfair. However, they are not inferior puzzles. Indeed, we could argue that compiling a conventional crossword is more difficult than compiling a cryptic puzzle. We admire the skill and patience of a constructor who can find words to fill a 4x7 or 5x6 rectangle and not need any black squares. So far as clues go, all we can say is that they follow different rules.

In general, solving humorous puzzles is like solving other types of crossword puzzles. Once you enter an answer into the diagram, try to use it to help find the crossing words.

Use chapter 4 as reference, even though the clues in humorous puzzles are both loose and tame compared to square-dealing cryptic clues. Here are some specific guidelines for solving the clues in typical humorous puzzles:

- A clue does not have to contain a dictionary definition of its answer. Clues usually contain at least one word that suggests a definition, but that word may not be the appropriate part of speech. J. F. Kelly once used "For aplomb, do pies." The answer was POISED, even though *aplomb* is a noun, not an adjective.
- Humorous puzzles tend to emphasize anagrams, and you should assume that the answer you seek is an anagram of one or more words in the clue (POISED is an anagram of "do pies" in the example in the previous paragraph). If two or more words in the clue make the anagram, they need not appear together in the clue. G. Buckler once gave "He goes to a resort near Reno" as the clue for TAHOE (rearranging the letters in "He . . . to a").

  Both this clue and the previous one illustrate an important point: Clues in humorous puzzles frequently dispense with signals, especially for anagrams.

  If the clue contains a proper name, you can be pretty sure that name is part of an anagram. Buckler once used "Tie Nell with this" for LINELET (you see the rearrangement of "Tie Nell," of course). You can be equally sure of an anagram when you spot initials in a clue. J. Arensberg's "What one M.D. is" led to the answer DEMON in one puzzle.

  Look for seemingly extraneous words or abbreviations. A common method of incorporating the letters *et* is to throw a gratuitous "et cetera" into the clue. The fact that the phrase is spelled out rather than abbreviated is a tip-off.
- Numbers play two roles in clues for humorous puzzles. The first is simple substitution for their letter look-alikes, as in Eugene Maleska's clue "Zoology 101A required Ph.D." Here "101" is a substitute for IOI. This clue reflects ideas in both the preceding guidelines, because the answer, OPHIDIA, comprises the numbers/letters "IOIA" and "Ph. D.," which are not adjacent. Ophidia is the zoological suborder to which serpents belong. That might be the subject of a course called "Zoology 101A," but it is not directly defined in the clue.

  As in cryptic crossword puzzles, numbers in clues may signal letters by way of Roman numerals. "5" may stand for V, for instance.

The second role numbers play is to indicate which letters of a long word in the clue are to be extracted for the answer. In the clue "Direction 242 swine headed," the numerals indicate that the answer involves the second, fourth, and second letters of "swine," giving WNW.

- Words such as *tea*, *be*, and *you* frequently stand for their spoken single-letter equivalents—*t*, *b*, and *u*, respectively. Most of the letters in the alphabet have similar representations. This substitution works both ways. Maleska's clue "Describing Dept. C" produced DEEPEST when the solver changed the *c* to SEE.

- Small answers in humorous puzzles occasionally are extracts from longer words. *Carton*, *direction*, and *brigade* break into smaller unrelated words. A composer could use "Rear end of a car" to clue TON, for example. "Kind of ion" could clue DIRECT. And so on.

  When the composer breaks a word at other than a natural point of syllabication the result is usually surprising and amusing. Would you realize that FRIENDS is a "Kind of hip"?

- Clues in humorous puzzles may contain partial anagrams. In other words, the clue contains letters that do not appear in the answer. This type of clue usually contains words such as *from* or *lots of* as signals. In the clue "Sugars exported from Odessa," the "exported from" signals that you should extract some letters from "Odessa" and perhaps rearrange them. The answer is OSES.

  Most of the time the containing word (here, "Odessa") bears no relation to the final answer. On rare happy occasions composers achieve literal sense. "He comes from a masculine background" might clue MAN or MALE; the letters that form either word appear in sequence in "masculine."[*]

- The clue may not indicate all the letters in the answer. R. Lake once presented "Something new in pens" for SWINE. The clue does not indicate the letters *is*.

- Fill-in-the-blank clues are rare in humorous puzzles because they are difficult to compose in the spirit of those puzzles. The best approach to deciphering such clues—which nearly always involve puns as opposed to anagrams—is to read them aloud several times, listening for what could be a common phrase in disguise. Often these clues provide a parenthetical phrase to help you form a secondary definition. In the clue "Justin ___ (careful chap)," repetition of "Justin" suggests two possibilities—TIME and CASE. "Careful" leads to CASE.

[*] Dmitri Borgmann coined the term *marsupial word* to describe this graphic curiosity, a word with a synonym "in its pouch."

These guidelines may make clues in humorous puzzles seem easy, and many are. The answers in good humorous puzzles are longer than those in typical conventional puzzles, more than compensating for some easy clues, though, and so these puzzles are about as hard to solve as any other variety. Try them. You'll like them.

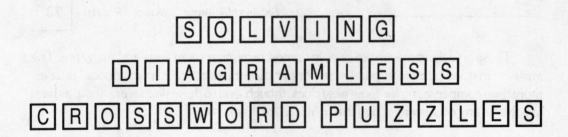

SOLVING DIAGRAMLESS CROSSWORD PUZZLES

6

Choice word and measured phrase . . .
—Wordsworth

Solving a diagramless puzzle is not nearly as hard as it may seem. You really have very much the same task you have with a conventional puzzle. If you need to be convinced of this, take an *easy* conventional crossword puzzle and cover or discard its diagram *after a brief glance.* Then solve the puzzle on another sheet of paper upon which you have drawn a square grid of the correct size. This should serve to get your feet wet. Don't worry if even this gives you some trouble. Remember, you're new at it, and diagramless puzzles usually have more helpful definitions and fewer obscure words than conventional puzzles.

HOW TO BEGIN

When you encounter a diagramless puzzle, you see all its definitions, correctly numbered, and its dimensions. Although you have no black squares and no numbers in the grid, in a sense all you are really missing is the lengths of the answers. If you had these you could soon complete the diagram. But you do know the length of 1 Across—its length is always one less than the number of the second Across answer! This is so, as you can verify in any conventional crossword, because each of the letters in the first Across word must be the first letter of a Down answer. If you followed (or anticipated) that little bit of reasoning, you're well on your way to becoming a devoted fan of these puzzles.

You've probably guessed that attempts to solve diagramless puzzles usually begin with the first few Across definitions. You have the information you need to deal with them.

Consider the second Across answer. Is the number of its definition the same as the number of the definition of a Down answer? If not, the second answer must begin directly under the first letter of the first Across answer. (See Figure 6.1.)

	ACROSS	DOWN
	1. ...	1. ...
	5. ...	2. ...
	6. ...	3. ...
		4. ...
		6. or higher

Figure 6.1. *Starting a diagramless puzzle*

Now assume the opposite is true, that the first letter of the second Across answer is also the first letter of a Down answer. Assume the second Across definition reads "4. Sea creatures" and the third is numbered 7. The alternatives appear in Figures 6.2 and 6.3.

Figure 6.2. *Two columns at the top of a diagramless puzzle*

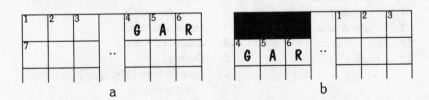

Figure 6.3. *Placing a diagramless puzzle's second Across word under the first, which is three letters shorter*

If fewer than three of the letters in the second Across answer had started Down answers—that is, if the next Across answer had been numbered 5 or 6, one of the configurations in Figure 6.3 would necessarily be correct because no answer, whether it starts a new column or not, may have fewer than three letters.

If the second answer starts a new column, that column is either to the right of and on the same row as the first answer (Figure 6.2a) or to the left of it and on the next lower row (Figure 6.2b). The same sort of reasoning holds for the remainder of the puzzle.

AN EXAMPLE

Look at a realistic example to see if everything is clear. Try to start the puzzle for which we give the first few definitions in Figure 6.4. If you do not get all the answers before getting frustrated, look at the solution in Figure 6.6 and then read the accompanying explanation. If the puzzle presents no problem, skip the explanation.

	ACROSS		**DOWN**
1.	Toward the stern	1.	Every
4.	Consumed	2.	S. neighbor of Ga.
7.	Claim to be true	3.	Lunar New Year
10.	Passed laws	4.	Jolson and Kaline
12.	Hitches	5.	Decade
		6.	*Liberté, Fraternité,* ___
		7.	Thing of value
		8.	Jewel
		9.	Dutch cheese city
		11.	18-mo. U.N. period

Figure 6.4. *The first few definitions for a sample diagramless puzzle*

The first Across answer must have three letters because the second definition is numbered 4. Even before looking at the definitions of the first Down answers, you may guess the answer is AFT. The next, 4 Across, might start a new column and be three letters long, or it might have six letters, of which three (excluding the first) lie directly under AFT.

In either case, 7 Across must either start a new column or fall below AFT, offset to the left at least one square (because there is a 7 Down). At this point, if you have two *I*'s below

AFT or suspect that the first letters of 7, 8, and 9 Down might be *a*, *g*, and *e*, respectively, you are likely to think of ALLEGE. That takes care of 7 Across and, with some Down answers, might even give you a fair picture of the puzzle's third row.

But 10 Across poses a new problem. Suppose your grid looks like the one in Figure 6.5. The answer to 10 Across is likely to be at least four letters long (because there's no 10 Down but there are definitions for 11 Down and 12 Across), but its definition suggests a longer answer.

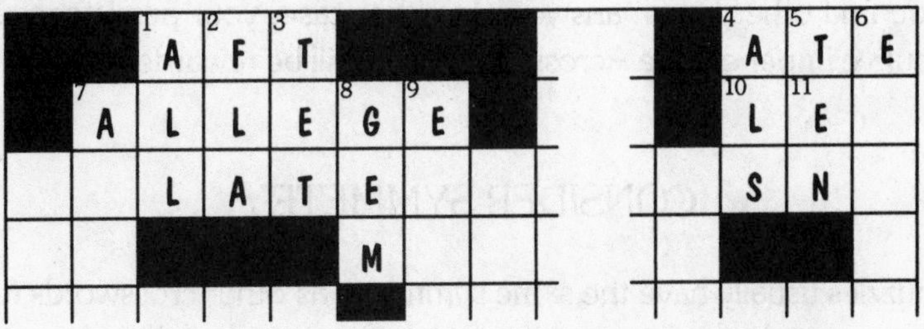

Figure 6.5. *Partial solution for the sample diagramless puzzle*

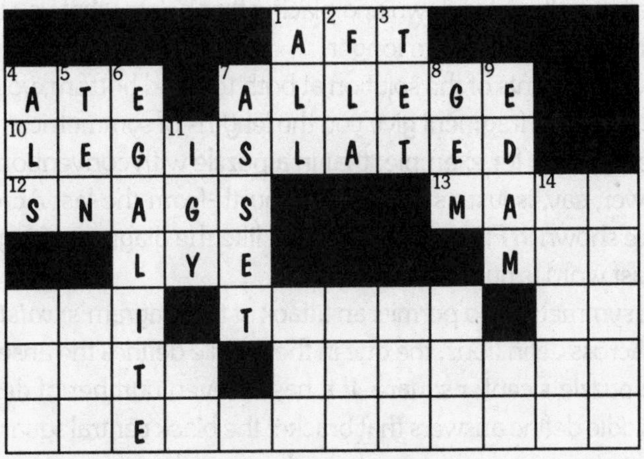

Figure 6.6. *Solution of the fragment in Figure 6.4*

If you have enough information to rearrange and reconnect your two columns with LEGISLATED, you are ready to start solving diagramless puzzles immediately. If not, you might want to study our example further and make sure you understand it all; then you will be ready. Figure 6.6 contains the solution to the puzzle fragment of Figure 6.4.

Persistence is important in solving a diagramless puzzle. If you have a few correct Down answers, they may help you find a correct Across answer several rows down, even though the intervening Across definitions have temporarily stumped you. That one answer may tell you that some of the words above are either shorter or longer than you thought they'd be or it may help you find other Down answers. In either case, your persistence in the face of several consecutive impenetrable Across definitions will be rewarded.

CONSIDER SYMMETRY

Diagramless puzzles usually have the same symmetry as other crosswords (the pattern of black and white squares looks the same if it is turned upside down), and most editors warn you if a puzzle has left-right mirror symmetry instead, or no symmetry at all. Even if the editor does not tell you, by the time you've completed almost half the puzzle, you should be able to tell whether the puzzle has any symmetry or if there's going to be a thematic picture.

If the pattern seems to have normal symmetry, you can often complete the diagram early by turning the top half upside down and placing that below what you have, as in Figure 6.7. The puzzle is then diagramless no longer.

Once you have fragments of the solution at both top and bottom, you can switch back and forth as answers in each fragment give you the lengths of symmetrically opposite words in the other fragment. (Note, for example, that in a puzzle with conventional symmetry, the fourth Across answer, say, is just as long as the fourth-from-the-last Across answer.) The bottom of the puzzle shown in Figure 6.6 must look like the diagram of Figure 6.7 (we have assumed that the last word is numbered 61).

Conventional symmetry also permits an attack at the diagram's *waist*. If the puzzle has an odd number of Across definitions, the one in the middle defines the answer whose central letter occupies the puzzle's center square. If it has an even number of definitions, the two definitions in the middle define answers that bracket the black central square(s) in the central row. You may be able to work up or down from the central row.

A pattern may feature left-right mirror symmetry if: (1) a row has more than one answer and the first and last answers on that row have the same number of letters; (2) a row has an odd number of answers and the middle answer has an odd number of letters with its middle letter in the puzzle's central column; and (3) an even number of Down words begin on each row, except when a Down word begins in the central column.

If you cannot solve the puzzle directly by starting at the top, consider other attacks. Since most diagramless puzzles have conventional symmetry, starting at the bottom is likely to be almost as easy as starting at the top, and easier definitions may make this approach even more fruitful.

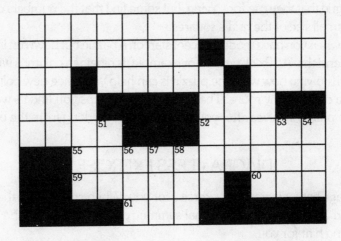

Figure 6.7. *The bottom of the puzzle started in Figure 6.6*

GRIDS

Magazines provide blank square grids for their diagramless puzzles. These are helpful, but you can obviously make your own easily. What you must keep in mind, however, is that even though the answer to 1 Across may be trivial, your first guess regarding its starting square on the top row is likely to be wrong (unless the publication gives, and you consult, a hint that tells you where 1 Across begins). This is also true of any subsequent Across answer if three or more of its letters are the first letters of Down answers. (Remember that this happens whenever two successive Across answers have numbers differing by three or more; those intervening numbers are used for Down answers.) To allow for error, you should not write the answer to 1 Across in the provided grid. In fact, you probably should not use that grid at all in the initial stages.

You should begin with a grid twice as wide as the finished puzzle will be. Write the answer to 1 Across starting in the center of the top row, and write each succeeding Across answer that seems to start a new column far to one side (perhaps first to the right, then one row below and to the left of, the previous Across answer, as in Figure 6.2) until you fix its actual placement by connecting it with the rest of your growing solution. The extreme placement ensures that even if you have to erase the new column, you will be able to transcribe it easily to its proper place a few characters at a time. Many solvers place small numbers in the grid that they use for solving, but some find that the numbers only get in their way due to the small size of the grid's squares.

Especially when you have made a decent start on a puzzle but have run into trouble, use the puzzle's dimensions. A 19x21 puzzle, for example, is nineteen columns wide and twenty-one rows deep. Knowing how wide the puzzle is can help you place new columns—or even prove that there can't be any more. The puzzle's depth helps you find its waist. Both help you connect the puzzle's halves after you've had to start working from the bottom.

DIAGRAMLESS EXERCISE

The following page has a diagramless exercise for you. When completed, the grid is 22x23 (22 columns and 23 rows) and has normal symmetry. The footnote at the bottom of this page has a solving hint for you.*

ALL ABOARD

You are now ready to embark on a new and more satisfying trip into the world of puzzle solving. Diagramless puzzles need never again intimidate you. *Bon voyage!*

---

* The answer to 1 Across begins in the second box on the top row.

ACROSS

1. Home of the Dolphins
6. Pilot lost over water
8. ___ a bell
9. Dec. 25, e.g.
10. Slangy affirmative
11. Out ___ limb
12. Land's ___
14. Partner of dash
16. Ship part
18. Hindrance
22. Agent's percentage
24. ___ clay (hero's defect)
26. To be, to Pedro
29. Bother
30. Goldwater's colleagues
32. Dolled up
34. Hwy. or tpk.
35. Torpedoed vessel: 1915
40. Northern ocean
41. Pair
42. Ending for Levant

43. With 41 Down, vessel in a mishap
45. Vessel in mishap with 43 Across
47. Peer Gynt's mother
48. Those who fire from cover
49. One after another
51. Ocean east of N.A.
52. "Help!"
53. Flinched
54. Luau dish
55. Turkish title
56. Compass pt.
58. Hearing organ
60. A DiMaggio
62. Prohibit
64. Berg material
67. Hurricane part
68. Actor Jason
70. ___ a whip
71. Bother

DOWN

1. Sweet Molly

2. Island nation
3. Cry of triumph
4. "The Wreck of the ___ Deare"
5. Dies ___
6. Solar phenomenon
7. Galley unit: Abbr.
13. Beetle
15. Vessel that sank in 1912
17. Adorns
18. Lair
19. Forte of some artists
20. Adjust
21. The Spruce ___ (Hughes seaplane)
23. Biblical land
24. Charge
25. Calendar abbr.
26. St.-Tropez is one
27. Strays
28. Right: Comb. form
30. Tolerate; endure

31. Elizabeth Cady ___
33. WWII arena
34. In power
36. Dye chemical
37. Canadian pol. group
38. Angers
39. Atmosphere: Comb. form
41. See 43 Across
44. Beast of burden
46. Cut down
47. Help
48. Tree fluid
50. Boston jetsam in 1773
57. Small mass
59. Clemente (lost over the Caribbean)
61. "Help!"
63. Loch of fame
64. Tax agcy.
65. Sleeplike state
66. Abba of Israel
69. Prince Valiant's son

ANSWER

The next page has the answer for the diagramless exercise, with an extra border provided to emphasize the grid's outline. Dr. Maleska, who was puzzle editor at *The New York Times* when Stan Kurzban's composition appeared in 1981, remarked that he deliberately broke puzzledom's traditional rule that material be upbeat because the diagram and puzzle theme were so elegantly matched.

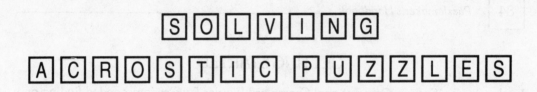

SOLVING ACROSTIC PUZZLES

7

The Times *and* Saturday Review *beguiled the leisure of the crew*
—Gilbert, *The Bab Ballads*

Acrostic puzzles may appear quite formidable when you first try them. There doesn't seem to be enough information for you.

The puzzle consists of a diagram vaguely like a crossword's, with numbered empty squares and black squares, and about twenty-four definitions followed by strings of dashes and numbers—and on first reading you know only two or three words that might satisfy the definitions. The instructions indicate, perhaps tersely, that when you solve the puzzle you will be able to read a quotation in the diagram (with black squares serving as spaces between words) and that you will be able to read the author's name and the title of the source of the quotation (or some other phrase) in an acrostic formed by the words opposite the definitions.

To solve an acrostic puzzle you need most of the same tools you use when working a crossword puzzle—an average working vocabulary, the ability to guess at words and word fragments, a sense of likely and unlikely letter combinations, a reference book or two, and the ability to get all there is to get from a definition. You also need the ability to extrapolate from a few words to a plausible clause in prose. And concentration, because acrostic puzzles seem to offer more ways to make careless errors than crosswords.

The puzzle constructor is, as usual, trying to challenge you. Definitions in acrostic puzzles are often wordier than those in crossword puzzles. They include more literary, historical, and biographical references than those in crossword puzzles. The constructors have at their disposal all the techniques for making definitions, even, in very limited markets, the devious wordplay of cryptic clues.

GETTING STARTED

In chapter 3, "Solving Conventional Crossword Puzzles," we recommended finding one starting place and building on it. That technique doesn't work well with acrostic puzzles—the letters don't make words reading vertically in the diagram. Get started simply by trying to think of as many words as you can that satisfy the definitions. Write your tentative answers above the dashes opposite the definitions, one letter per dash. Write lightly or heavily depending on how sure you are of your guess. Figure 7.1 shows one definition and its answer.

G. Contribute   <u>D</u> <u>O</u> <u>N</u> <u>A</u> <u>T</u> <u>E</u>
                  78   9 115 182 83 40

Figure 7.1. *Sample definition and answer*

If you can guess as many as three or four answers, chances are excellent that you will finish the puzzle. If you can guess only one or two answers, don't give up; you may still be in the running.

Let's say you are able to think of words that satisfy four definitions. As with crossword puzzles, your answers are hypotheses, and you will test them later. What you must do, after writing the answers over the dashes, is copy each letter into the diagram square containing the number that appears under the dash. Working from Figure 7.1, you would write D in square 78, O in square 9, and so on. Part of the diagram would then look like the one in Figure 7.2.

78G	79K		80A	81L	82P	83G
D		■				T

Figure 7.2. *Part of a diagram with letters copied from the answer in Figure 7.1*

In Figure 7.2, notice the small letters printed in the diagram squares. They indicate the definition whose answer supplies the letter for that square. (Notice, too, the G opposite "Contribute" in Figure 7.1.) For now, just use these indicators to make sure you have copied each letter into its proper square in the diagram.

After copying all of the letters in your tentative answers into their respective squares, you may have filled in as much as ten percent of the diagram.

DEDUCTION

The detective work begins now. Your goal is to reveal the quotation in the diagram. You have begun to piece it together already by inserting a few isolated letters. (They are isolated because one satisfied definition will not supply two letters in one word of the quotation.)

The key to solving an acrostic puzzle is remembering that the words in the diagram make sense together.

You can, and should, apply deductive reasoning to several aspects of acrostic puzzles: words by themselves, word fragments, words in combination, and total context. We describe each of these aspects below.

WORDS BY THEMSELVES

Try to guess individual words whenever you have some of the letters. For instance, TH_ is probably THE, although it could be THY. WA_ is likely to be WAS or WAY, although WAN, WAG, WAD, and WAR are also possibilities. _RIDG_ must be BRIDGE or FRIDGE, and, in any event, the last letter is E. A_D could be AND, ADD, or AID. A one-letter answer is usually I or A. The choice is very limited when you try to guess a two-letter word and you already have one letter. (But every once in a while a quotation pertains to TV or uses someone's initials. When this happens even the best solver is temporarily thrown off. Don't worry about this challenge—you will overcome it.)

If you can guess one or more words in the quotation, even if you are not very sure, write the missing letters in their proper squares in the diagram. Hedge your bet by writing lightly so that if you later change your mind the eraser won't rub through the page. Suppose you have completed _RIDG_ to form BRIDGE. (See Figure 7.3.)

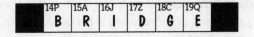

Figure 7.3. *Use of identifiers*

Your next step is to copy the letters B and E to their proper spots in the list of words opposite the definitions. The B in Figure 7.3 goes above the dash with the number 14 under it, in the word defined by definition P. The E goes above the dash opposite definition Q with the number 19 beneath it.

As you copy a letter from the diagram to a dash in one of the words, look again at that word's definition. A single letter, even if it's not the initial letter, can bring a answer to mind, and sometimes one more answer is all you'll need.

After some good guesses on your part regarding both the definitions and the words in the diagram, you should have completed one or two more words in the acrostic. As you did at first, copy the letters from these words to their correct squares in the diagram, and look to see if the addition of these letters helps you guess still more words in the quotation.

Don't be afraid to take some wild stabs. You can go a long way on intuition when solving these puzzles, even guessing a long word from only a few letters. It is perfectly reasonable to guess that _E_ _E_E is BELIEVE, for instance, or that _E_P_ _ is PEOPLE. (Of course, many other words might be correct. The fun and pride of solving acrostic puzzles come from taking chances, trying to make as much as you can out of the least amount of information. Besides, the word *people* shows up a lot more often in quotations than does, say, *bedpan*.) Even if your guess is wrong, some letters may be right because of the way they combine in English. If BELIEVE is wrong, RELIEVE may be right. (Watch your spelling— DECEIVE is not an alternative.)

WORD FRAGMENTS

In chapter 3, "Solving Conventional Crossword Puzzles," we discussed the technique of surmising bits and pieces of words from context and from definition. Apply the same technique to acrostic puzzles. If a definition implies that a plural word is in order, try an *s* at the end of the answer. Similarly, you can infer a verb in the past tense from an equivalent form of definition. (But be careful, because many definitions that appear to lead to verbs in the past tense are in reality adjectives. "Frightened" may define PHOBIC, not SCARED—an example of the composer's use of ambiguity.)

Be alert to the possibility that word fragments will emerge in the quotation as well as in the word list. The letter *g* at the end of a long word is probably preceded by *in*. If the next to the last letter of a word is *v*, the last letter is likely to be *e*. Going one step further, you should assume that any three-letter word with one letter in the right place is the word THE. You can deduce other, longer word fragments, such as ING from _ _G, TION from T_ _N and ICAL from _C_L.

Last, don't overlook the fact that the initial letters of the word list form an acrostic. You may deduce the author's name, or you may recognize a word in the title of the source material. Every letter you place can be a source of inspiration.

WORDS IN COMBINATION

Just as you can guess individual words from a few letters, so you can guess whole phrases from a few words, or even from partial words in some cases. As you gain experience and confidence in solving acrostic puzzles, you will take more and more chances, trying to build longer and longer strings of words that fit in context. Here too, a wrong guess may include some right words or letters. Here are the basic ways to deduce word combinations:

- Sudden recognition of a common phrase. It would be impossible to list here all the short phrases you might recognize. It would also be pointless since our intent is to make you aware of the possibility without doing the work for you. In any event, here are a few combinations you should look for: IN THE, ON THE, TO THE, ONE OF THE, A LONG TIME, AS WELL AS, IT IS.
- Analysis of grammar and context. Again, it is not practical to attempt to compile an all-inclusive list, but we have some ideas to start you off.

  - Nouns and pronouns (used to) agree with their associated verbs. A two-letter word followed by WERE is probably WE. It can't be IT, *as it were*. In the same way, a two-letter word followed by WAS is likely to be IT or HE, not WE.
  - Some words don't belong together. In the last example, a two-letter word followed by WAS cannot result in IN WAS or OF WAS.
  - In ordinary English sentences, nouns precede verbs and adjectives precede nouns. Faced with the combination in Figure 7.4, we might reason as follows: SOME should be followed by a plural noun. Put an *s* at the end of the long word. Copy the *s* to where it goes in the acrostic. Any help there? No? Back to the quotation. What comes after SOME things? A verb, possibly HAVE or WERE or COME, but write in an ending *e* anyway.

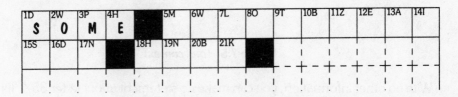

Figure 7.4. *Analysis of words in combination*

Remember, we're describing a process of supposition here. It's entirely possible the correct solution in Figure 7.4 is SOME UNDISCIPLINED KIDS, or any of a multitude of similar constructions. When you leap to conclusions, as we have done here, you will sometimes regret your hastiness, as we have at times. So hedge your bets. Write lightly until you are sure of your guesses.

When you guess a phrase in the quotation, follow the same procedure you use when you guess a single word. That is, transcribe the letters in the completed phrase to their proper locations in the acrostic and check the definitions again to see if lightning is about to strike.

TOTAL CONTEXT

By "total context" we mean use of three dimensions to test a hypothetical letter. In particular, each of the initial letters of the answer words actually belongs to three words: a word in the quotation, a word in the acrostic, and a word in the author's name or the title of the source material. To a lesser degree, the second letters of the words in the acrostic also have a three-dimensioned characteristic. This means that you have three points of information to use when conjecturing tentative answers. Consider, first, just the portion of a puzzle shown in Figure 7.5a.

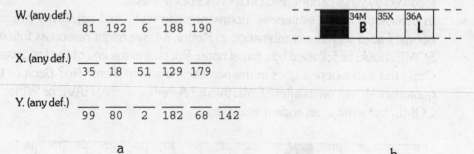

Figure 7.5. *Total context*

With no other information, you can make no statement about letter 35X. It may be a consonant or a vowel. But if you also have the information in Figure 7.5b, you should conclude that 35X must be a vowel. This certainty should permit you to concentrate on, and ultimately to select, one of a small number of likely answers for definition X.

OTHER THOUGHTS

The very nature of the quotations selected for acrostic puzzles is of value to you as solver. They are chosen for their humorous, lyrical, or evocative properties—or for philosophical succinctness. We have noticed some common attributes of these quotations:

- More often than you might expect, a word, especially a long one, is repeated within the quotation. This means that if you have two long words of equal length with some letters common, and with other letters corresponding to blanks, you should visualize the result if all the letters you have were present in both words. If the merger is plausible, both words may be the same. Suppose, for example, that your emerging quotation contains these two eight-letter words: SU_ _IV_ _ and _U_VI_ _ _R. If you mentally superimpose the two, the result is SU_VIV_R, which must be SURVIVOR. Repetition may involve word roots rather than whole words. CARELESS and CARELESSNESS may both appear, for instance.

     Less commonly, a word appearing in the quotation also appears in the title of the source material.
- The constructor, having to deal with someone else's words, cannot inject unusual letters into the puzzle. Therefore, in a quotation of about two hundred letters, you should expect the common letters (ETAOIN SHRDLU, according to one list) to be present in natural proportion. The letters *w* and *h* always seem to show up frequently due to words such as *who* and *how* that appear frequently in quotations.
- Quantifying words such as *some*, *most*, *never*, *every*, and *always* appear often. The words *America*, *people*, *believe*, and *experience* show up out of proportion to their occurrence in everyday conversation (unless you are running for political office).
- If a long word begins with *e*, the second letter may be *x*. This is particularly so if the second letter is also the second letter of a long word in the acrostic list.
- Many quotations are autobiographical reminiscences. Therefore, if the first word of the entire passage is a one-letter word, it is more often *I* than *A*.
- Assume that all one-letter words are the same.

AN EXERCISE

The following two pages present a complete acrostic puzzle for you.

1C	2R	■	3Q	4I	5H	6F	■	7Q	8F	■	9N	10P	11L	12I	13C	14R	■	15F	16N
17M	18W	19X	20A	■	21R	22I	23D	24A	25U	26F	■	27J	28T	29R	30B	■	31H	32P	
33X	34C	35E	36T	■	37F	38F	■	39T	40X	41I	42O	43K	44F	■	45U	46V	47R	48Q	
49G	50F	51B	52P	■	53W	54M	55N	56P	■	57F	58D	59U	60O	61L	62J	■	63K	64L	
65T	66E	67G	■	68Q	69E	70A	71B	72P	73V	74O	■	75X	76W	■	77L	■	78E	79O	80U
81X	82C	83N	84P	85S	■	86M	87H	88P	89B	90I	■	91D	92U	■	93M	94T	■	95B	96S
97T	98I	99R	100F	101O	102D	103X	104E	■	105U	106J	107F	108O	109N	110E	111X	■	112L	113W	114P
115E	■	116X	117P	118A	119C	120L	■	121H	122E	123I	■	124S	125N	126R	■	127K	128J	■	129T
130G	131N	132V	■	133D	134F	135Q	■	136V	137X	138L	■	139F	140J	141T	■	142B	143C	144F	145E
146R	147V	148S	■	149P	150A	151K	152U	153O	154R	155E	156L	157N	■	158F	159U	160T	161H	162A	
163D	164L	165E	■	166I	167J	168G	■	169K	170I	■	171X	172E	173G	174N	175V	176P	177B	178M	179A

Clues

Words

A. Knock down; destroy

$\overline{20}\ \overline{145}\ \overline{24}\ \overline{70}\ \overline{150}\ \overline{118}\ \overline{179}\ \overline{162}$

B. River of sorrows

$\overline{51}\ \overline{95}\ \overline{142}\ \overline{30}\ \overline{89}\ \overline{177}\ \overline{71}$

C. What "nth" lacks

$\overline{34}\ \overline{143}\ \overline{1}\ \overline{82}\ \overline{13}$

D. Safe from prosecution or infection

$\overline{91}\ \overline{163}\ \overline{23}\ \overline{102}\ \overline{133}\ \overline{58}$

E. Extreme indulgence in sensuality

$\overline{115}\ \overline{110}\ \overline{155}\ \overline{122}\ \overline{78}\ \overline{69}\ \overline{66}\ \overline{35}\ \overline{172}\ \overline{165}$

F. Start of a diction exercise (4 wds.)

$\overline{50}\ \overline{8}\ \overline{6}\ \overline{44}\ \overline{134}\ \overline{158}\ \overline{15}\ \overline{57}\ \overline{139}\ \overline{144}$

$\overline{26}\ \overline{100}\ \overline{37}\ \overline{107}$

G. Speak up; complete

$\overline{130}\ \overline{49}\ \overline{168}\ \overline{67}\ \overline{173}$

H. Sponge (off someone), like Minnie

$\overline{121}\ \overline{5}\ \overline{31}\ \overline{161}\ \overline{87}$

I. Possession and use; pleasure

$\overline{170}\ \overline{4}\ \overline{98}\ \overline{22}\ \overline{123}\ \overline{41}\ \overline{90}\ \overline{166}\ \overline{12}$

J. Play New Age music, perhaps

$\overline{140}\ \overline{106}\ \overline{167}\ \overline{62}\ \overline{27}\ \overline{128}$

Clues (continued)	Words (continued)

K. Monastery leader

$\overline{151}$ $\overline{169}$ $\overline{127}$ $\overline{43}$ $\overline{63}$

L. Put out with the trash (2 wds.)

$\overline{11}$ $\overline{120}$ $\overline{61}$ $\overline{64}$ $\overline{53}$ $\overline{77}$ $\overline{112}$ $\overline{164}$ $\overline{138}$

M. Oneness

$\overline{178}$ $\overline{93}$ $\overline{54}$ $\overline{86}$ $\overline{17}$

N. Hoover's successor

$\overline{83}$ $\overline{125}$ $\overline{174}$ $\overline{131}$ $\overline{157}$ $\overline{109}$ $\overline{16}$ $\overline{9}$ $\overline{55}$

O. Governmental forgiveness

$\overline{60}$ $\overline{42}$ $\overline{79}$ $\overline{108}$ $\overline{153}$ $\overline{101}$ $\overline{74}$

P. Earth's crust

$\overline{114}$ $\overline{10}$ $\overline{52}$ $\overline{117}$ $\overline{72}$ $\overline{84}$ $\overline{149}$ $\overline{56}$ $\overline{176}$

$\overline{32}$ $\overline{88}$

Q. Is odorous

$\overline{135}$ $\overline{48}$ $\overline{68}$ $\overline{3}$ $\overline{7}$

R. Ready for service

$\overline{14}$ $\overline{38}$ $\overline{47}$ $\overline{99}$ $\overline{21}$ $\overline{126}$ $\overline{154}$ $\overline{146}$ $\overline{2}$

S. Unsociable one

$\overline{156}$ $\overline{96}$ $\overline{124}$ $\overline{85}$ $\overline{148}$

T. Placing of a satellite into orbit; shot

$\overline{160}$ $\overline{36}$ $\overline{129}$ $\overline{141}$ $\overline{39}$ $\overline{65}$ $\overline{28}$ $\overline{94}$ $\overline{97}$

U. Fiendishly evil

$\overline{59}$ $\overline{159}$ $\overline{25}$ $\overline{152}$ $\overline{45}$ $\overline{80}$ $\overline{92}$ $\overline{105}$

V. Involuntary resident

$\overline{46}$ $\overline{175}$ $\overline{73}$ $\overline{136}$ $\overline{132}$ $\overline{147}$

W. Place of business; elected position

$\overline{18}$ $\overline{29}$ $\overline{76}$ $\overline{113}$ $\overline{119}$ $\overline{104}$

X. Eleventh-hour phrase (3 wds.)

$\overline{137}$ $\overline{40}$ $\overline{116}$ $\overline{75}$ $\overline{103}$ $\overline{19}$ $\overline{33}$ $\overline{81}$ $\overline{171}$ $\overline{111}$

FINAL WORDS

You will discover a tempo to the process of solving acrostic puzzles. At first the paucity of known letters allows you to make only snail-like progress. But with a few correct assumptions and some lucky wild guesses, a faint glimmer of recognition breaks the stalemate and the pace quickens. At some point you will be absolutely certain that you can finish the puzzle.

You work frantically, trying to write in several letters at the same time, each addition triggering the answer to a previously unsolved definition, each new letter added to the diagram inspiring your brain to produce still more phrases out of the remaining unfilled letters. Finally comes the denouement. You put down the pencil and read for the first time the complete solution—the quotation, a list of words (only some of which you knew at all a short time ago) and, haltingly, the name of an author and the title of a book.

What fun!

ANSWER TO PUZZLE

"We know so little beyond common life, or even of common life, that, with regard to the economy of a universe, there is no conjecture, however wild, which may not be just; nor any one, however plausible, which may not be erroneous."

WORD LIST:

Demolish	**U**nity
Acheron	**R**oosevelt
Vowel	**A**mnesty
Immune	**L**ithosphere
Debauchery	
	Reeks
How now, brown cow	**E**ffective
Utter	**L**oner
Mooch	**I**njection
Enjoyment	**G**houlish
	Inmate
Noodle	**O**ffice
Abbot	**N**ow or never
Throw away	

The quotation is from philosopher David Hume's *Dialogues Concerning Natural Religion*. We shortened the title for this exercise, so the acrostic reads: DAVID HUME NATURAL RELIGION. You'll see this quotation again in chapter 12, "Composing Acrostic Puzzles."

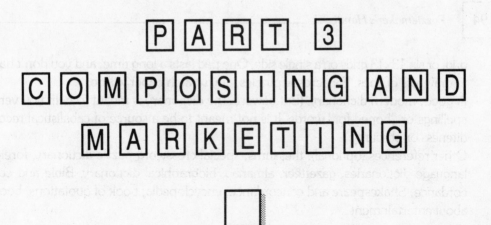

PART 3
COMPOSING AND
MARKETING

Perhaps you are starting to read this part of the book with misgivings. You feel that you could never compose a crossword puzzle. Please put your doubts aside. If you can solve puzzles, and maybe even if you try but cannot finish them, you can compose them. All you need is a little instruction and some resoluteness of purpose. You may not sell your first puzzle; few have done so. But the first sale will swell your heart with pride when it comes, and it will soon be followed by many others. Will it be followed by riches? No, hardly that. Fame? In a *very* small circle, perhaps. But satisfaction will certainly come from knowing that millions of people want what you can produce for them.

Even before you sell puzzles, you can create them as gifts for the solvers among your friends and relatives. What gift could better express your love and consideration than your own creation, a personalized puzzle? (See chapter 13, "Marketing," for a reference to a business venture based on this idea.)

The chapters that follow treat the same types of puzzles mentioned in Part 2 of this book. Again, conventional puzzles, those likely to be most familiar to you, are at the top of the list. These may be the easiest to compose and they may offer the best monetary reward, but once you've got the knack, you may want to experiment with the other forms. Now, it's time to begin. Here is a list of the basic equipment you'll need.

- Basic writing tools: pencils with hard lead, a block eraser, a good writing surface, and good lighting.
- Scratch paper. For crossword puzzles, we recommend pads of graph paper ruled into quarter-inch squares. You can fit four 15x15 grids, or two 15x15 grids and one 23x23

grid, or six 13x13 grids on a single side. One pad lasts a long time, and you don't have to draw lots of lines. For acrostic puzzles, any scratch paper will do.

- A good, modern dictionary. (But beware, the dictionary is meant to help you verify spellings or "hoped-for" words. It is not meant to be a source of cabalistical reconditeness or obscurity.)

- Other references (optional): thesaurus, special crossword puzzle dictionary, foreign language dictionaries, gazetteer, almanac, biographical dictionary, Bible and concordance, Shakespeare and concordance, encyclopedia, book of quotations, books about entertainment . . .

Computers are not essential tools of this trade, although they offer space-saving, convenient alternatives to all the items on the list.

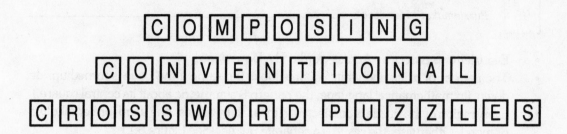

COMPOSING CONVENTIONAL CROSSWORD PUZZLES

8

Proper words in proper places.
—Jonathan Swift

Conventional crossword puzzles have three components of nearly equal importance: *theme*, the unifying idea behind the overall construction; *fill*, the smaller words that make up the majority of answers; and *definitions*, or clues. In those markets that demand them, the themes catch the editor's eye first; a good, consistent theme predisposes the editor to look with favor on the rest of the puzzle. The fill often distinguishes a premium puzzle from a so-so work—or even an also-ran. The definitions slant the puzzle for a particular audience, help make a puzzle easy or difficult, and enliven the solver's overall reaction.

This chapter tells you how to compose conventional crossword puzzles. It contains:

- Exercises for an orderly initiation into the mysteries of composition.
- Observations about a simple, nonthematic puzzle.
- Explanation of some rules you will have to obey in composing marketable puzzles.
- Step-by-step analysis of the composition of a sample thematic puzzle.
- Examination of different kinds of definitions.
- Discussion of sophisticated techniques used in composing puzzles of higher quality.

BASIC RULES AND TRADITIONS

Most conventional crossword puzzles conform to these rules and traditions:

- The diagram is square, with an odd number of squares in every row and column.
- Every answer is at least three letters long.

- Every letter is part of an Across word and a Down word.
- The pattern of black and white squares looks the same if the page is turned upside down. (In mathematical language, the pattern is symmetric about its central square.)
- Every region of the puzzle is connected to the next by at least one word (preferably, two or more). Otherwise, the result is a separate puzzle. (See Figure 8.1.)

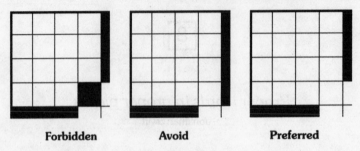

Forbidden   **Avoid**   **Preferred**

Figure 8.1. *How a corner connects with the rest of a diagram*

- No more than about a sixth (1/6) of a diagram's squares should be black, about thirty-eight for a 15x15 puzzle (15 x 15 = 225; 225 ÷ 6 = 37.5).* Some editors adhere rigidly to this limit. Others relax it often, especially for puzzles of great appeal.
- A 15x15 diagram should have no more than about seventy-eight answers. This total comes about, in part, as a natural consequence of the black-square limit. We can also ascribe this rule to the amount of space available for printing clues. Grids' limits increase with size, of course, but not linearly; that larger puzzles should pose tougher challenges is understandable. Again, some editors relax this rule on occasion.

The following table summarizes both the black-square and word-count conventions for grids of different common sizes.

Grid Size	Black Square Limit	Word Limit
15x15	38	78
17x17	48	100
19x19	60	120
21x21	74	142
23x23	88	170

---

* Margaret Farrar may have formulated this convention to make composers work harder in an environment with more puzzles being submitted than she could print. By the second *Cross Word Puzzle Book* she, Hartswick, and Buranelli counseled: "A too black pattern means the constructor was a bit lazy."

THE FILL

Experienced crossword writers typically start with a potential theme. They develop it into something useful, fill the grid, improve what they've got, then prepare definitions. For now, though, postpone the investigation of themes until you gain some mastery of the craft of the fill. In any case, writing definitions comes last.

FIRST EXERCISE

Figure 8.2 is a simple 3x3 diagram.* Fill it with six different, ordinary, three-letter English words. (We recommend you do this and all subsequent composing exercises on separate sheets of paper. Composers without computers use about a quarter of an inch of eraser for every two inches of lead, and you don't want to erase through a page of this book.) Stop reading until you complete the exercise.

Figure 8.2. *A 3x3 diagram for the first exercise*

The acceptable fills for this diagram surely number in the thousands. We'll show you a little later how to tell which ones are better than the others. What's important right now is for you to replay the steps by which you chose letters, square by square. If you don't remember, try again using six completely different words.

Here's how an experienced composer might think when beginning to tackle even this simple problem: (1) It's easiest to fill a space using words with alternating vowels and consonants. (2) Most three-letter words begin with consonants. (3) Therefore, the letter in the top left-hand corner should be a consonant and the overall pattern of vowels and consonants should look like that in Figure 8.3.

---

* When you set out to make a crossword, you will not number the boxes until the composition is done. We've numbered boxes here and in some subsequent diagrams so we can refer to them conveniently.

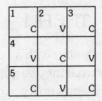

Figure 8.3. *Best places for vowels (V) and consonants (C) in a 3x3 diagram*

The vowel most often found at the end of words is *e*, so make 2 Down and 4 Across end with *e*'s. The vowels that most often appear inside words are *a*, *o*, and *i*. Make the second letter of 1 Across an *a*. If the second letter of 1 Down were also *a*, 2 Down and 4 Across would be identical, so make that letter an *o* instead. Letters that begin large numbers of three-letter words are *s*, *t*, *r*, and *d*. Let 1 Across start with an *s*. (See Figure 8.4.)

	2	
1 S	A	**3**
4 O		E
5	E	

Figure 8.4. *Vowels that let you complete the 3x3 diagram most easily*

The letter *d* or *t* (but not *r*) could end 1 Across and start 3 Down, or end 1 Down and start 5 Across, so use *t* for I Across and 3 Down, *d* for 1 Down and 5 Across; 3 Down and 5 Across must end with the same letter, and *n* goes nicely. The center square could be *r*, *d*, or *w*. Finished! (See Figure 8.5.)

1 S	**2** A	**3** T
4 O	R	E
5 D	E	N

Figure 8.5. *A simple 3x3 composition*

Before going on, fill that same diagram again using words that haven't shown up yet, either in your first version or in our example. You should sense a mental pattern developing.

GENERAL OBSERVATIONS

Figure 8.6 makes a big jump—to a 15x15 diagram. It is, nevertheless, a relatively simple composition.

S	H	A	D		S	T	A	R	T		R	O	M	P
L	A	M	E		P	O	L	E	R		E	M	I	L
A	T	O	P		E	L	I	T	E		P	I	L	E
B	E	R	A	T	E	D		R	E	L	A	T	E	D
		R	O	D		D	O	S	E	S				
S	L	A	T	E		T	I	S		A	T	T	I	C
P	O	M	S		S	O	L		S	N	E	E	Z	E
O	R	B		T	I	R	A	D	E	S		P	A	L
T	R	I	C	O	T		T	A	X		R	E	A	L
S	E	T	O	N		D	O	N		P	E	E	K	S
		N	E	V	E	R		P	A	T				
S	P	E	N	D	E	R		E	R	M	I	N	E	S
T	A	K	E		N	I	T	R	E		R	O	B	E
A	L	E	C		O	V	A	L	S		E	T	O	N
R	E	S	T		M	E	T	E	S		D	E	N	T

Figure 8.6. *A simple 15x15 composition*

The puzzle has no theme, no answer more than seven letters long, *few* of the rare letters (*q, z, x, j, w, v, f*) and *many* of the common ones (*i, e, s, r, a, t, l, d*). The puzzle may therefore lack appeal to the connoisseur, but it serves our purposes well because it provides extreme examples of the characteristics of crosswords that are easy to solve and not too difficult to compose, namely:

• The only vowel in the rightmost column and bottom row is *e*. In fact, only one word in the whole puzzle (ALI) ends in a vowel other than *e*.

- The six words in the top row and leftmost column comprise only eleven different letters. Five begin with two consonants; none has more than one vowel.
- Many other answers have alternating vowels and consonants. Only two answers, both plurals, contain three consecutive consonants. Many diagonals contain only vowels or consonants.

How can you apply these observations when you fill parts of a diagram? First, try to place an *e* wherever a vowel must end an answer. Second, try to use consonants to begin answers. Third, except for the top row and left column of corner regions, try to avoid words with strings of consecutive vowels or consonants. (Note, however, that an *s* at either end of a word, even if it is next to another consonant, will help you more often than it hinders you.)

You've probably noticed that some words occur more often in crosswords than in prose or conversation. That's because answers fully interlock. If you alternate vowels and consonants on the top row or leftmost column, for example, about half of those letters will be vowels, and they must start crossing words. Nowhere near half our words begin with vowels, though, so there are fewer to choose from—and they show up repeatedly. Or, you can pick words for the top row and leftmost column with few vowels. On the other side of the grid, conversely, words whose only vowel is *e* are common in the bottom row and rightmost column.

The end of this chapter has lists of four- and five-letter words in three categories: those starting with vowels, those that are comparatively easy to use in the top row and left column, those having no vowel except *e* for the bottom row and the rightmost column. They should help you complete the exercises that follow.

SECOND EXERCISE

Before you try your first composition of consequence, there is another important principle you should understand: The first place you should attack (the key square) is the square where the diagram and the letters already in it give you the least freedom—that is, the square that simply must contain one of only a few letters. For example (see Figure 8.7), if a square follows an initial *d* in a vertical answer and it is surrounded by vowels in the crossing horizontal answer, you practically must place an *r* in the square (*dhows* aside).

In general, two things restrict your choice of letters for a particular square: (1) The neighboring letters and the rules of English spelling dictate that only a few letters are candidates for the square, as in the example in Figure 8.7, and (2) There are few acceptable answers that can be placed in either the horizontal or the vertical string of squares including the one in question. For example, if you need a four-letter answer of the form O_ _L, to avoid obscure words the third letter must be *a*. The second letter might be *p*, *r*, or *v*.

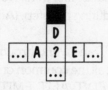

Figure 8.7. *A square that must hold a particular letter,* r

If the square you are filling is restricted for the second reason above, but more than one answer might work in the crossing direction, list them all, then try each one in turn, starting with the ones that seem to fit best with the letters already placed in nearby squares, until you fill an entire region of your composition satisfactorily. The tables at the end of this chapter can help you decide in what order to try the words on your list.

Now move on to the significantly more difficult problem in Figure 8.8. Try to complete the exercise before reading further.

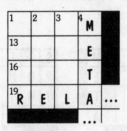

Figure 8.8. *Second exercise: a typical corner*

The first key square of the problem is the initial letter of 16 Across. Because this square precedes a final *r* in 1 Down, the rules of English spelling practically require that it contain either a vowel or the letter *r*. If it's an *r*, the next letter across must be a vowel (for similar reasons), which would mean that the word at 2 Down ends with two vowels. For the time being, ignore this possibility and proceed on the theory that 16 Across begins with a vowel. (You can briefly postpone choosing which vowel you use.)

If 16 Across begins with a vowel, the next key square is the second letter of 16 Across—and it must contain a consonant. Mentally go through the consonants alphabetically to find words that might fit at 16 Across. That is, first think (vowel)-B-(vowel)-T. You don't have to think too hard about "which" vowels during this step. (After all, there were no written vowels in ancient Hebrew.)

If you say to yourself, "Uh**B**uh**T**," and work through the alphabet, you should think of half a dozen words soon enough. List all the common ones you find in alphabetical order by second letter: ABET, ABUT, OBIT, EDIT, ALIT, EMIT, OMIT, UNIT, and EXIT. You may even come up with some *partials* (short for *partial phrases*, snippets from sayings, song titles, or quotations): A HOT (". . . Time In the Old Town Tonight"), I GET (from "I Get Ideas," another old tune), and I MET (". . . a man with seven wives"). Next, try to arrange your list according to which items might be easier to use in the crossing words.

Since more common four-letter words end in *il* than in *el* or *ul*; more in *le*, *de*, *ne*, and *me* than in *be* or *xe*; and more in *ar*, *er*, and *or* than in *ur*, a reasonable, if somewhat arbitrary order for this exercise is: ALIT, EDIT, EMIT, OMIT, OBIT, UNIT, ABET, ABUT, EXIT. Partial phrases are less desirable than single-word entries and full phrases, so put them at the end.

Try each word on your list at 16 Across and next concentrate on the letter at the intersection of 3 Down and 13 Across. Continue the process as long as necessary for each crossing until you complete the exercise.

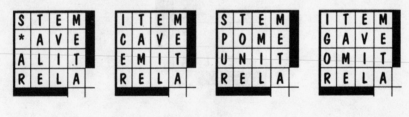

* = C, P, or E

Figure 8.9. *Some solutions to the second exercise*

Figure 8.9 shows four solutions to the problem of Figure 8.8. The first two contain only common English words. Each of the other two contains one proper name. We avoided phrases and foreign or obscure words.

How did you do? Don't be discouraged even if you gave up after an hour. You will improve with practice and we chose our example more for realism than simplicity.

MORE CHALLENGING EXERCISES

Now look at the 9x9 diagram of Figure 8.10. Can you think of four intersecting nine-letter answers for 4 and 5 Down and 13 and 16 Across? Try to find answers that will make it easier for you to complete the composition:

- Words with alternating consonants and vowels.
- Answers with *s*, *t*, *r*, *p*, or *d* in each square that will contain the first letter of a crossing word (marked with asterisks in the sixth column and the sixth row).
- Answers with *e*, *s*, *r*, *t*, *d*, or *l* in each square that will contain the last letter of an intersecting word (marked with daggers in the fourth column and the fourth row).

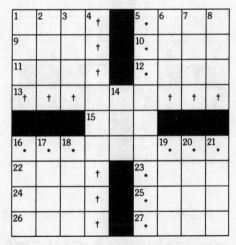

* = first letter of a four-letter word; † = last letter of a four-letter word

Figure 8.10. *A 9x9 diagram*

Early compromises are usually necessary, so don't hold out for perfect answers. Our choices are shown in Figure 8.11, but they are not the only possibilities by any means.

The diagram in Figure 8.10 has four *corners*. In fact, we use *corner* for any almost rectangular collection of white squares. A long answer crossing a corner's apparent boundary "bridges" corners. Each nine-letter word in this exercise bridges two corners.

Now, fill in the diagram of Figure 8.11. Attack first the corner that seems to you to present the greatest difficulty. Why? For the same reason you choose a key square within a corner: You should try to find out quickly if you're going down a blind alley. If you discover that you are, you can go back to the last letter or answer you chose as "probably but not necessarily the best" and discard it in favor of another. If you have tried all possible letters or answers in that place, you must go still further back and discard a letter or answer chosen even earlier.[*] In the present problem, if you cannot complete a corner, you should discard one of the nine-letter words and replace it with another. When you run out of replacements, you should replace a different nine-letter word. When you run out of nine-letter words, you should modify the diagram, and so on.

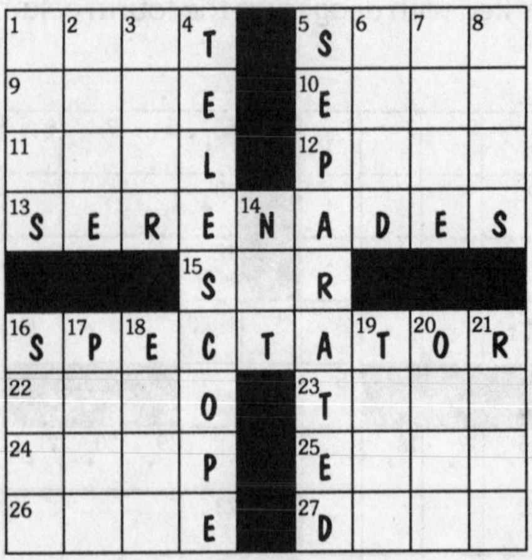

Figure 8.11. *A 9x9 diagram with helpful nine-letter answers*

Figure 8.12 shows one solution for the problem of Figure 8.11. The numbers at the corners of the diagram show the order in which we attacked them. The numbers in the lower right-hand corners of individual squares show the order in which we attacked them in completing each corner.

Figure 8.13 shows another solution for the problem of Figure 8.11 with another goal: to use as many different letters of the alphabet as possible. To derive this more interesting solution, we first placed rare letters (x, k, z, y, and v) where they seemed most likely to fit and proceeded as before. (IS UP answers the clue "The jig ____.")

---

[*] Backtracking is a technique used intuitively in problem-solving and it is applicable to all sorts of problems, including solving crossword puzzles (and mazes, by the way). Its use is very important in tasks such as puzzle composition, which leans so heavily upon many interrelated assumptions. Analysis improves backtracking efficiency.

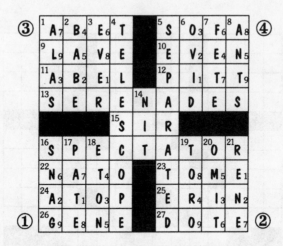

Figure 8.12. *How the authors filled the previous 9x9 diagram*

Figure 8.13. *A more elegant composition based on the diagram of Figure 8.11*

Now that you've had some realistic practice in the art of composing puzzles, you should try your own version of the relatively undemanding 15x15 diagram we started with. Figure 8.14 is a blank diagram you can copy. The starred squares are your first key squares because the diagram's longest answers intersect there.

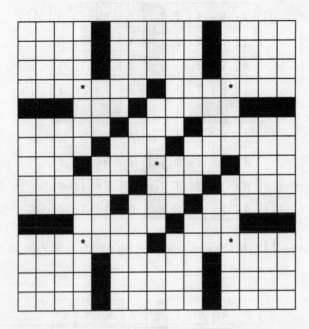

Figure 8.14. *The empty 15x15 diagram from Figure 8.6*

As a next exercise, fill in simple diagrams similar to the one in Figure 8.14. Diagrams for easy puzzles in newspapers and in newsstand publications will do nicely. Ignore the published definitions and compose your own puzzle. You can even do that while you are solving! If a corner stumps you, simply ignore the offending definitions and treat that corner as just another composing exercise.

RESTRICTIONS ON ANSWERS

If you hope to sell your puzzles some day, you should be aware of some restrictions beyond those listed early in this chapter. Some apply to diagrams, others to answers. Some are universal, others are relaxed by some editors.

- Answers must be in good taste (remember Lewis Carroll's guidelines about the Doublets puzzles). Most editors won't allow RAPE as an answer even if you define it as grape pomace. Similarly, most editors accept only the most mundane, non-life-threatening diseases and refuse even clinical names for certain body parts and functions.

- Answers must be findable in some respectable reference work—a dictionary, atlas, encyclopedia, or the like[*]—or be justifiable as an idiomatic expression or an excerpt from some well-known phrase, lyric, or documented quotation.
- Some editors forbid brand names.
- No two answers should contain any form of the same root word unless they carry out the puzzle's theme as a result. For example, use both ROCKY and ROCKING only if ROCK is the theme of your puzzle.
- Many types of answers are acceptable only in very limited quantities—say no more than ten percent of a puzzle's words altogether, and some editors are much more restrictive than this guideline. The categories are listed here in order from most to least objectionable, but the first eight types are essentially undesirable to the same degree; moreover, words from those eight types should never cross or lie adjacent because the result usually leaves one or more squares most solvers won't be able to complete.

   a.   Foreign words having no English cognates (related words) or usage.
   b.   Foreign words having English cognates.
   c.   Crosswordese.
   d.   Plurals of family names; plurals of unique first names (EARTHAS).
   e.   Variant spellings, dialectic words, obsolete words.
   f.   Uncommon words having a prefix of *re-*.
   g.   First names of little-known people.
   h.   Uncommon abbreviations.
   i.   Partials, especially of more than four or five letters.
   j.   Combining forms.
   k.   Plurals formed with a final *s*.

We'll return to the subject of the fill later.

THEMES

Most editors occasionally accept unthemed crosswords. Indeed, some syndicators of puzzles for daily newspapers seem to prefer them. Some editors, conversely, accept puzzles without themes only if the word count is very low. Overall, the market for themed puzzles is greater than that for unthemed ones, and we believe themed puzzles are more fun to create.

---

[*] Even so, you can still get into trouble. *GAMES* once rejected an otherwise good puzzle because an impressive array of authoritative reference books split evenly on the spelling of Mama Cass's last name: Elliott vs. Elliot.

Listing the best themes for puzzles is like listing all inventions yet to be patented: It is impossible by definition. Originality, of course, is the reason. The best themes are the ones the solver has not yet encountered.

Crossword themes have two aspects: subject matter and design—what you do with the subject matter to turn it into a puzzle. For example, "numbers" is a subject and "films with numbers in the title" is a design. Or, "films with numbers in the title" is a subject and "subtracting one from each number" is a design. Other factors we'll address include consistency, completeness, profusion, selecting candidate answers, why theme answers affect grid size, where to place theme answers in a grid as you begin, and changing theme answers to fit a work-in-progress.

SUBJECT MATTER

The key to subject matter is widespread familiarity. Literature, music, sports, dance, art, plants and animals, geography, academic subjects, minerals, history and public figures, politics and current events, religion, literature, all facets of the entertainment industry, transportation, and amusing relationships among words are all appropriate subjects.

Subject matter should not feature obscure knowledge. Butterflies, stamps, and fencing fascinate many people, but puzzles about these topics could probably appear only in magazines with specialized readerships or as one entry in a book. A puzzle featuring the name of one disgraced aide in a former presidential administration is probably unmarketable without some other consideration. A puzzle featuring eight or ten of them might be quite another story, however.

Timing is another factor. Most markets accept puzzles related to national holidays or other familiar annual events, but puzzles on the four-minute mile or Watergate may be tough to sell today.

Thoughtful or humorous quotes can also be puzzle themes, provided (1) the entire quote fits in the grid, (2) filling about as much of the grid as theme answers usually do, (3) exactly as said or written, (4) arranged symmetrically (including the source, if necessary), and (5) without splitting words across diagram entries.

DESIGN

A puzzle's subject is often less important to the solver's satisfaction than what you make of it. Your design may be as simple as profusion—ten state flowers, for example. Maura Jacobson's puzzle in which over one-quarter of the definitions read "Author" brought great pleasure to successful solvers. Even those of little literary bent had to admire it. Puzzles in television magazines always feature a heavy concentration of thematic answers.

In rough order from simplest to most complex (or, if you prefer, from easiest to think of and carry out to hardest), here are some (but certainly not all) design ideas:

- Repetition in answers (for example, STONEHENGE, REDSTONE, and LEAVE NO STONE UNTURNED). Some editors frown on repeated-word themes precisely because they *are* easy to think of and, consequently, are seen often.
- Related whole words in answers (STONE MOUNTAIN, PEBBLE BEACH, and ROCK CLIMBER).
- Repetition in definitions (five definitions reading "Hudson," with answers such as A BAY DISCOVERED BY CABOT and UPSTAIRS, DOWNSTAIRS MAN), also called *relocated theme.*
- Related parts of words in answers (REDSTONE, WHITEWASH, and BLUEBONNET).
- Related words in definitions (another form of relocated theme) leading to totally unrelated long answers. ("Bacon" clued SHAKESPEARE CONTEMPORARY and "Waffles" clued EQUIVOCATES ON AN ISSUE in a breakfast-theme puzzle.) "Two kings" as a definition (for ALAN AND RICHARD I) may appear with "Two princes" (HAL AND CHARLES) or "Two Jacks" (BEAU AND KENNEDY) in relocated themes involving royalty or playing cards, respectively.
- Seemingly unrelated words and phrases tied together in some unexpected way (the answers CARBOLOADING, HITTING MY STRIDE, and THE END IS NEAR in a puzzle about the Boston Marathon).
- Puns. Many editors accept random wordplay, but the best crosswords featuring puns have a unifying element—namely, a single subject (SCENE STEELERS and COLT-BLOODED MURDER punning on Super Bowl winners).
- Switches (CHARLES HORSE and CHARLENE HORSE for CHARLEY HORSE, in puzzles titled "STRICTLY FORMAL" and "WOMEN'S LIBERATION").
- Use of a rebus, that is, the substitution of a symbol for a sound or combination of letters: Greek letters, digits for their names, *x* for *cks* (CHEX AND BALANCES), geometric shapes for their names (BERMUDA ▲ and TRAFALGAR ■), and even an empty square to represent the word *space* or *blank*.

Don't copy someone else's design unless you know you can put a new wrinkle on it. Especially, don't copy someone else's entry, even under the pretext of paying homage. Either the editor or the solvers will remember it.

A design must not disguise the subject matter so subtly that it eludes the puzzle editor or typical solver. An editor who doesn't recognize a subtle theme is likely to reject the puzzle.[*] You might view TIRES ONESELF OUT, CAMPING GEAR, and PLUGS AWAY AT as "obviously" related, but a typical solver might not make the connection unless you carry out the automotive theme elsewhere in the puzzle. You may recognize Pierce and Arthur as presidents' names out of context, but a solver may not connect an answer such as PIERCED EAR without a pointed definition or thematic profusion.

CONSISTENCY

Consistency is an absolute requirement, even for puzzles with simple designs.

To begin with, you must incorporate your design only in the answers or in the definitions. You must not, for example, carry out a numerical theme by using "Twelve O'Clock High" as the definition for GARY COOPER FILM with "Shirley MacLaine film" elsewhere as the definition for TWO FOR THE SEESAW.

Next, answers having related words must use the identical relationship throughout. That is, TWO FOR THE SEESAW and TWELVE O'CLOCK HIGH are part of a design with cardinal numbers, but SECOND IN COMMAND and TWELFTH STREET RAG belong in one with ordinal numbers. A puzzle featuring people whose surnames also happen to be cities could use JOHN DENVER, JACK LONDON, and IRVING BERLIN, but not JILL IRELAND (country, not city), RUTH ROMAN (adjectival form, not the city name per se), or FLORENCE NIGHTINGALE (first name, not last name).

A design built on puns must use them consistently. They must all be of the same form (homophones, deliberate misspellings, and so on) and, once again, all in the answers or all in the definitions.

A design based on switches must apply one type universally and with narrow focus. The gender switch WOMAN OF LA MANCHA does not go with WOMANDARIN ORANGE because the latter switch affects an accident of spelling, not the word *man*.

Similarly, you must use rebuses consistently when they have more than one interpretation. If Φ appears in a puzzle using Greek letters, it may stand for either the sound or the letters *phi* but not both: ΦLIP (for *Philip*) and ΦNANCE (for *finance*) are inconsistent.

The point is: Elements of your design may be very clever indeed, but most editors reject inconsistent execution.

---

[*] Rarely, it can work the other way. A former puzzle editor at *The New York Times* didn't catch the theme concealed in RUMPUS ROOM, CIGAR BUTTS, and two more entries(!), and published the crossword.

COMPLETENESS

Good thematic puzzles also exhibit completeness. That is, a puzzle whose theme incorporates the names of continents must use them all; a puzzle featuring zodiac signs or Snow White's dwarfs must use them all. (There's a practical limit to this notion, of course. You wouldn't be able to use all the Kentucky Derby winners' names in a single grid.)

PROFUSION

Other things being equal, use as many thematic answers as you can. They should occupy at least fifteen percent of all squares, although some editors may accept less, and at least four percent of the answers. A reasonable way of expressing criteria editors commonly apply to thematic puzzles is shown in this table.

Puzzle Size	Minimum Number of Squares (using 15% guideline)	Minimum Number of Thematic Answers
15x15	34	3
17x17	43	4
19x19	54	5
21x21	66	6
23x23	79	6

Observe the end of that last bit of advice: Use as many thematic answers *as you can*. If you are too ambitious, you may not be able to complete the fill without resorting to obscurities, crosswordese, and all the other nonsense we've counseled against. Most experienced constructors don't try to work more than ten thematic answers into a 21x21 or 23x23 grid, and there are a few patterns that show up over and over with occasional minor adjustments.

This is an appropriate time to mention that this book has an appendix with a sampling of empty diagrams, in two popular sizes, with commentaries. Just as we previously advised you to practice filling grids by ignoring the definitions in your daily newspaper crosswords, we'll now remark that many experienced puzzle writers find it easier to seek previously published grids that accommodate their candidate thematic answers than to invent their own grids. Furthermore, they may go so far as to seek candidate answers of certain lengths because they know in advance which familiar pattern they hope to use. Don't be anxious about copyright problems; empty grids are not protected.

All answers longer than, say, nine letters should carry out the theme. When shorter answers are thematic, the puzzle's symmetry should match them with one another.

SELECTING THEME ANSWERS

After you have selected subject matter and a potential design, list candidates for thematic answers—terms (or names or phrases) pertaining to the subject. For example, flowers with names of animals embedded in them (DANDELION and SNAPDRAGON), state capitals, names of composers, presidents—whatever you're working on. Write down as many as you can without using a reference book, then write down more.

In making this list, think about the task ahead of you. Answers with rare letters or long strings of consonants or vowels may kill your project before it is well under way. You won't see many puzzles with Dag Hammarskjöld's name in them, no matter how famous he was. If your design involves a rebus, remember that every instance of a picture will be part of two answers, so you'll need lots of candidates.

If your design involves puns on thematic words, you should next jot down, for each item on the list, words related to important parts of it in your chosen approach. If you're working with Super Bowl winners, for example, your list includes the Pittsburgh Steelers and the Baltimore Colts, and you probably notice that *Steeler* sounds like *stealer* and *Colt* is close to *cold*. From there, go to expressions that contain those words—say, *scene stealer* and *cold-blooded murder*, then restore the original words from your list.

For gimmicks involving other kinds of switches (grownup animals instead of young ones, gender changes, adding one to phrases whose key words are numbers . . .), proceed in the same way.

Except for one or two answers going through the puzzle's center square, symmetry will force you in the end to select pairs of answers of equal length. You can manipulate the length of theme answers to achieve matching lengths by using inflected forms and pronouns—for example, KEEP TO YOURSELF, KEEPS TO ONESELF, and so on.

Finally, check your sources, especially for spelling, before investing great mental energies. A composition based on a false assumption may waste many valuable hours.

THEME ANSWERS AND GRIDS

Theme answers have substantial influence over the size of the puzzle you can make from them. If you jot down four sixteen-letter candidate answers, you obviously cannot use them in a 15x15 grid. Conversely, if your goal is a 21x21 grid, your candidates must facilitate that task, and four sixteen-letter entries could be useful.

For every grid size, some lengths are more convenient to use than others. In general, theme answers that are, in order of preference, zero, three, five, or four letters shorter than the puzzle's width usually bridge corners neatly and make it easier for you to complete the fill. One letter less than half the puzzle's width is also a good length. By contrast, answers that are one or two letters shorter than the puzzle's width often force you to use *cheaters* (extra black squares that have no effect on word count), which are considered flaws and which cheapen a composition.

Where should long theme answers go? Three or four rows or columns away from the grid's edge are good starting places. The sample grids in our appendix use one or the other location for long entries.

Every editor at least occasionally accepts noninterlocking thematic answers strung out across a puzzle's width, but we think solvers notice and admire interlocking thematic answers more. Furthermore, interlocking answers often permit denser packing of thematic material. Finding places where you can make long answers interlock is a purely mechanical process, but we provide an illustration below with a more detailed discussion of placement of theme answers.

AN INSTRUCTIVE EXAMPLE

The next section of this chapter describes the composition of a typical thematic puzzle. We'll document our reasoning as the puzzle moves from inspiration to completion. The basic steps along the way are:

- Selecting a theme
- Listing candidates for thematic answers
- Setting thematic answers in the diagram to form a *skeleton*
- Placing black squares provisionally
- Developing a first fill
- Polishing the fill

Your first puzzles will probably lack themes. Themes constrain puzzles and make composition more difficult. Yet that is precisely why we have chosen a thematic puzzle as our example—because themes pose problems with interesting and instructional solutions.

THEME

One day we were struck by the fact that many American cities' names are names or phrases in other languages (for example, Baton Rouge means "red stick" in French), and we set out to build a puzzle around those names.

We began with a list of suitable names, ordering the list by the lengths of the names:

Name	Length
BATON ROUGE	10 or 5 + 5 (that is, could be two five-letter answers)
LOS ANGELES	10 or 3 + 7
SAINT LOUIS	10 or 5 + 5
SAN ANTONIO	10 or 3 + 7
DES MOINES	9 or 3 + 6
LAS CRUCES	9 or 3 + 6
PALO ALTO	8 or 4 + 4

More theme answers can often be made to fit into a grid if they intersect, so we decided to make our own pattern instead of using a stock one. We sought pairs of entries that could intersect without violating the symmetry rule. Figures 8.15 through 8.18 show four of the possibilities.

Figure 8.15. *One way to place thematic answers in a 15x15 diagram*

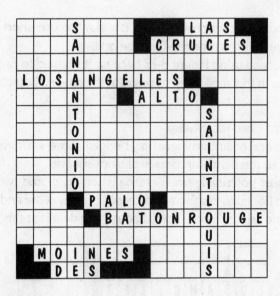

Figure 8.16. *Skeleton with short thematic answers added symmetrically*

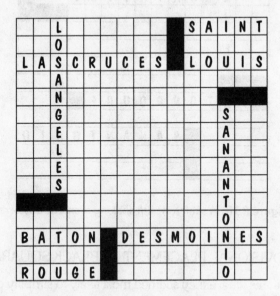

Figure 8.17. *Another possible skeleton*

Figures 8.16 and 8.17 demonstrate that it's okay to use short entries as thematic answers if you arrange them symmetrically in the grid.

We chose to proceed using Figure 8.18 because it seemed to present the fewest and least difficult problems. In this version, as opposed to the others, thematic answers had these characteristics:

- They were not bunched too closely.
- They fell in rows and columns where they bridged corners conveniently.
- They led to no requirements for masses of black squares.
- They left the most potentially troublesome letters (*c*, *g*, and two *u*'s in this case) in places where we hoped to use them fairly easily. (Tables at the end of this chapter help you make such decisions. Don't worry about these details at this point.)

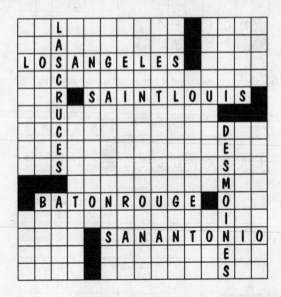

Figure 8.18. *A skeleton with six long thematic answers*

PROVISIONAL PLACEMENT OF BLACK SQUARES

We next put black squares where they seemed most likely to simplify our remaining tasks. We started by bounding the corners of our grid with *fingers*, strings of black squares protruding from the diagram's borders. We placed them, as Figure 8.19 shows, to equalize the areas of the corners (because large corners are difficult to complete) and to leave the letters *m* and *n* at the ends of answers and *g* and *u* at the beginnings of answers, because we can use these letters easily in these positions.

Fingers added

Black squares nearest theme answers

Last black squares places

Figure 8.19. *Black squares placed provisionally in the diagram of Figure 8.18*

The next black squares we placed were those nearest the theme answers. These gave us small answers of reasonable size, with fairly convenient starting and ending letters elsewhere (initial *o* in SAINT LOUIS, *d* in DES MOINES, *r* and *o* in BATON ROUGE, final *o*, *s*, *r*, and *n* symmetrically opposite). The last black squares were placed to leave us with a word count of seventy-eight and no nonthematic answer of more than seven letters. We now had thirty-eight black squares and a manageable *field of white* (a rectangle without black squares) in each corner of the grid.

The starred square of Figure 8.19 clearly needed first consideration because so few five-letter words end in *u*. Before you read on, try to find your own first fill for Figure 8.19.

FIRST FILL

Our quest for a first fill progressed through the stage shown in Figure 8.20 to Figure 8.21.
BANTU, CORFU, and PERDU came to mind for the key square. PERDU had the fewest
troublesome letters, so in it went. The *d* in PERDU started a five-letter word ending with *m*.
We couldn't think of anything better than DATUM. That gave us a start on the 5x5 corner
in the lower right-hand side of the diagram. We then placed some very common and, we
hoped, convenient letters where other sections of the puzzle met (*s* as first letters above the
a in DATUM and the *t* in BATON ROUGE, *l* or *n* as a last letter [expecting GRAIL or GRAIN
down from the *g* in LOS ANGELES] *s* or *t* as another last letter [anticipating an *ous* or *out*
ending crossing the *u* in SAINT LOUIS]).

① Salvador and family
② Jump through ___
③ ___ small voice

Figure 8.20. *The emerging first fill after about two hours*

Next we tackled each corner in turn, the largest and most troublesome ones first. The
following table summarizes our thoughts on this puzzle.

Corner	Approx. Size	Biggest Problem
bottom right	5x5	consecutive *io*
top left	5x5	letter under *a* in LOS ANGELES
bottom middle	4x5	word crossing *n* in BATON ROUGE and *s* in SAN ANTONIO
top middle	4x5	word crossing end of LOS ANGELES and *l* of SAINT LOUIS
top right	4x5	*i* near the end of SAINT LOUIS
bottom left	4x5	none anticipated
mid. right	4x3	none anticipated
mid. left	4x3	none anticipated
center	3x3	none anticipated

Each puzzle and each corner has its own personality, but the most difficult problems tend to be (in order):

1. The longest nonthematic words, especially near the center.
2. Remaining bridges between corners.
3. Largest corners or sections.
4. Clusters of consecutive consonants or vowels.
5. Rare letters.
6. Less rare letters in unfortunate positions.
7. Remaining isolated corners.

Solve each problem the same way: first choose letters, then whole words that place letters where you can use them easily. Start with *s* in a single square linking sections. If you need a vowel near the center's two words, try an *a*. If a letter must end two words, use *s* or *e*. (You can often eliminate a surplus of common letters later. Don't let such a consideration delay your first fill.)

After you have attacked the first few problems, successfully or not, take stock. Are your goals attainable? Should black squares be added, moved, or deleted to increase or decrease the total word count? Should the form of a thematic answer be changed, for example, from

KEEP IT UP to KEPT IT UP or KEEPS IT UP? Should two nonintersecting thematic answers be interchanged? Should you have used a larger diagram? Should you have stuck to solving puzzles?[*]

D	A	L	I	S		B	A	A	L		S	E	R	E
O	H	A	R	A		E	L	B	A		P	L	O	D
L	O	S	A	N	G	E	L	E	S		R	E	T	E
L	O	C	K	E	R		A	A	A		O	M	E	R
S	P	R		S	A	I	N	T	L	O	U	I	S	
		U	N	T	I	L			L	I	T			
P	U	C	E		L	O	P	P	E	D		D	R	U
S	T	E	V	E		V	I	E		S	T	E	E	P
T	E	S		C	H	E	E	R	S		A	S	T	O
		S	T	A		D	A	T	U	M				
	B	A	T	O	N	R	O	U	G	E		O	A	F
C	A	N	E		D	E	W		A	S	T	I	L	L
E	S	T	E		S	A	N	A	N	T	O	N	I	O
I	T	E	R		A	V	E	R		E	D	E	N	S
L	E	S	S		W	E	D	S		D	O	S	E	S

Figure 8.21. *A first fill*

Note the flaws commonly found in first fills:

- Many of the common letters (*e*, *r*, *n*, *s*, *t*).
- Abbreviations (SPR, UPO, PST, STA, AAA), crosswordese or odd words (ELEMI, RETE, SERE), foreign words (TES, ARS), variant spellings (IRAK), particles (OIDS, ECTO), and so on.
- More than a few partials (jump through A HOOP, just A LINK in the chain, to skip A BEAT, I LOVE a parade, AS TO, A STILL small voice).
- A plural of a family name (DALIS).

Still, an acceptable composition is probably not far away. All we have to do now is improve the fill, step by step, by applying a few basic techniques to the most unsatisfactory corners and answers.

---

[*] No. If you have gotten this far you can succeed, and successful composing will satisfy you far more than successful solving ever has.

POLISHING THE COMPOSITION

Our finished composition is shown in Figure 8.22.

■	S	L	A	V	■	M	E	A	L	■	B	A	L	K
S	H	A	M	E	■	A	L	V	A	■	E	L	A	N
L	O	S	A	N	G	E	L	E	S	■	D	I	N	O
A	N	C	H	O	R	■	E	R	A	■	A	B	E	T
P	E	R	■	S	A	I	N	T	L	O	U	I	S	■
■	■	U	P	E	N	D	■	■	L	A	B	■	■	■
V	A	C	A	■	T	A	P	P	E	T	■	D	I	Z
O	X	E	Y	E	■	H	O	E	■	S	T	E	N	O
W	E	S	■	C	H	O	I	R	S	■	A	S	T	O
■	■	■	A	H	A	■	■	D	A	T	U	M	■	■
■	B	A	T	O	N	R	O	U	G	E	■	O	A	R
J	I	L	T	■	D	E	W	■	A	E	D	I	L	E
E	L	L	E	■	S	A	N	A	N	T	O	N	I	O
E	B	A	N	■	A	V	E	R	■	E	D	E	N	S
P	O	N	D	■	W	E	R	E	■	R	O	S	E	■

Figure 8.22. *A polished composition*

Here are some guidelines, illustrated by references to our example, for moving from a first fill to a final composition:

- A common shortcoming of first fills is an abundance of words ending in *s*. Where two such words meet at the last letter, you can often find a plausible change. For example, change SPINS and LADS to SPINY and LADY. We changed WEDS (at the bottom center of Figure 8.21) to WERE without difficulty. This change was also good because it turned the foreign word ARS into the common English word ARE.
- Change frequently occurring letters to rarer letters. Notice the left side of Figure 8.21. We changed PUCE, STEVE, and TES to VACA ("Cabeza de ___"), OXEYE, and WES in Figure 8.22. Similarly, we changed DRU and STEEP, on the right side, to DIZ ("Nickname for trumpeter Gillespie") and STENO.
- Eliminate abbreviations. The changes described in the previous item share this virtue. PST ("Pacific Standard Time") became VOW.
- Change crosswordese into ordinary words. Look at the top right-hand corner of our

first fill. Six puzzle words are crammed into that small area: SERE ("Withered"), RETE ("Network"), OMER ("Hebrew measure"), ELEMI ("Varnish material"), ROTES ("Fixed routines"), and EDER ("German river"). Our rewrite is a big improvement.

- Eliminate partial phrases. Notice A BEAT starting on the top row in Figure 8.21. Revising that portion of the composition allows the substitution of AVERT, as shown in Figure 8.22.

- Eliminate clusters of proper nouns. The upper left-hand corner of Figure 8.21 has five proper nouns, including the variant spelling IRAK. One way to break up the cluster is shown in Figure 8.22. Note, however, that we added a cheater, and AMAH replaced IRAK. (Current dictionaries have AMAH, so it's not awful.) We balanced the cheater by another in the bottom right-hand corner.

- Keep foreign words and variant spellings to a minimum. We replaced several in the course of the improvements.

You may have noticed that the center of the composition changed as we moved from first to final fill. This is due to a ripple effect. When we changed SANEST (starting on the top row in Figure 8.21) to VENOSE we had to replace UNTIL on the sixth row. UPEND worked, but then the partial I LOVE in the seventh column had to go. IDAHO filled in nicely, but that caused CHEERS in the ninth row to make way for CHOIRS. The point is that a single change may have far-reaching consequences. Conversely, don't be dismayed by how much you have to do to improve a first fill. Any time you take to polish and refine a puzzle is rewarded many times over by the increased probability of sale.

You should now take a critical took at your own first fill. Identify and try to correct its flaws, one by one, until you are satisfied.

DEFINITIONS

In general, write definitions only after your composition is complete and polished. The obvious exception to this rule occurs when you select theme answers with definitions already in mind.

There are several basic types of definitions for conventional crosswords. The primary dictionary definition (in which, for example, "Woody plant" defines TREE) is the most common. Solvers are tired of a steady diet of these definitions, however, unless their sole interest is in writing a lot of letters without regard for entertainment or mental exercise. The puzzle editors don't want these definitions if interesting alternatives exist.

Stanley Newman has observed that the definition of *puzzle* includes words such as *perplex* and *test*, and that "rote filling-in of answers to dictionary definitions" doesn't fill the bill. In other words: There's got to be a puzzle in the puzzle.

Furthermore, to sell a lot of puzzles to different markets you'll need to write a variety of definitions, both easy and hard, and slant them appropriately. This aspect of puzzling is as important as discovery of fresh themes.

How do you achieve variety? How do you spice definitions? The general approach is to stay away from the primary dictionary definition. Ironically, this means you must use a dictionary and other reference books. A basic library also includes a thesaurus, an encyclopedia, a biographical dictionary, a gazetteer or geographic dictionary, and a book of quotations. If you rely only on your memory you will miss many good definitions, and you will miss an excellent chance to broaden your own knowledge as well as that of the solver.

FIRST EXERCISE

Before reading on, return to your polished fill of the BATON ROUGE skeleton and write definitions for the words in the top two rows and the left two columns. That's twelve in all.

EASY DEFINITIONS

Primary dictionary meanings and straightforward synonyms usually make easy definitions for ordinary words. Writing these is also easy—just look up the answer word in your dictionary or thesaurus and record the main definition or obvious synonym. (We're back to "Woody plant" for TREE.)

Secondary dictionary meanings may provide easy or hard definitions. For example, TREE is also a verb, meaning "to back into a tight spot"; hence, "Corner." TREE also means "to stretch shoes on a last," yielding the definition "Stretch shoes."

Fill-in-the-blank clues (also called *missing word* clues) are typically easy, too. They are not definitions, because you're not literally defining the answer word, but they've been around for a very long time ("___ of life" and "___ of knowledge" both lead to TREE).

Definition by example is another common form. You could use "Oak or elm" as an easy definition for TREE.

Related to fill-in-the-blank clues is the use of proper names. TREE could be clued as "Theatrical figure Sir Herbert Beerbohm," for instance, and you can build easy or hard definitions this way.

The remaining definition forms represent *extra-effort clues* and share this trait: Even though they may be easy to solve, they bring something extra to the page. What's the point? To make the solver think, not just remember.

You can treat a word as an attribute of some other word, either a person or an ordinary noun. This is *definition by description*. For instance, "Kilmer's symbol of beauty" is TREE. So is "Surgeon's patient, perhaps." "Family, for one" reverses the attribution.

Definition by description is a cousin of fill-in-the-blank in that it does not offer a definition, per se; instead, it challenges the solver's knowledge of related facts.

Literary and similar allusions can make easy or hard definitions. "It grew in Brooklyn" is an easy one for TREE (if you remember the 1945 film *A Tree Grows in Brooklyn*). "Forest feature" and "Sherwood sight" suggest TREE as a response. "Leopard's perch" is a little more direct, but compensates in that it calls up an image in the solver's mind. The encyclopedia tells us that the bristlecone pine may live 4,500 years; hence, "Oldest living thing" can clue TREE.

Imagery is important in these clues. "Picnic umbrella" evokes thoughts of pleasant outings. "Shade giver" is less evocative.

Definition by model is another important technique and is applicable to foreign words, abbreviations, and combining forms (prefixes and sufixes). As you'll see, the traditional ways of defining these kinds of answers are parallel, and so are the modern techniques.

The traditional way to tell the solver to expect a foreign word or an abbreviation is straightforward, and it works. Just tack a colon and a standard signal onto the end of a standard definition. "Fr." for French, "Sp." for Spanish, "Abbr." for abbreviation. Nothing to it. And no variety.

The modern approach is more subtle, yet it is easy to learn and you can incorporate the idea at once. To signal a foreign word, for example, just use one in the definition. Instead of writing "Aunt: Sp." for TIA, you can write "Pedro's aunt" or "*Madre*'s sister." Do the same for abbreviations—instead of "Communications company: Abbr." for ITT (or GTE, or MCI), write "Communications corp." Instead of "Hallowed French female: Abbr." for STE, use "Jeanne d'Arc, e.g."

This approach has a corollary: If abbreviations in definitions signal abbreviations in answers, then definitions should have abbreviations only when their answers are abbreviations. With freedom comes responsibility.

Similarly, the traditional way to tell the solver to expect a prefix or suffix is to end a definition with ": Prefix" or ": Suffix." Two modern approaches deserve your consideration. First, use alternatives for the standard format. "Recent, in combos" and "Combining form for recent" are perfectly fine replacements for "Recent: Prefix." Second, challenge the solver's vocabulary and lateral thinking skills with a bit of wordplay . . . something such as "Classical lead-in" for NEO (which is, after all, a prefix seen at the front of *classical*).

Finally, some editors allow definition by model when speech patterns are involved. "Thpeak like thith" might be allowed for LISP, and "Cockney's abode" for OME or OUSE, perhaps. (One editor allows OME only in conjunction with the line from Kipling's poem "Fuzzy Wuzzy": "So 'ere's to you, Fuzzy Wuzzy, at your 'ome in the Soudan.") A friendly editor might conspire with you to allow "Da digit afta two?" for TREE.

HARDER DEFINITIONS

Hard definitions for ordinary words may:

- Use unusual dictionary meanings.
- Rely on obscurity.
- Demand unusual knowledge of the solver.
- Be ambiguous.
- Be vague.
- Be misleading.
- Use words in surprising ways, in *tricky clues*.

An old unabridged dictionary includes "take refuge [in a tree]" as an intransitive verb meaning of *tree*. ("The raccoon treed" is its elaboration.) A new dictionary offers "computer data structure" at *tree*. Neither meaning is very common, so either's appearance constitutes a more difficult definition.

Consider definition by example again. "Apple or pear" is perfectly good for TREE, but can be ambiguous and potentially misleading for a while because POME is another possible four-letter answer. "Banyan, for instance" stretches the solver's knowledge somewhat; "Baobab" is less familiar to many; and most solvers would consider "Lebbek" to be an obscure example of a tree.

Obscurity and unusual knowledge often go together. Sir Herbert Beerbohm Tree was married to Helen Maud Holt, who was an actress. He managed Her Majesty's Theatre after 1897 and wrote a book called *Thoughts and Afterthoughts*. Using any of those facts as the basis for defining TREE would severely challenge a solver.

Vagueness is not the same as ambiguity. Ambiguous definitions are reasonably precise, but two or more answers might work. "Close" is a simple synonym for unrelated four-letter answers: NEAR and SHUT (or SEAL). Vague definitions, on the other hand, supply very little information, so the solver must complete crossing words first. In the extreme, a vague definition is but a mechanism the solver can use to confirm, not deduce, an answer. "It lives in the forest" might suggest TREE, but BEAR and DEER are equally plausible answers until several crossing words provide confirmation. "British theatrical figure" for TREE (without including any part of Sir Herbert's name) is extremely vague, and more likely to annoy solvers than please them.

Tricky clues are often akin to definitions by description. They "add puzzle to the puzzle" by making solvers (and composers!) think in new directions, and they have become increasingly popular over the last fifteen years. They probably first appeared in *Judge* magazine. Farrar allowed them in puzzles in *The New York Times* and Weng encouraged them. The idea is to incorporate an unexpected, but absolutely legitimate, sense of a word, often in a colloquial phrase. One of Maleska's original tricky clues was "They go to blazes" for (fire) HOSES. Many ordinary English words have unrelated senses; clever puzzlemakers invent tricky, misleading, surprising clues using those senses every day. "Leaves home" seems to mean something quite different from "a home for leaves"—that is, TREE. "Newspaper source" has nothing to do with people who supply news tips, it's TREE, again.

If you have a choice, avoid obscurity and arcane knowledge in favor of trickiness and moderate vagueness. You should strive to make the solver proud to have thought of the right word, not relieved after thumbing through six reference books.

MORE EXERCISES

Return to that BATON ROUGE construction. Write new definitions for the same twelve words. If you think your first definition for a word was on the easy side, write a harder one, and vice versa.

Now pick any one of the twelve words and write several more definitions. Use different kinds of definitions and at least two different meanings of the target word.

Next, look at the newspaper crossword you solved most recently. Write a three-word definition for each of the first ten answers that originally had one-word definitions, but don't "settle" for just paraphrasing primary dictionary meanings. Use any of the forms we described earlier.

WARNINGS

- Be careful about parts of speech. "Climbs the walls" is a verb. It can define GOES DAFT, but not IVY, which is a noun.

- Be precise. A definition must *define* the answer. "Quest" can define SEARCH, not FLEECE or GRAIL, the objects of famous quests.
- If your answer is plural, make sure the definition implies so. Likewise, make sure present-tense verbs match present-tense answers, past-tense verbs match past-tense answers, and so on.
- Don't use any form of a word in your composition in any of the definitions unless it's part of the puzzle's theme.
- Don't write definitions with the same number of letters as their answers. If you do, the puzzle is less challenging because solvers have fewer answers to consider.
- Don't offend the solver. Increasingly, people on the receiving end of words they perceive as insults or disparagements are declaring "I won't take it anymore." It is not for us, as puzzlemakers, to argue against those perceptions. So:

  a.   Write gender-neutral definitions. "Firefighter's gear," not "Fireman's gear," for HOSE. "One with a trying job," not "He may be trying," for JUDGE. "Actor Streep," not "Actress Streep," for MERYL (or, for variety, "Filmdom's Streep" or "*Out of Africa*'s Streep").

  b.   Be very cautious about ethnic, religious, and racial references. Some are obvious slurs, and you know to shun those in answers and definitions alike. Some are less obvious, however, and even if a current dictionary does not carry a warning and you think them neutral, other people may consider them offensive or disparaging. You know, of course, that many people prefer "Native American" to "Indian" (or even "American Indian") as the designation for someone whose ancestors were here before 1492; you may also be aware that "Asian" is replacing "Oriental" as another encompassing descriptor.

Technical writers have a saying, typically applied to grammatical details such as passive voice and the awkward "his or her" phrasing: Real writers rewrite to avoid the problem. You can apply that saying to the writing of definitions. If space for clues is at a premium and you cannot afford the long definition "Native American in Arizona" for HOPI, try "Kiva worshiper," or "Pueblo dweller," or "Kachina maker."

REFINEMENTS

When you have completed all the definitions, review those for words that bridge into isolated corners. It's difficult to judge this point with any great precision, but you should do your best to ensure that the solver has a fair shake at accessing every part of the diagram, especially those that contain any tough words or definitions.

In any event, don't panic about having to prepare definitions; do the best you can. Editors are free to make improvements, and patient ones will help you do it their way the next time.

THE FINER POINTS

When you are satisfied that you can turn square grids into things people recognize as crossword puzzles, you will want to raise your sights—to seek more interesting subjects and designs for your creations; to hone your skills for placing theme answers, black squares, and letters in skeletal compositions; and to use appealing filler answers and inventive definitions to enliven your composition and tailor it for a specific market. The following material should help once you've chosen a theme.

SKELETAL COMPOSITION

After you have listed many more candidates for theme answers than you expect to use, you are ready to build a skeletal grid. (A lot of the work is done for you if your list of theme answers happily matches the scheme accommodated by one of the grids in our appendix.)

Long theme answers never appear on the grid's edge, because answers in the second row or column must be at least as long to avoid unchecked letters. Similarly, they rarely appear exactly one row or column in from the edge, because answers in the third row or column must be at least as long to avoid two-letter words. Even if, say, two four-letter answers with a single black square between them lie along a side and a nine-letter answer lies next to them, another answer of at least nine letters must lie next to it closer to the puzzle's center to avoid two-letter answers. In Figure 8.23, for instance, the word at 17 Across must be at least nine letters long because 14 Across is that length.

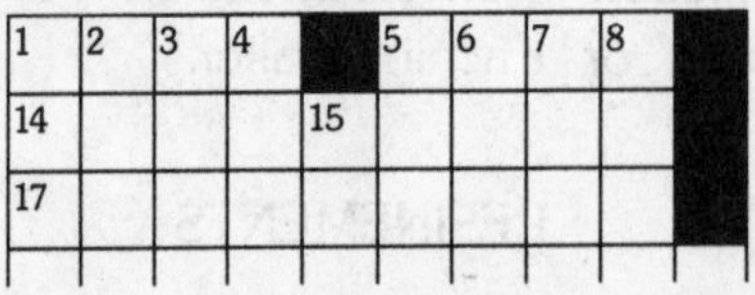

Figure 8.23. *The effect of a nine-letter answer in a diagram's second row*

Where, then, do theme answers go? One simple option is to set them horizontally in widely spaced rows of the diagram. 15x15 puzzles with full-width thematic answers on the fourth, eighth, and twelfth rows are quite common. Such a layout offers a lot of leeway in completing the diagram; with it you may easily avoid obscure, foreign, or uninteresting words. This technique, however, penalizes both you and the solver. It removes the challenge of crossing thematic answers and restricts the number you can put in the grid.

Making long adjacent thematic answers behave (as in, say, Figure 8.23 if both 14 Across and 17 Across were thematic) is very challenging for you and the solver. Even achieving close proximity is often difficult. Placement of three thematic answers within five consecutive rows is rare indeed, and often troublesome, but then rarity is a criterion of worth. You should probably resort to it only seldom, if ever.

Intersection of thematic answers is the subject of the remainder of this topic.

First, note that long answers intersecting near (but not at) their centers demand a second pair of symmetrically crossing answers, constrain large regions of the diagram, and often complicate placement of other long answers. Thus, as you seek to intersect pairs of theme answers, concentrate on the letters third, fourth, and fifth from each end of the answers on your candidates list. Answers crossing at those letters fall naturally in rows and columns where they conveniently bridge corners.

Here is our list of American cities from the earlier example.

position from nearer end of answer

	3	4	5	5	4	3	
BA	T	O	N	R	O	U	GE 5+5=10
LO	S	A	N	G	E	L	ES 3+7=10
SA	I	N	T	L	O	U	IS 5+5=10
SA	N	A	N	T	O	O	IO 3+7=10
DE	S	M		O		I	N ES 3+6=9
LA	S	C		R		U	C ES 3+6=9
PA	L	O			A	L	TO 4+4=8
	3	4	5	4	3		

We listed the longest ones first and arranged answers of the same length alphabetically. Follow our lead when you seek useful intersections in your own list: Space out the answers' letters as shown so you can more easily find points where two pairs of answers might intersect at symmetrically opposite points three, four, or five squares from the puzzle's borders. The ten-letter answers present the two possibilities shown earlier in Figures 8.15 and 8.16. These results are fortunate. You'll usually need a far longer list of candidates.

Have you seen how to determine whether or not the crossings you seek exist? Let's treat the problem in concrete terms. If the same letter is the third of a nine-letter entry and the third in a ten-letter entry, as with the *s*'s of LAS CRUCES and LOS ANGELES, then a symmetric intersection is possible if the third-from-last (if you want to be fancy, antepenultimate) letter of another nine-letter entry matches the third-from-last letter of a ten-letter entry, as with the *n*'s of DES MOINES and SAN ANTONIO. See Figure 8.17, to which we added the other ten-letter entries symmetrically as four five-letter words.

In looking for intersections, examine pairs of letters equally distant from opposite ends of answers of the same length. In the case of DES MOINES and LAS CRUCES, the pairs (see Figure 8.24) are *d/s, e/e, s/c, m/u, o/r, l/c, n/s, f/a,* and *s/l.* A potentially useful crossing exists if two other equally long answers have the identical letter pair. On our list the candidates SAN ANTONIO and LOS ANGELES also have an *n/s* pair. This coincidence accounts for Figure 8.17.

D	E	S	M	O	I	N	E	S
S	E	C	U	R	C	S	A	L

L	A	S	C	R	U	C	E	S

⇐ spelled backward

Figure 8.24. *Finding pairs of letters equidistant from opposite ends of two long thematic answers*

Another way of achieving intersections is to place one long answer with an odd number of letters in the central column (or row) of the grid, to be your puzzle's *spine* (or *waist*). Two answers of equal length can intersect it if their nth and nth-from-last letters, respectively, match letters occurring in the spine equidistant from its middle letter, as with:

```
                        D
                        E
          L O S A N G E L E S
                        M
                        O
                        I
        S A N A N T O N I O
                        E
                        S
```

That is, *s,* the third letter of LOS ANGELES and *n,* the antepenultimate letter of SAN ANTONIO, are equally far from the center (*o*) of DES MOINES.

Even if you succeed at crossing several theme answers, you'll probably have room in the grid for more, and they won't be able to intersect any others. How should you place them? Answer: They should bridge corners.[*] That is, place them on the third or fourth row or column in from a border, meeting an edge, or equidistant from two edges in a large puzzle. These positions form natural borders internal to a puzzle.

To determine which corners any particular nonintersecting thematic answer should bridge, examine its letters. If it has many letters that often appear in the third, fourth, or fifth positions of words or rarely appear in those positions,[†] then place the answer accordingly:

	Common	Rare
Third position	*t l d a r i o n*	*h x q j z*
Fourth position	*t e d s r*	*h c i o q j z*
Fifth position	*r s e*	*v u q j z*

Avoid the third row or column in from an edge if the answer has letters from the set *q*, *j*, *z*, *h*, *x*; seek such a row or column if it has many of the letters *t*, *l*, *d*, *a*, *r*, *i*, *o*, *n*.

Similarly, some letters are common toward the end of a word while others are rare, and you should seek or avoid rows and columns near the bottom and right side of the grid as the case may be. Common and rare letters at the end of words are shown below.

	Common	Rare
Third from end	*a r d l c p v*	*q z y f*
Fourth from end	*r t a o i l*	*x u y f*
Fifth from end	*s t d e*	*x z y n k v o*

Of course, some letters are rarer than others, irrespective of their positions in words. Letters such as *q*, *z*, *j*, and *x* will rarely occur in your thematic answers, so knowing where *not* to place them will be of little value. More interesting are the examples of those places where common letters are rarely found, and rare letters are most commonly found. Key facts, then, are that *v* is easy to incorporate third from the end of a word and *o* may be difficult when it is fifth from the end, etc. Remember these facts when you place thematic entries. (See the tables at the end of this chapter for more data of this sort.)

---

[*] Remember, we call a rectangular section a corner, even if it isn't in a corner of the diagram.

[†] The judgments in this chapter concern only words that are easily placed in puzzles. Rare words and those with rare or troublesome letter combinations do not enter into our consideration, nor does the frequency with which words appear in ordinary writing. Our tables were not compiled by counting words in dictionaries or on pages of prose. Finally, the short tables here in the text are included in more comprehensive tables at the end of the chapter.

PLACING BLACK SQUARES

You are now ready to place black squares provisionally. The thematic answers' locations have fixed some of these already. The next ones you place will be the fingers that mark the corners. (See Figure 8.25.)

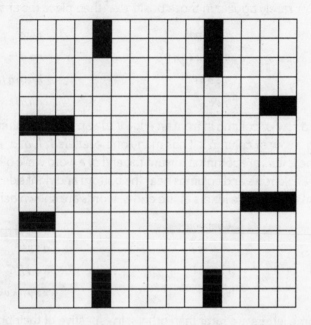

Figure 8.25. *Fingers in a 15x15 grid, creating three corners along each edge*

Most 15x15 puzzles have three corners per side, although many, especially "Puns and Anagrams" puzzles, have only two per side. The configuration of three corners along the top row and two along the leftmost column (or vice versa) is fine but uncommon. This may be due to the difficulty of finding an answer to emerge from the middle of an elongated corner as a bridge to another corner. Three corners per side may suffice for diagrams up to nineteen or twenty-one squares to a side. Four corners per side should be plenty even for 23x23 grids.

Place the next batch of black squares in the rows and columns on either side of the thematic answers by reference to those answers.

Some letters commonly and easily begin words, and some end words most frequently. Some rarely begin words, while others hardly ever end words. These letters are:

	Common	Rare
Start words	*s t r o p f q j g*	*x n y e v*
End words	*s r d e t n l y*	*q j z v i u b*

The locations of these letters in thematic answers influence your placement of black squares. You must not forget other criteria, however. Words must have at least three letters, for example, and the puzzle must not contain so many short words as to exceed the editor's maximum word counts.

A row or column of black squares within a puzzle often creates a rectangular field of white on either side, with which you must be prepared to deal. (See Figure 8.26.)

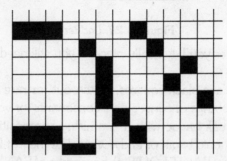

Figure 8.26. *Field of white created by a string of black squares*

Conversely, *ladders,* diagonal runs of black squares, simplify your task, as Figure 8.6 earlier in this chapter shows. Further, in ladders running from the upper right to the lower left (NE–SW, if you will) the same square is the first (or last or second . . .) of each of two different words. Some letters, such as *p*, are good "first letters," and others, such as *e*, are good "last letters," so you can place them quickly. The first and third squares of answers in NE–SW ladders are good places for rare letters, as Figure 8.27 demonstrates.

Another batch of black squares often appears two and three rows from thematic answers. To place these, you should know which letters are easiest or most difficult to use when they are two or three letters from the beginnings and ends of words. These are:

	Good	Bad
Two from start	*a o i r t u*	*j z q k w v f*
Three from start	*t l d a r i o n*	*q j z x h v*
Two from end	*e d r t n p l*	*q j x z f i u*
Three from end	*a r d l c p v*	*q z y f*

Figure 8.27. *Ladder*

The last black squares you'll typically place, if you still need any, are those near the center of the diagram.

As you tentatively place black squares, watch out for rare letters and consonantal clusters. Rare letters and strings of consecutive consonants (or vowels, for that matter) in thematic answers can wreak havoc with a promising composition. At least one of the consecutive consonants should begin or end a word, like the *r* of LAS CRUCES, the *m* of DES MOINES, the *n* and *t* of SAINT LOUIS, the second *n* of SAN ANTONIO, and the *g* of LOS ANGELES in Figure 8.19. Pay special attention to rare letters and clusters, giving them priority when you place black squares nearby.

When you've placed the black squares provisionally, check your word count. If your work has led to an acceptable diagram, proceed; if it has not, rework is in order.

We should comment here on how to determine a diagram's word count efficiently. You could count each answer, of course, but symmetry offers a shortcut. To find out how many horizontal answers there are, count the answers in the rows above the central row (that takes care of the top half), double that number (for the bottom half), and add the number of words in the central row. To find out how many vertical answers there are, count the words in the left-side columns, double to include the right half, add the center. Then add the two results together. The grand total will always be an even number.

If your provisional black squares lead to a pattern with too many words, consider removing a black square to turn four short answers into two longer ones that cross at their centers, or moving a black square sideways to further open a region of the puzzle (and, if you must, adding a cheater to keep the lengths of the intersecting words more manageable). (See Figure 8.28.)

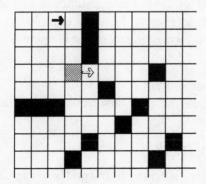 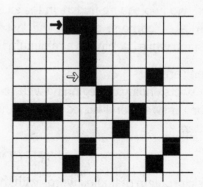

Figure 8.28. *Lowering word count by moving an existing black square (hollow arrow) and, perhaps, adding a cheater (solid arrow)*

Delete cheaters to raise the quality of your puzzle. If you have black squares configured like this you can delete either square in the middle row (but not both) without altering the word count.

Reduce the number of corners either horizontally or vertically, especially where no thematic answer acts as a bridge, even though you'll have a lot of rework to do. You can often fill larger corners unconstrained by thematic answers.

Use nonthematic answers that are as long as the shortest thematic ones. They can be puzzle-saving bridges, but you should use them symmetrically. Some editors dislike nonthematic answers that are as long as any thematic answers, however.

REVIEW

Look back at Figure 8.19 to see how it illustrates the points we've made. We placed the nonintersecting thematic answers in the only locations left for them and they served as bridges into the remaining corners. These answers could have been set one square closer to the puzzle's borders, but the *u*'s near the ends of the answers favored the placements shown.

We used two two-square fingers in the sixth and tenth rows and columns to establish the boundaries of corners, and set the last black squares to facilitate completion of the composition while keeping to a minimum the numbers of the following elements:

- Long answers.
- Answers ending or beginning with vowels other than *e*.
- Long answers sandwiched between thematic answers or near troublesome clusters or letters.

THE COMPOSITION

The basic problem of finding words with the "right" letters to fill the grid is susceptible to a number of attacks. However, we urge you to adopt this short catchphrase: Don't settle. In other words, don't wait until you've pieced together a first fill before starting to refine the composition. Refine as you go along, Every time you reach for a foreign-language dictionary or a mammoth atlas, or pencil in an uncommon abbreviation, a three-toed sloth, or that good-old ESNE, an alarm bell should ring. Here are some resources you should consider:

- *Funk and Wagnalls Crossword Word Finder,* by Schwartz and Landovitz, lists (without definitions) words of six letters or fewer that have two specific letters in specific positions. If you cannot locate it, try for one or another of the references British solvers and composers favor: *Cassell's Crossword Finisher* or any book based on *Chambers 20th Century Dictionary*. These books are either out of print or unavailable at retail stores in the United States, but you may find them at stores specializing in used books.

    Take care, however, to avoid strictly British variant spellings for your American audience.

- Battery-powered, handheld spelling checkers are inexpensive electronic equivalents of the books just mentioned. A typical one has a miniature keyboard and a small display screen. To find four-letter words beginning with *a* and ending with *t*, you'd type A??T and press the Enter key. Some models have huge word lists; others have fewer words but offer definitions or synonyms as compensating features.

    Franklin Electronic Publishers may be the most prominent of several companies making similar gadgets, which you can find at electronic supply office supply stores.

- If you have a computer, you may already have a word-finder at hand—your word processor's spell-checking module. Use it just like a handheld gadget: Type a search pattern and press Enter. If you also have a dictionary on your computer, it probably offers a similar search procedure.

- Keep inflected forms and common prefixes in mind. Plurals, third-person singular forms, verbs in the past tense, and words beginning with *re-* or *in-* should be used sparingly, but they can be very valuable in difficult situations.

- Keep an eye out for places where phrases and partials may save the day. If you can place a preposition, article, or pronoun at the beginning or end of an answer of intermediate size, you may be able to find another word to fill out the answer and form part of an acceptable title, saying, or quotation. A Bible concordance and a copy of *Familiar Quotations* can help, even though *familiar* is not an editor's synonym for "automatically acceptable."

  Most editors frown on partials longer than four or five letters.

- Expand or update your home library. Get a biographical dictionary and an atlas. Reference books focus on specific aspects of our world in ever-increasing numbers. One publisher, for example, publishes dictionaries and guides to opera, ballet, and popular music. Many film reviewers produce annually updated movie books; similar references report on hit songs and television shows. Almanacs list recent award winners and sports leaders, and sports almanacs offer even more complete listings in that field.

  Some of these books provide extensive cross-reference indexes, by the way, which makes them even more useful. Amende's *Legends in Their Own Time* (a biographical dictionary) includes an index of first names. So, if you need to clue ANNE, and you don't want to use "Boleyn" or "Bancroft" yet again, you can choose from more than twenty others.

- A desktop computer can be a great convenience. If your computer has a CD-ROM reader, you probably already have a decent encyclopedia and you can add some intriguing databases to your arsenal at very modest expense. For example, one disk has the full text of nearly 1,900 literary works, including the Bible and all of Shakespeare. Others offer extensive film, music, history, sports, and technology references. One even has the whole text of the 1840 set of Audubon's *Birds of America*, with pictures, and the entertaining (but not helpful in this context) bonus of many recorded bird calls.

  Characteristically, these programs provide fast searches for names, words, or phrases. Tired of "Smell ____" to define A RAT? Look up "a rat" in Shakespeare and find three lines for variety.

  If your computer has a modem you can read data stored around the world—probably without so much as a long-distance phone call. For example, encyclopedias accessible on on-line services such as Prodigy, America Online, and CompuServe are updated more frequently than you would buy a new encyclopedia for yourself. On-line movie references and similar files may be updated every day. Want to confirm the exact form of a book's title in the Library of Congress catalogues? Use Internet, either directly or through one of the on-line services.

- Consider words in foreign languages. Tap them only sparingly, but you can occasionally get out of a jam by using one. Lean to cognates, words that resemble their English equivalents, to give the monolingual solver a fair chance. Familiarize yourself with inflectional endings and letter patterns that appear in various languages—for instance, *aa* occurs in words of Dutch origin, *ich* occurs in words of German origin, and some Italian plurals end in the letters *oli*. The *Random House Unabridged Dictionary* offers an appendix with small French-, Spanish-, Italian-, and German-English dictionaries, so you may not need to buy special books.

- Be mindful of the patterns in which letters appear. What do all of these words and phrases have in common?

one-time	delegates
Camelot	paramedic
avocado	inoperative
ecumenical	misused
not on a bet	coverage

Answer: they all have alternating consonants and vowels, which makes them extremely useful. You can fill in relatively large fields of white, and ladders of even six- or seven-letter words quite rapidly by manipulating such words.

- A gimmicky device, which you should resort to only in an emergency, is use of a single symbol for an alphabetic O in one word and a numeric 0 in the crossing word, for example. In the extreme, IOLITTLE can be defined by "___ Indians." Be warned, however: Editors generally disapprove of this bit of chicanery, and many refuse to accept it.

- Finally, if you do have a desktop computer, there's another resource available: a crossword-generating program. There are several on the market, for IBM (and compatibles) and Macintosh systems. Investigate them before you buy, though, because some of them claim to produce crossword puzzles but turn out to make what you may now know as a skeleton or kriss kross puzzle, not a crossword puzzle.

Most work essentially the same way: You set up a grid, fill in some thematic answers, and say "Go." If your grid isn't too extremely open, and if the program's word stock is large enough and to your liking, you should get a completed grid you can live with—or, at least, one you can polish to your satisfaction. After all, if the word stock is good, computer-generated crosswords are good. If the word stock has no obscurities, unheard-of abbreviations, or crosswordese, the resulting grid simply cannot contain any of those deprecated items.

Most of these programs let you adjust the word stock to suit your own wants and needs. At least one offers a "preferred" word list, in which you put thematic answers besides those you prefill in the grid—the idea is to increase the number of thematic answers in the fill, even though they'll probably not be placed symmetrically.

The programs guard against duplicate answers (but plurals are tough to catch, especially when the spelling changes even a little, say from WOLF to WOLVES).

Some of the programs provide canned definitions or let you save and conveniently reuse your own if the same answers show up in subsequent grids. All can ensure that your grids are symmetric. All can properly number them for printing; some are set up to "typeset" puzzles for your friends to solve, while others print material in a form suitable for freelance submittal to an editor.

One editor pays a convenience bonus for accepted puzzles supplied on computer disk. At least one other editor encourages puzzles sent on disk, also for convenience.

You may view such programs as heretical or as practical technology. Either way, they're here—and a growing number of composers are using them effectively. If you choose not to explore this option, that's perfectly fine, but you need to know what the competition is doing to supply the crosswords most of today's editors buy.

Many competitive situations are spoken of using sports metaphors. We use the phrase "level playing field" to describe fair competition. If you don't use a computer to help build crossword grids, maybe that part of the field isn't quite level for you. However, if you take extra care to execute themes very consistently, and if you write interesting, intriguing definitions using a variety of techniques, you can make the rest of the field level, or even tilt it your way a little.

POLISHING THE FILL

There are good reasons for including and for rejecting words—if you can find alternatives. A composition filled with uninteresting answers will bore the solver. *Interest* is an uninteresting word. No matter how clever the definition is, the solver will gain little satisfaction from thinking of *interest*. Here are a few attributes of words we find interesting:

- Lots of consonants. Words with a high percentage of consonants may be difficult to incorporate, but they keep the solver's attention: *frenzy, bum's rush, schnapps*.

- Presence of rare letters. To add specific rare letters to a composition, first look in a comparatively problem-free corner for a convenient square for a given rare letter, say the upper left-hand square for a *q*, one row and one column in from the lower right-hand square for a *z*. Then try to complete the corner with the rare letter in place. A grid as small as 9x9 can be pangrammatic—that is, can contain every letter of the alphabet—if that's the only objective. See Figure 8.29, for example.

Figure 8.29. *A 9x9 grid containing every letter of the alphabet*

- High imagery. Adjectives and adverbs, which evoke images, are pleasant words to encounter. *Purple, crisp, sultry,* and *dowdy* are examples of evocative words.
- Onomatopoeia and cacophony. Words such as *clamor, smooth, mouthy, buzz,* and *barnacle* can almost be heard as well as seen.

Here, for contrast, are some kinds of words that, to us, are not interesting in a puzzle:

- Ordinary words from technical and bureaucratic circles. These words often have vague or lifeless definitions. *Parameter* and *individual* come to mind.
- Proper names. However, one way to refer to today's world is to incorporate the names of today's prominent people. The challenge, of course, is to guess which prominent people will be remembered tomorrow. Before Mikhail and RAISA Gorbachev came to public attention, puzzle writers had only soprano Rosa RAISA available for that letter combination. It may be so again, before too long.

- Words loaded down with prefixes and/or suffixes. The word *unretentiveness* does nothing for us. And don't coin words by tacking on prefixes. *Rehesitate* is, as Will Weng once wrote, "a poor word."
- Words composed almost solely of the letters *e*, *n*, *r*, *s*, and *t*: *sternness*, *nest*, *entree*.

CATERING TO A MARKET

Some publications offer a range of puzzles from very easy to very hard; others offer only one or the other end of the spectrum. But there's more to it than just "easy" or "hard," and, so, catering to a market means catering to a particular editor's wishes across several different aspects of puzzle writing:

- Are nonthematic puzzles acceptable?
- Are themes allowed that rely on repeated words in long entries?
- Are minor thematic inconsistencies seen regularly?
- Are quotations allowed as themes?
- Are obscure words, crosswordese, or odd abbreviations allowed in the grid?
- Are brand names allowed in the grid?
- Are puzzles often allowed that exceed the traditional black-square limits?
- What's the maximum allowable word count?
- Do definitions explicitly declare prefixes, abbreviations, and the like, or does the editor prefer the contemporary approach?
- Do definitions contain a lot of ambiguity? What about vagueness?
- Is there much wordplay for short answers?

You can do two things to gain an insight into an editor's style. Read and study the puzzles that editor publishes, and mimic their style when you send puzzles to that market. And solicit that editor's *style sheet* for whatever statement exists regarding philosophy, preferences, limits, and so on. Chapter 13, "Marketing," has style sheets from several publications. Use them as reference, but write for the editor's most recent version.

A SUBTLE REFINEMENT

You should be aware of one last subtle refinement: rewriting the entire composition so that all the horizontal words become vertical words, and vice versa. Probably because we read and write English horizontally, rows' contents register more fully on editors and solvers than columns' contents. Modify your completed composition if:

- The vertical thematic answers are more interesting than the horizontal ones.
- The theme is carried by the definitions (as opposed to the answers) and the thematic answers are all in widely separated rows. Placing them in columns—even though that may seem counterintuitive—may move the definitions closer together, catching the solver's attention.
- The first several horizontal words are less interesting than the vertical words in the two leftmost columns.
- The bottom row contains more *e*'s and *s*'s than the right-hand column.
- In your opinion, the arrangement of black squares looks more cluttered than it does when you turn the pattern on its side.

CAREER PLANNING

What types of puzzles should you now compose? We suggest that you start by composing puzzles for your own amusement. Then compose puzzles as gifts for puzzle fans among your relatives, friends, and acquaintances. What present could show more thoughtfulness?

After you've reached the point where your pride and confidence in your skills are unshakable, try to sell a puzzle. Let chapter 13, "Marketing," be your guide. Start with periodicals devoted to puzzles, because they buy more puzzles of all types and levels of difficulty, then move to markets with fewer opportunities. Few composers reach the top of the trade, and even those who do don't become wealthy as a result, so don't give up the joys of composition because you still see a few puzzles better than any of your own.

LISTS AND TABLES

Earlier in this chapter we mentioned there would be some lists of words meeting different criteria. Here they are.

WORDS THAT BEGIN WITH VOWELS

ABASE	ABUT	ADELA	AFAR	AGENA	AGORA	ALIBI
ABATE	ACAD	ADEN	AGAR	AGER	ALAN	ALIEN
ABED	ACED	AD IN	AGATE	AGES	ALAS	ALIT
ABET	ACES	ADORE	AGED	AGILE	ALES	ALOHA

ALONE	AROMA	EGAD	EMOTE	EWES	ODER	OVAL
ALOP	AS IS	EKED	ENATE	EXILE	ODIN	OVATE
ALUM	ATONE	EKES	ENEMY	EXIT	ODOR	OVEN
AMATI	ATOP	ELAN	ENOLA	IBAR	OKAPI	OVER
AMAZE	AVAIL	ELATE	ENOS	IBIS	OLIVE	OVINE
AMUSE	AVER	ELIAS	EPIC	ICON	ON ICE	ULAN
ANILE	AVON	ELIHU	ERAS	IDEA	ONUS	UNIT
ANODE	AWAKE	ELITE	ERASE	IDOL	OPEC	UNITE
APACE	AWARE	ELOPE	ERATO	IMAM	OP ED	UNIV
APED	AWED	EMAIL	ERODE	I MET	OPEN	UPON
APER	AWES	EMERY	EROS	INURE	ORAL	URAL
APES	EBONY	EMORY	EROSE	IRAN	ORAN	USED
AREA	ECOL	EMIL	ETON	IRAQ	ORATE	USER
ARECA	ECON	EMILE	EVEN	IRATE	OREL	USES
ARENA	EDEN	EMIR	EVER	IRENE	ORES	UTAH
ARES	EDIT	EMIT	EVIL	IRON	OTIC	UTES
ARIA	EELS	EMORY	EWER	IVAN	OTIS	

WORDS FOR TOP OR LEFT PLACEMENT

Words easily used at the top or left of a puzzle (or corner) share some traits. They have two or three consonants together, their consonants appear often with other consonants (as *p* can precede *h*, *l*, and *r*), and their vowels don't include *e*. Here are some:

BALD	CHAP	CROP	FRAT	PATS	RAFT	SCAN
BAND	CHAR	CROW	GRAM	PLAN	RAPT	SCAR
BARN	CHART	DARTS	PADS	PLAT	RASH	SCARF
BASH	CLAP	DOST	PALS	PLOP	RASP	SCAT
BASIS	CLASP	DRAG	PANS	PORT	RATS	SHIRT
BLAND	CLAW	DRAM	PAWS	POST	ROTO	SHORT
BRAN	CLIP	DRAT	PARD	POTS	ROTS	SHUN
BRAND	CLOP	DRAW	PART	PRAT	SARA	SHUNT
CASH	CRAM	DROP	PAST	PROTO	SASS	SLAM

SLAP	SOFT	SPAT	STATS	SWIFT	THAN	TRAP
SLAW	SOLO	SPLAT	STOP	SWIG	THAW	TRAY
SLIP	SORA	SPLIT	STOW	TADS	THIN	TRIM
SLOP	SORT	SPORT	STRAD	TAGS	THING	TRIP
SLOT	SOTS	SPOT	STRAP	TAPS	THROW	TROY
SLOW	SPAD	SPRIG	STRIP	TARA	TOPS	TSAR
SODA	SPAN	STARS	SWAG	TARS	TOSS	WRAP
SOFA	SPAR	START	SWAN	TART	TRAM	XRAY

WORDS FOR BOTTOM OR RIGHT PLACEMENT

Conversely, words with many letters from the set *d*, *e*, *r*, *s*, and *t* are relatively helpful in the bottom row and in the rightmost column. Here are a few.

DEED	DRESS	ESTES	REED	SEEP	STEEL	TEEN
DEER	EDEN	ETES	REEDY	SEER	STEEP	TENET
DELE	ESSEN	EYES	SEDER	SERE	STEER	TREES
DESERT	ESSES	KEEN	SEED	SEVER	STERE	TRESS
DETER	ESTER	REDS	SEEN	STEED	TEDS	

LETTER-SELECTION TABLES

In the following three tables we present our opinions regarding placement of letters in words in crossword puzzles. You will have many occasions to disregard the information in these tables to satisfy the constraints of puzzles in progress. We believe, however, that on many more occasions these tables will simplify your task by helping you eliminate problems before they arise.

Table 1 provides information to help you select rows and columns for thematic answers and to place black squares near thematic answers. For example, try to avoid placing a black square so that *x*, *n*, *y*, *e*, or *v* must start a word, or so that *q*, *j*, *z*, *v*, *i*, *u*, or *b* must end a word.

Table 2 provides information to help you complete corners. It tells you what letters are likely to help you find crossing words. If you have a choice of letters for a square, look at table 2 for letters that will give you the most freedom in selecting a crossing answer. For example, if you must complete the word A_ED, table 2 will help you choose from among *c*, *g*, *p*, *w*, and *x*, depending on the position of that letter in the crossing word.

Table 3 may help you finish an area where some constraining letters already exist. Consider the corner in Figure 8.30.

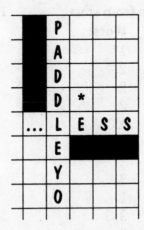

Figure 8.30. *An example of how you might use table 3*

That long Down entry might be part of the phrase "paddle your own canoe," and the incomplete crossing entry is just for illustration. Fill the starred square in Figure 8.30 by using table 3 to find a letter that easily follows *d* near the beginning of a word and precedes *e* near the end of a word. The only one is *r*.

Table 1. Positions in five- to seven-letter words where particular letters are especially easy or hard to deal with.

| Position of letters from start | | | | Position of letters from end | | | |
Easiest		Hardest		Easiest		Hardest	
strdpfqjg	1	*xnyev*		*srdetnly*	1	*qjzviub*	
aoirtu	2	*jzqkwvf*		*edrtnpl*	2	*qjxzfiu*	
tldarion	3	*qjzhx*		*ardlcpv*	3	*qzyf*	
tedsr	4	*qjxzshcio*		*rtaoil*	4	*xuyf*	
rse	5	*qjzxvlaiuo*		*stde*	5	*xzynkvo*	

Table 2. Position in five- to seven-letter words where it is best or worst to find particular letters.

Letter	Position from start		Position from end	
	Best	**Worst**	**Best**	**Worst**
a	2, 3	1*	3, 2	1**
b	1, 3	2	3	1, 2
c	1	2	3	1, 2
d	1, 3	2	1, 3	
e		1, 3	1, 2	
f	1	2		1, 3, 2
g	1	2		2, 3
h	2, 1	3		2
i	2, 3	1	3	1
j	1	2, 3		1, 2, 3
k	3	2	2	
l	1, 2, 3		3, 2	
m	1, 3		2	1, 3
n	3	1	2, 1	3
o	2, 3		3	1
p	1, 3	2	3, 2	1
q	1	3, 2		2, 1, 3
r	1, 2, 3		1, 3	
s	1	2	1	
t	1, 3, 2		2, 1	
u	2	3		1, 2
v	3	2, 1	2, 3	1
w	1	2		2
x	2	1	1	2
y		1, 2	1	3, 2
z		2	1	

   *   That is, as first letter of answer.
 **   That is, as last letter of answer.

Table 3. Letters that most often precede or follow given letters in four- and five-letter words

| Letters that often precede | | Given | Letters that often follow | |
Near beginning	Near end	letter	Near beginning	Near end
r, l, m, b, t, h, s	e, r, l, n, m, t	A	r, l, n, m, t	s, n, l, r, t, d
a, o	a, m, r, o, u	B	a, o, e, r, u, i, l	s, a, e, o, i
s, a, i, o	vowels + n, r	C	o, a, h, r, l, u	h, k, e, a, t, o
a, i, o, e	e, i, a, n, o, r	D	o, e, i, a, u, r	e, s, y, a
r, l, d, h, t, s	l, r, t, n, d	E	n, r, l, a, e	s, d, r, a, n, l, t
a, e, i, o	f, i, a, e, o, l, r	F	l, a, i, e, r	s, f, t, e, y
a, o, i	n, a, o, i, r	G	a, r, o, l	e, s, o, a, i, h, y
s, c, t, w, p	c, t, s, p	H	vowels	e, a, i, s, y
r, l, d, h, m, t, p	r, l, a, n, t, d	I	n, l, t, r, s, d	n, l, s, e, t, d, r
e	n, a, o	J	a, o, e	a, i, o
a, i, o, s	n, r, o, a, s	K	i, e, a	e, s, y, a
vowels + s, b	a, i, l, e, o	L	vowels	s, e, l, a, y, t, o
vowels + s	vowels	M	vowels	e, s, p, a, i, y
vowels + s	vowels + r	N	vowels	s, t, e, g, a, d
r, t, l, d, m, p, n	r, o, l, t, n, i, g	O	r, l, n, u, v, t, m	n, r, s, l, t, w
s, a, o, u	a, o, m, e	P	vowels + l, r	s, e, a, t, y, h
s, a	a	Q	u	u
a, o, t, p, d, g, i	vowels	R	vowels	e, a, s, t, i, o, y
vowels	vowels + t, n	S	vowels + t, p, l	e, t, s, h
vowels + s	a, s, n, o, i, r, e	T	vowels + h	s, e, y, a, h, t
l, r, t, p, s, d	o, r, l, a	U	r, n, l, s	s, r, n, l, e
vowels	a, i, e	V	vowels	e, a, i, o, y
o, a, s, t	o, a, e	W	a, i, e, o, r, h	s, e, n, l
e, o	e, i, a, o	X	e	e, i
a	l, r, t, n, a	Y	a, o, e	s, e, l
a	a, z	Z	a, o	e, y, z, a

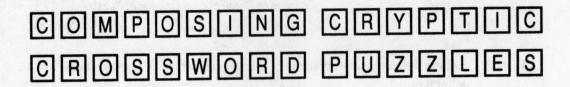

COMPOSING CRYPTIC CROSSWORD PUZZLES

9

To . . . the man who searches painfully for the perfect word . . .
there is . . . the constant joy of sudden discovery.
—H.L. Mencken, *A Book of Prefaces*

As a constructor of cryptic crosswords, you'll face problems quite unlike those posed by conventional puzzles. Certainly the nature of cryptic clues constitutes the major distinction and challenge; less important, but best discussed first, are the diagrams and answers.

DIAGRAMS

From a shared invention, American crossword composers migrated to complete word interlock, eliminating letters with no intersection (unchecked letters, or unches), while British composers exploited unchecked letters to have greater freedom in completing the diagram with fewer obscure answers.

Cryptic puzzles inhabit many types of diagrams. The type we focus on is symmetric in the same way as conventional crosswords. Furthermore, no more than half of the letters in any one answer are unches, no word has fewer than four letters (in American cryptics, although some British cryptics permit three-letter words), and the average word length runs close to half the puzzle's width (and length, since the diagram is square). A 15x15 lattice, or black-square, puzzle might contain twenty-four to thirty-two answers; a 12x12 bar-diagram puzzle, thirty-six to forty-two. Numbers are placed as they are in conventional puzzles.

In black-square diagrams, alternate letters are checked as a rule. In American cryptics, at least, the appearance of two consecutive unchecked letters is now taboo, and in any case three unches never occur together. Furthermore, some British publications permit three-letter words, but in American black-square cryptic puzzles the minimum length is four letters. The easiest way to guarantee checking of alternate letters and of at least half each word's letters is to start the first Across and Down answers in the top-left corner of the grid, rather than one row or column away. (See Figure 9.1.)

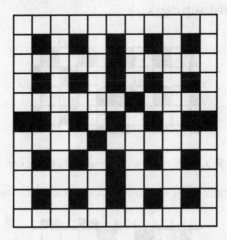

Figure 9.1. *Checking at least half of each answer's letters*

Figure 9.2 shows what not to do. Answers lie one row or column away from the border; as a result, fewer than half their letters are checked.

Figure 9.2. *Too many unchecked letters*

Isolated corners, it should be clear, are forbidden in cryptic puzzles—as they are in conventional puzzles. Furthermore, it should never be possible to divide one puzzle into two by blacking out a single square.

Figure 9.3 demonstrates both consecutive checked letters (marked with asterisks) and consecutive unches (marked with daggers).

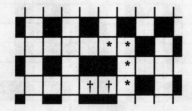

Figure 9.3. *Consecutive checked and unchecked letters*

The intersection in Figure 9.4 also offers consecutive checked letters.

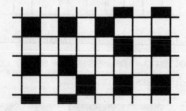

Figure 9.4. *Another arrangement of consecutive checked letters*

ANSWERS

Because cryptic puzzles constrict your answers less than conventional puzzles do, selection of interesting answers is important.

Good 15x15 cryptic puzzles usually contain at least two, and preferably four, or even six (nearly-)full-width answers. They may be related in some way but unlike conventional puzzles, cryptic puzzles commonly have no themes.

As you'd expect, you should choose and place the longest answers first, as anchors. Choose them in such a way as to make it easiest for you to complete the composition. Don't choose for 1 Across or 1 Down a long answer whose odd-numbered letters (the ones that will start intersecting answers) rarely begin words. Similarly, long answers terminating in the bottom right-hand corner should have few letters in odd-numbered positions, counting from the back, that rarely end words.

Clues will involve plays on words, so choose answers that readily lend themselves to such antics. Such words and phrases (1) contain particles with multiple meanings, such as *pine*apple, re*store*, and dand*elion*; (2) conceal shorter and *totally unrelated* words within them, forward, backward, or scrambled, such as or*din*ary (*din*), fami*lia*r (*lima*), and p*en*et*r*ate (*rent*); (3) have a fair number of common letters from which you can easily form anagrams; (4) sound like other words; (5) have idiomatic meanings as well as plausible literal interpretations; and/or (6) offer other approaches as suggested by the types of clues described here and in chapter 4, "Solving Cryptic Crossword Puzzles."

The letters at intersections should generally be fairly common consonants or vowels in positions they occupy less often. Why? To aid solution without impeding your completion of the composition. Knowledge that the first and last letters of a five-letter answer are *s* and *e* hardly helps the solver, yet making the same letters *n* and *w* unacceptably constrains you. (Compromise choices might be *w* and *d*, *b* and *r*, or *c* and *l*.)

Much of what we said about conventional puzzles applies to cryptic puzzles as well, at least in catering to American cryptic markets: Obscurity is bad; long intersecting answers challenge and ultimately reward the solver; patterns of vowels and consonants are significant. All in all, though, achieving a first fill is much easier for cryptic puzzles than for conventional puzzles, but producing an interesting and entertaining final fill is at least as difficult and poses many of the same problems. The *clues* make the puzzle cryptic, but the answers determine to what the clues must lead. There may be no interesting way to clue UNDER, for example.

You can add black squares as you go or immediately after establishing the anchors. In any case, fill the grid by working away from the anchors toward isolated regions. Use words about half as long as the puzzle's length and width, with common consonants in the odd positions, if possible, to promote interesting and helpful crossings. By the time you get to the last region, difficulties may have arisen. Solve them by redoing whatever you must. Don't become so enraptured with a particular answer that you hesitate to change it to complete a puzzle.

Within each section of the grid, resolve the most difficult problems first—probably the longest remaining words and those that link to the rest of the pattern. By the time you near the end of your task and have several letters seeking a word to hold them, the letters may well be convenient ones like S_ A_ T_ and may leave you many words from which to choose, such as SPARTA, STARTS, SHANTY, and so on.

Many answers that would be acceptable in conventional puzzles are unacceptable in cryptic puzzles—partial phrases that can exist only in fill-in-the-blank definitions and words requiring long definitions, for example. Cryptic clues usually won't work with such answers.

Quick reference sources for answers are *Cassell's Crossword Finisher* and any of the books built by computer from the Chambers dictionary. Of course, you must match your vocabulary to your intended audience; don't take clearly British words from either book for an American publication.

CLUES

The cross-checking provided by total interconnection permits composers of conventional puzzles to use difficult words and ambiguous definitions to challenge solvers' vocabulary skills. For cryptic puzzles, you need clues that lead to ordinary words and phrases, but so subtly as to retain and actually heighten challenge. You must be devious, employing wit rather than mere vocabulary, the needle and not the sword.

There is much to be said for this, but fans of cryptic puzzles may say too much. Subtlety is sometimes gained at the expense of challenge in the diagram's construction. In the end, solvers will forever take up the verbal cudgel for the type of puzzle they most enjoy. *De gustibus non est disputandum.*

SQUARE-DEALING CLUES

There are a few rules to "square dealing" that we want to emphasize here. Several are embodied in Afrit's words. A good cryptic clue, according to Afrit, contains three things: (1) a definition of the answer; (2) a second definition or some (square-dealing) wordplay leading to the answer by another route; (3) nothing else!

Furthermore, as Afrit also wrote (and which has become known in the puzzle-writing craft as Afrit's Law): While a clue may not mean what it seems to say, it must say exactly what it does mean.

DEFINITION

Every clue contains a definition of its answer. Except for some variety cryptic crosswords, the answer is what goes into the grid. (When instructions in variety cryptics alter the answer, what goes into the grid is called a light.) Although cryptic puzzles entail greater latitude than conventional ones, the definition should usually be reasonably straightforward and, as in conventional crossword puzzles, it must agree in number and part of speech with the answer.

The definition begins at the beginning of the clue or ends at its end, and does not overlap any part of the wordplay except for & lit clues, in which both definition and wordplay occupy the whole clue.

SECOND APPROACH

Every clue also contains either a second definition (which may involve a pun or an elliptical or literary reference) or a hint, which is wordplay often needing a signal to tell the solver what's going on. This part of the clue does not overlap the definition except for & lit clues.

In chapter 4, "Solving Cryptic Crossword Puzzles," we wrote about different kinds of clues from the solver's point of view: double definitions, hidden words, anagrams, reversals, charades, containers, homophones, homographs, additions and deletions and changes, abbreviations and selections, and "& lit." If you need a refresher, refer to chapter 4.

NOTHING ELSE

There are no extra words. For example, in a clue reading "Step off a rumpled cape (4)," with answer PACE, the "a" is extra; it plays no part in either definition or wordplay and does not improve surface reading. Here's an extreme example: "Fountain in which, if coins are thrown in it, revisiting's likely (5)." The clue's ordinary sense (the *surface reading*) seems to make the answer TREVI. Its letters span "iT REVIsiting" to be sure, and the second word of the clue signals a hidden word to be sure, but six words come between that signal and the crucial words and there's another pointless word afterward.

A minor exception to this tenet involves the linking word or phrase. If you view a clue as an equation of definition and wordplay, good surface grammar may employ something to function as the equals sign in that equation. In the clue "Brace for a terrible age (3)," the word *for* is like an equals sign separating two definitions of the answer, TWO.

AFRIT'S LAW

Afrit's Law has two parts. Here it is again: A clue may not mean what it seems to say, but it must say exactly what it does mean.

First, a clue's surface reading may have nothing to do with the cryptic instructions. In fact, that's a lot of the fun. In the clue "Butcher takes beef for dinner (5)," the surface reading seems to say nothing more than that a seller of meat trusts the merchandise well enough to use it personally. The cryptic instructions, however, tell the solver to scramble ("butcher") the letters in "takes" to get an answer meaning "beef for dinner" (STEAK).

Second, the clue must describe precisely how to acquire (each component part of) the answer. Precision is often what distinguishes a good clue from a bad one, and we believe many lapses of precision arise because of a mistaken belief that surface reading is more important than cryptic instructions. To write precise instructions:

- Use language precisely. Suppose you decide to write a container clue for LEERIEST, with ERIES inside LET, and you hit on "Great Lake's inlet making you most wary." The problem is, "inlet" and "in let" are different. There is a great temptation to use "indeed" when "in deed" is what you really mean. Don't give in. A variation of this flaw involves letter addition or subtraction. "Bout" and "B out" are not the same.

  Correct use of language also pertains to the straight definition. It's perfectly fair to use a word that appears to be a noun but that also has a verb sense, and vice versa, as with *butcher* in the clue above, but when all is said and done, the answer and clue must agree in number and part of speech. "Climbs the walls" is a verb; IVY is a noun.

  There's some subtlety to this part-of-speech notion. Consider the clue "It's stupid trapping him in financial disasters (7)." The intended answer is CRASHES, and the hint is supposed to be CRASS around HE. The problem is that *him* is an objective-case pronoun and *he* is a nominative-case pronoun. They are related, but different. Substituting "that man" for "him" would be satisfactory.

  Finally, you can add some difficulty by using a word's synonym. If you try for extra difficulty by using a synonym of a synonym, though, the result can easily be off base. *Visit* and *see* are synonyms, and so are *see* and *perceive*, but *visit* is not a substitute for *perceive*. And remember that you cannot use indirect anagrams—that is, synonyms for words whose letters participate in anagrams.

- Don't overwork a word. Suppose you decide to write a hidden-word clue for NAME. The clue "Reputation, in a meaning (4)" looks plausible, but the cryptic instructions fail because "in" both signals a hidden word and contains one of the letters in that word.

- Pay attention to detail when single letters (especially *I*) participate. If you want to get from CAN to CAIN by inserting the letter *I*, you must do it in a way that makes grammatical sense, both as regards instructions to the solver and as the clue purports to be a sentence or clause. "I is in fire [CAN as a verb] for biblical brother" builds the answer, but the surface reading is impossible as a correct sentence in English. "I go through fire for biblical brother" makes a plausible sentence, but it doesn't tell the solver what to do in a grammatical way. One way to deal with the letter *I* is to change verb form: "I will be found standing in fire for biblical brother."

You need to take similar precautions when you add or subtract other single letters. If you refer to those letters cryptically, make sure the reference is cryptically precise. "Top of morning" is not the same as "Top of the morning"; the former is M, the latter is TAM ("top of the" = T; "morning" = AM).

CLUE BALANCE

Write clues after you have completed the composition. Actually, the composition may well have grown from one or more answers for which you already had choice clues in mind.

You should deliberately allocate some number of the clues to multiple definitions, hidden words, whole anagrams, and charades not involving anagrams for word parts. The easiest clues to solve involve only one kind of wordplay, and the idea is to provide a few places at which the solver can attack the puzzle. Sprinkle them about the grid rather than concentrating them in one area. The number to allot depends on your audience's presumed skill level. Make the remaining clues more complex by using two or more kinds of wordplay and synonyms for parts of charades, containers, and reversals.

First, compose clues for the answers likely to give you the most trouble: the longest ones and those with rare letters. When you get down to the last few, you'll know what types of clues you need for balance and you may have great freedom to exercise your wit.

If the first set of clues you derive seems unbalanced, look for easier clues for answers with common letters or, conversely, harder clues for answers with rarer letters. Don't be reluctant to change parts of the composition to get more interesting clues or a better balanced set of clues.

Remain observant as you write a clue. Look for totally unrelated words concealed in the answer or hiding at its ends. Would you notice THE in BATHER, or PETER around the outside of PERIMETER? If not, you couldn't compose "Tribunal imprisoning the beach enthusiast (6)" or "Peter embraces uplifted [that is, reversed, in a Down clue] desert prince [EMIR] outside (9)."

Anagrams are good things to look for next. To find these easily and rapidly, shuffle tiles or cubes from a word game—not randomly, but by placing common prefixes (such as *re-*, *in-*, *de-*, *ex-*), suffixes (such as *-er*, *-ed*, *-es*, *-ing*), roots (such as *-ect-*, *-plain-*, *-vis-*) and letter pairs and letter triplets (such as *er*, *at*, *est*, *ent*, *ant*, *tle*) together in groups. Other sources for anagrams include *Chambers Anagrams*, handheld electronic gadgets, and computer software. However you do it, you're sure to notice that ELEGANT has the same letters as TEEN GAL and come up with something like "Awkward teen gal is stylish (7)."

The most challenging anagrams to solve pair long words with few bigrams and trigrams in common. Thus, a clue for BEARING that leaves the RING intact ("Ring Abe, perhaps, to get direction") is poor. The anagram LATENT for TALENT has the virtue of pairing words that often go together, thereby making cluing easy. On the other hand, the words have the vices of a shared trigram, *ent*, and a shared pattern of vowels and consonants.

A superior anagram is something like ENUMERATION for MOUNTAINEER, because the two words are long with only one common bigram (*er*), and have no common linguistic root. "Clumsy mountaineer produces list (11)."

Most editors prefer to minimize the number of clues involving only anagram wordplay, so don't overdo it.

Recomposition (such as FOREST ALL for FORE-STALL) and simple changes with great consequences (HIDEOUS to HIDEOUT) are useful kinds of bases for good clues. "Stop in woods, everybody (9)" and "Refinish unsightly den (7)" do the job with few words.

In looking for charades, force yourself to forget etymology and pronunciation. Otherwise, you might never notice that BEGONE = BEG + ONE or that COOPERATION = COOPER + AT + ION, and you'd miss: "Plead to get one's leave? (6)" and "Barrelmaker near ion exchange (11)."

If the basic approaches don't seem to be getting you anywhere, consider wordplay involving letter addition or subtraction. Almost every letter or pair of letters offers several promising treatments. Here are some abbreviations and cryptic instructions illustrating what you might do for single letters. We've also provided a few incompletely spelled-out homophonic approaches, which demand the utmost care:

A— one, top grade, middle-man, from French, note (in music)
B— boy's first, Ben initially, bee, note
C— see, 100, sea, about (circa), note, center
D— land's end, 500, note, dawn's first, day
E— end of the, point (of compass), note, string (of a violin)
F— bad grade, loud (in music), note
G— gee, note, string
H— goalpost (from its shape)
I— one, I (first person), eye
J— jay, little John, first of January, the capital of Japan
K— Kay, quai, King
L— 50, left

M— 1000, measure (of type), first of May
N— point, measure, pole
O— nothing, circle, boy at heart, loop, love (tennis), egg, ring, boundless joy
P— soft (in music), pea
Q— queue, cue, Queen
R— are, right, Rabbi, run
S— point, pole, head of state
T— tee, tea, start of the
U— school (univ.), you
V— five, victory
W— point (compass), watt
X— ten, cross, kiss, heart of Texas
Y— why, end of day
Z— Zaire's capital, zoo's head

You can also incorporate any single letter with a phrase like "a bit of ___" where the word in the blank starts with the letter you need. For example, "a bit of jam" is J. Similarly, "duck's tail" is K.

Pairs and triplets of letters are also easy to handle, especially if you dip into abbreviations, chemical symbols, and foreign articles, namely:

Abbrev—   NA (North America), IE (*id est*, or that is)
Chemical—   NA (sodium), CL (chlorine)
French—   LA, LE, UN, UNE, LES
Spanish—   LA, EL, LAS, LOS, UNO, UNA
German—   DER, DIE, DAS, EIN

Of course, once you settle on a pleasing approach to the wordplay, you still have work to do. You still need a witty clue with a good, preferably misleading, surface reading. It is probably impossible to teach wit. For the most part, wit depends upon vocabulary, creativity, and, most of all, practice. The only general advice apt to be of use is this one: Read all the definitions of the answer and parts of the wordplay for those you can define in the most ways. These second-level definitions may include words such as *set*, *put*, *let*, or *note* that you can easily use in a single sentence with the desired effect. If the implications of this advice are unclear, try to see how each of the clues used as examples in this chapter and in chapter 4, "Solving Cryptic Crossword Puzzles," might have been derived using this procedure.

If a clue involving a container, reversal, or charade looks too easy for your intended audience, try replacing a word in that clue by a synonym. The added level of indirection can challenge and please a competent solver. It might frustrate a novice, however, so don't add indirection capriciously. After all, it's the solvers who pay you, ultimately. (Again, current practice is to show all the letters in an anagram directly in the clue. Using *climber* to replace *mountaineer* in our earlier example is unacceptable.)

An appealing device to make a clue more challenging is this one: Use for the dictionary definition a word or phrase whose meaning in context in the clue appears to be altogether different from the one the solver must discover. The clue "Light, wicked thing (6)," for CANDLE has this virtue because *light* seems to mean "not heavy," rather than "a device that illuminates." Furthermore, *wicked* seems to mean "evil," not "having a wick."

Another way to throw solvers off the track temporarily is to apply a word that often serves as a signal to some other purpose—in an anagram or charade, for instance. Consider "Dynasty hiding in explosive emplacement (6)." The "hiding in" implies there may be a string of letters spanning the last two words that has something to do with a dynasty. Not this time! The *real* clue reads something like "[A particular] dynasty hiding IN [yields a word meaning] explosive emplacement." In other words, M-IN-ING.

Use punctuation precisely, both as regards surface reading and cryptic instructions. "Robin's-egg" is a shade of blue. A "robin's egg" is found in a nest. The "robins' egg" contains a chick. Where you can most often be deceptive involves the *'s* combination, for it can stand for "it is," signify a possessive, or just supply the letter *s*.

One last thing you must remember in devising a cryptic clue: Don't leave the identity of an unchecked letter ambiguous. For example, "Refer to backing around movie rating with nothing exciting (6)." (*Cite* reversed around a movie rating and *o*) won't do if the second letter of EROTIC/EXOTIC is unchecked.

POLISHING CLUES

When you have a complete set of clues, polish them as follows:

- If two adjacent clues have a related theme, rewrite them to emphasize the relationship. See 21 and 23 Across in Figure 4.3 on page 64. As with conventional puzzles, you can exchange rows and columns in cryptic puzzles if doing so will juxtapose related clues.
- Where possible, use words with multiple meanings or words that might be signals (in place of their synonyms).

- Unlike Naomi, but like the New York Yankees after 1934 (in other words, Ruthlessly!), strip from each clue any words that are not essential to its fairness.
- Tailor the level of difficulty to your market. If your solvers expect real challenges, replace words in wordplay with synonyms wherever permissible; to make a puzzle easier, do the reverse. Use blatant signals to simplify a puzzle, fiendish ones to do the opposite.

CONCLUSION

To gain a better appreciation of how to construct a cryptic puzzle, study Figure 9.5, the puzzle clued in Figure 4.3 on page 64. We began with the four semirelated fourteen-letter answers that frame the puzzle and their intersecting answers that end in vowels other than *e*. The nine-letter answers were next. Then we filled the composition from upper left to lower right, refined it, and wrote clues.

Figure 9.5. *The composition clued in Figure 4.3*

Oh, as to cluing UNDER in an interesting way, how about "Beneath French and German articles (5)"?

COMPOSING HUMOROUS CROSSWORD PUZZLES

10

A man who could make so vile a pun would not scruple to pick a pocket.

—John Dennis, *The Gentleman's Magazine*, Vol. LI

You already know that the two elements of crossword puzzle construction are the composition itself and the set of definitions—and that you should tackle them in that order. The procedures and guidelines presented for the composition of conventional crossword puzzles generally apply to such humorous offshoots as "Puns and Anagrams" as well. The market for these puzzles is very small. Nonetheless, we would be remiss if we didn't discuss them, and there are some special points to consider.

Editors place heavy emphasis on low word count in humorous puzzles. Themes occur only rarely. In practical terms, this means that you have to use patterns with plenty of white space, like the one in Figure 10.1, and let the words fall where they may.

Almost all humorous puzzles use 15x15 patterns, so we discuss only puzzles of this size.

Minor variations on the pattern in Figure 10.1 are common, usually involving diagonal triplets of black squares in the interior of the grid, and they do not affect the total word count of seventy. Other alterations include cheaters in the corners, flanking the fingers, or in the interior. The critical feature of the pattern is that it contains only two words in the first row and two words in the leftmost column. Most crossword patterns with three words in the top row and in the leftmost column have word counts that are unacceptably high.

Composition of a crossword puzzle with only seventy words is a very challenging mental task. (All the answers, of course, must be real words or phrases—no nonsensical letter combinations escape the editor's scrutiny.) We recommend that you refer to chapter 8, "Composing Conventional Crossword Puzzles," for help in composing the puzzle itself. The remainder of this chapter discusses techniques for making clues for humorous puzzles.

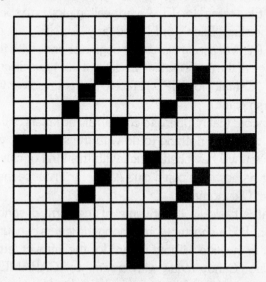

Figure 10.1. *Typical pattern for a humorous puzzle. Blackening the center square simplifies the task of composing the puzzle, while raising the word count only from seventy to seventy-two*

You are not bound to follow any rigid rules when writing clues for humorous puzzles. If for no reason other than space requirements in publications, puzzle editors cannot afford the luxury of verbose cryptic clues that "play fair" in all respects. Don't be afraid to be inventive. Who knows? Maybe you'll discover a new kind of clue.

The guidelines that we give solvers of humorous puzzles in chapter 5 are essentially the same ones that apply to the writing of clues:

- Clues should, but need not, supply primary definitions for answers. If necessary, a clue can suggest a definition in a roundabout way.
- While most editors would rather emphasize puns and other wordplay, anagrams are the most abundant resources. Words in anagrams do not have to be together in the clue. Avoid the signals that make anagrams so obvious—namely, proper names, rare words, abbreviations, and numerals. A forced anagram may be the least desirable clue, and you should use one only as a last resort.

- Some numbers have alphabetic lookalikes. You can also imply some letters by Arabic equivalents of Roman numerals.

- Spell letters by short words: "Tea," "are," "eye," and so on. You can also spell plural letters: "ease" for EE, "tease" for TT. An appealing ploy is to spell two different letters by one word in the clue: "Ellen" for LN and "any" for NE.

- For short words: Think of a long word that begins or ends with the word you're cluing and take advantage of the coincidence. (In clues of this type, disguise what you've done as best you can. "Cat tail" for NIP will nicely distract a solver who cannot reject the image of the marsh plant.)

- Think of a longer word that happens to contain all the letters of the word you're cluing. Even if the long word has nothing to do with the short one, you can usually make something of it. You will have better luck with this kind of clue if you look for place names or proper names. You could clue ADA, for instance, as "Town in Nevada?" even though it's in Oklahoma.

- Make a clue that is basically the inverse of the form described in the preceding suggestion. That is, find a *shorter* word among the letters of your answer. Incorporate the shorter word in the clue without regard for the leftover letters. G. Buckler once presented the clue "Candy made with cream" for CARAMEL. You should try to achieve literary sense in clues of this form, and you should use more than half the letters in the answer word in the clue.

- You can occasionally incorporate fill-in-the-blank clues in humorous puzzles. Such clues invariably involve puns. You can get an idea by repeating aloud the word to be clued. Think of phrases that use the word. Invention of a clue such as "Bronze ___ Ages (fireside topic?)" for ANDIRON ("and Iron") is very satisfying. Strive to be fair when preparing one of these clues. Supply a short parenthetical phrase that sheds light on your dark humor.

- Write a straight clue that appears to be cryptic. Frank Lewis used "Talk about a friend!" for GOSSIP, and Harvey Estes used "Place in front of church for promises" for ALTAR.

Someone once remarked, speaking of the game of chess, "When you have found a good move, look again. There's probably a better one." The same philosophy applies to writing clues for humorous puzzles. A clue may be mediocre, adequate, good, or outstanding. It may also not be to the taste of the puzzle editor, but that's another story.

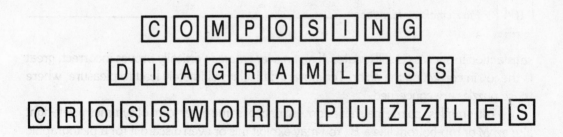

COMPOSING DIAGRAMLESS CROSSWORD PUZZLES

11

A shapeless mass and a book of rules
—R. L. Sharpe, *Stumbling Block or Stepping Stone*

The diagramless puzzle offers much opportunity for visual creativity. The stifling square borders and constraints of symmetry are gone. You become an artist, creating a silhouette on a blank canvas.

Yet, like any art, the composition of diagramless puzzles has its discipline. Diagramless puzzles must be no larger than 23x23 for American markets. They should have about eighty-two words, unless they are 17x17 or smaller and destined for periodicals, not *The New York Times*. Two-letter words remain *verboten*. Obscure words and crosswordese are even less welcome in diagramless puzzles than they are in conventional crosswords.

Your objectives as the composer of a diagramless puzzle are to stimulate and challenge, but not thwart, the solver. These objectives should sound familiar by now, but they have unique implications in the present context. The solvers of a diagramless puzzle are challenged if they cannot complete the puzzle without restarting it at a point other than the beginning. There should be Across answers, besides those in the first row, that lie under no previous answers; that is, each letter of those answers starts a Down answer. Solvers cannot place such answers in the grid definitively until they can link them with whatever has gone before.

The more rows needed for reconnection, the greater the solver's satisfaction in accomplishing it. If the solver cannot finish the puzzle without working from the bottom up—or even, in the extreme case, from the waist of a conventionally symmetric puzzle—the satisfaction in success is still greater. If an answer entered vertically proves incorrect, great is the joy in correcting the error. Temporary difficulties ultimately lead to pleasure, where these puzzles are concerned.

A diagramless puzzle may have conventional or some other form of symmetry: left-right like an *M* or top-bottom like a *B*. You may exploit this or even discard it for a pictographic representation of a thematic object. Published puzzles have featured symmetric diagrams representing valentines, jack-o'-lanterns, and a six-pointed star, while a map of New York State had no symmetry.* In 1994, *GAMES World of Puzzles* published a diagramless puzzle in which a picture of a hammer was formed, not by the perimeter of the words but by an interior empty space completely surrounded by the words. Pictures cannot have sharp points, due to the limitation on how short an answer may be. You can, however, simulate an arc of a circle by steps, as shown in Figure 11.1.

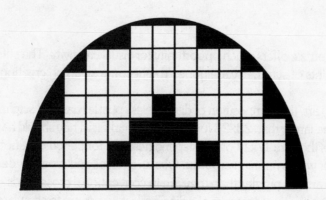

Figure 11.1. *A simulated arc*

Avoid long straight lines unless you have suitable long words in mind. You can break long lines with fingers, strings of black squares, in some cases without losing the pictographic effect. Thus, a puzzle shaped like the letter *W* is easy to construct, but the letter *T* is best forgotten. (See Figure 11.2 for an illustrative *K*.)

---

* Of the latter puzzle, Gene Maleska wrote in *Across and Down*: "The ultimate in shaping diagramless puzzles was reached by Stanley A. Kurzban. The outline of New York State appeared and inside the puzzle chief cities like Utica . . . and New York were located exactly where they are on a map."

Any theme suitable for use in a conventional puzzle can be used in a diagramless puzzle as well, but a diagramless puzzle is more appealing if its diagram carries out its theme. An outline can represent a map (a state's border), a symbol ($, ℞, ♡, or ✿), letters or numbers (such as 76, which was used to commemorate our Bicentennial, or SA for South America), or a picture (a bunny's head, a telephone, or the Taj Mahal). Each outline readily suggests a related theme.

Because connecting separate columns is a rewarding feat for solvers of diagramless puzzles, many such puzzles have collection of ladders (like *W*)—and you'll find them easy to construct. The diamond is another convenient shape, for the same reason. Conversely, composition of a pictographic puzzle with a long first word across is always a remarkable puzzlemaker's accomplishment.

Remember that the absence of a diagram may be but a slight impediment to seasoned solvers, but even they are due compensation. You must avoid obscurity and you should write straightforward and reasonably unambiguous definitions to hold the solver's attention and to be fair.

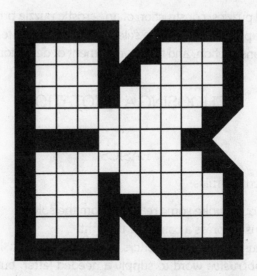

Figure 11.2. *A diagramless puzzle in the shape of the letter* K

Gimmicks in the form of a few punny answers are acceptable, and certainly themes unrelated to a diagram's shape are common. Extreme deviousness, such as the use of symbols in answers, is unfair.

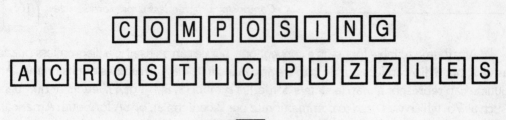

COMPOSING ACROSTIC PUZZLES

12

Put them all together, they spell MOTHER
—H. Johnson, "M-O-T-H-E-R, a Word That Means the World to Me"

Just as with crossword puzzles, construction of an acrostic puzzle proceeds from solution to definitions. In this chapter we discuss the selection of appropriate source quotations, the technique of puzzle construction, and the development of definitions.

CHOOSING A QUOTATION

BASICS

There are three elementary rules:

1. The selection should evoke some reaction from the solver.
2. The selection must express a complete thought.
3. The quotation must contain all the letters used in the acrostic. It is sometimes possible to inject an *unobtrusive* word to supply a needed letter, but you should avoid this particular act of creativity if at all possible.

NATURE OF MATERIAL

The quotation may be purely objective or descriptive, such as this excerpt from Ambrose Bierce's "A Horseman in the Sky":

On a colossal pedestal, the cliff,—motionless at the extreme edge of the capping rock and sharply outlined against the sky,—was an equestrian statue of impressive dignity.

A humorous passage, especially one that combines humor with philosophy or description will usually be a good choice. This is from Mark Twain's "The Celebrated Jumping Frog of Calaveras County":

The new frog hopped off, but Dan'l gave a heave, and hysted up his shoulders—so—like a Frenchman, but it wasn't no use—he couldn't budge; he was planted as solid as an anvil, and he couldn't no more stir than if he was anchored out.

A quotation may also express some nugget of philosophy, as in the following words by David Hume, from *Dialogues Concerning Natural Religion*. If they seem familiar, you solved our example acrostic in chapter 7, "Solving Acrostic Puzzles."

We know so little beyond common life, or even of common life, that, with regard to the economy of a universe, there is no conjecture, however wild, which may not be just; nor any one, however plausible, which may not be erroneous.

The possibilities are legion. Nontechnical descriptions of technical processes are suitable. Biographical and autobiographical anecdotes usually work well. Fiction and nonfiction, prose and verse, subjective passages, and criticisms—all may serve.

LENGTH

You must consider the quotation's length. An excerpt should be between 150 and 250 letters long, not counting punctuation (or spaces between words). The first of the three selections above is not long enough.

The length of the acrostic is also important. It should be between eighteen and twenty-nine letters. If you have to, you can usually shorten the acrostic by using only the last name of the author, or by omitting an unimportant part of the title of the source material. Here are a few examples of shortened names and titles:

W. Shakespeare
Shakespeare
Adventures in Wonderland (The full title is *Alice's Adventures in Wonderland*.)
Philadelphia Story (The full title is *The Philadelphia Story*.)

The full acrostic for the second quotation would be far too long. We could shorten the title to "The Jumping Frog," which would result in a twenty-three-letter acrostic—but the selection contains no *j*, and that letter is necessary even for the shortened acrostic.

The full acrostic for the quotation from Hume is forty-three letters long. We will use this quotation as a basis for technical discussion through the rest of the chapter, however, and so we will shorten the acrostic by omitting the first two words in the title so that the acrostic will spell: David Hume, *Natural Religion.*

You should take into account the ratio between the total length of the quotation and the length of the acrostic. Divide the number of letters in the quotation by the number of letters in the acrostic to find the length of the average word in the acrostic. If the result is less than six letters, the puzzle will probably be too easy to solve. If the result is greater than eight letters, you may have difficulty finding words you need. Our Hume quotation has 179 letters. With a twenty-four-letter acrostic the average word will be about 7.5 letters long, nearly ideal.

SOURCES OF MATERIAL

Quotations can come from many sources. Most come from books, of course, but articles in magazines and published journals are acceptable sources, as are titled speeches. Almost any published reading matter can supply appropriate quotations.

You must not overlook another source—your own imagination. Most editors accept original material. Pointed, humorous verse is probably the most popular form of original writing for acrostic puzzles . . . short filler paragraphs of the type used to pad newspaper columns usually aren't interesting enough to the solver. (If you do use original writing in an acrostic puzzle, the acrostic will spell your name. You will also have to supply a title for inclusion in the acrostic.) We need to make some technical points here regarding sources.

- The copyright laws generally permit the inclusion of brief excerpts in book reviews, and they also describe "fair use" so as to allow use of short selections for other purposes. They say nothing, however, about this specific use of copyrighted material (especially regarding a poem or other short, complete work), except that you should obtain written permission. You can avoid this minor inconvenience, both for yourself and for the publishers, by sticking to material for which copyright has expired, or that is in the public domain. Don't worry, this limitation is not severe. Of course, if the publisher's style sheet permits or encourages current material, then use it.
- Be cautious about using "condensed" material. Go to an unabridged version and satisfy yourself that you have chosen the full version of a passage.

- Don't use well-known excerpts. Solving should be a challenge up to some climactic moment. There's not much challenge in solving well-known lines such as "To be or not to be."
- Newspaper articles, editorials, and wire service accounts do not normally qualify as sources for acrostic puzzles because you cannot identify the author.
- If you're going to use original writing, make sure it is just that—your own work. Don't get accused of plagiarism.

PUZZLE CONSTRUCTION

FOUNDATION

Your first step in constructing an acrostic puzzle, after selecting the quotation, is to copy the passage onto a blank piece of paper in large print. While you're at it, write down the author's full name, the complete title of the quotation's source, the publisher's name, the city of publication, and the number of the page on which the quotation is found. (The last three items are necessary when you submit the puzzle for sale.)

Next, count the letters in the quotation and jot down the total. Now make a tally for _each_ letter. As a double-check, add up these tallies and compare the total to the one you've already written. If they don't match, find and correct the error.

Now scan the individual tallies to see if there is a high incidence of any of the less frequently encountered letters. If so, it's important that you recognize the situation early; otherwise, you will have a lot of backtracking to do later. You should also look at the ratio of vowels to consonants to know whether the words you use in the acrostic must have a preponderance of either one.

The Hume quotation has 179 letters. The most frequent are: _e_—26, _o_—23, and _n_—15. There are 10 _h_'s, 8 _w_'s, 4 _v_'s, and 2 _j_'s. There are 103 consonants and 76 vowels, counting _y_ as a vowel. Although _o_ is a common letter, the tally is high and we will have to incorporate many of them early. The ratio of vowels to consonants is about three to four, not so uneven that we need to worry about it.

FRAMEWORK

The next step is to write in a vertical line on another sheet of paper the letters that will start the acrostic. Adjust the letter tallies to account for these removed letters. (The only _g_ in the Hume quotation is used in this step.)

BUILDING

The most difficult step in composing an acrostic puzzle is the formation of words for the acrostic list using the letters in the quotation. Here are some basic principles for you to consider:

- You do not have to work sequentially through the acrostic. Skip around if that *seems easier*.
- Morbid medical terms, and all the other words to avoid in crossword puzzles, are out!
- Keep in mind how long the average word must be, and make the first several words you form two or three letters longer than average. (Remember that the average word in the acrostic for our Hume quotation must be about 7.5 letters long.)
- In the initial stages hold back on *a, e, i, o, t, s,* and *d,* unless you have an abundance of them. You can always use *s* to make a noun plural or to change a verb to third person singular; *d* puts a verb into the past tense.
- Use the unusual letters early, particularly any that occur often in your quotation. Some letters, especially *h* and *w,* occur more often in running prose than they do in a list of randomly chosen words. Prose ordinarily contains a few words like *the, where,* and *who* in comparative profusion, which accounts for this phenomenon.[*]
- The first acrostic puzzles were presented as literary challenges. The words in the acrostic were often lines from poems, from the Bible, and from similar sources. Titles and idiomatic phrases are generally welcome, but you must shun obscurities, nonstandard words, and variant spellings.

KEEPING SCORE

As you form each word for the acrostic list, adjust the letter tallies to keep track of how many of each letter remains to be used. When you have made about half the number of words in the acrostic list, divide the remaining letters by the number of remaining words to recompute the length of the average word you will need to extract from those remaining letters. Recompute again when you're about three-quarters done. You should notice the average dropping each time. Of course, at the end you had better come out even.

---

[*] Usually about half the letters that begin the acrostic will be vowels or the letters *h* or *n.* Since far fewer than half the words in the English language begin with these letters, those that do and that contain goodly numbers of unusual letters (including *h* and *w*) are very useful. Some of these are: *highhanded, anyhow, inchworm, nohow, Erewhon* (Samuel Butler's novel), *everywhere, however, hothouse,* and *unwholesome.*

ALTERNATIVE SCORE-KEEPING METHOD

You may prefer this method of keeping track of the letters: Use tiles from a word game or make your own as we describe here.

Copy the quotation onto paper that you have ruled off into one-inch squares. After proofreading carefully to insure that you have copied the passage correctly, cut along the ruled lines to separate the individual letters. Now sort the squares into groups by letter and count each group to see if you need to use up any abundant unusual letters. To make words for the acrostic, start by laying out the letters that will be the initial letters of the word list. All you need do to form words is slide the remaining pieces of paper around until you make a satisfactory list. (If you're a saver, you can keep the letters for use on your next puzzle.)

THOUGHT PROCESS

Figure 12.1 presents the Hume quotation, the letter tallies, and the acrostic we made from those letters. Here is the step-by-step reasoning that led to formation of the first few words we made.

1. There are twenty-three *o*'s and eight *w*'s. (OW!) HOW NOW BROWN COW would get rid of four of each. Okay. ROOSEVELT uses up two more *o*'s. NOW OR NEVER and THROW AWAY get rid of more of each.

2. There are two *j*'s to dispose of. That's a lot in a quotation of this length. Put down ENJOYMENT, which also uses one of the five *y*'s, and INJECTION.

3. Put down LITHOSPHERE to use up two *h*'s and another *o*. Try EFFECTIVE to work on the four *f*'s and to use one of the four *v*'s.

The last several words we made were UNITY, REEKS, INMATE, and LONER.

FINISHING THE ACROSTIC LIST

If you follow our principles—especially the advice to make the first several words longer than the average, to hold back on the easiest letters to use, and to use the unusual letters early—the last few words you need to form will perhaps be only three or four letters long and should contain a high percentage of easy-to-use letters. Thus, your task should get easier near the finish. If you should get stuck, look back at some of the *earliest* words you made and regroup. Be extremely careful at this stage if you are using pencil and paper to keep track of the letter tallies. It is incredibly easy to make a mistake and wind up with an extra letter, or one too few. In fact, if you use pencil and paper to keep track (as opposed to letter tiles), you should double-check your work after you have made the complete acrostic. Do this by reading through the acrostic list and tallying individual letters, just as you first counted the letters in the quotation. The two sets of tallies must agree.

```
We know so little beyond common life, or even of common
life, that, with regard to the economy of a universe,
there is no conjecture, however wild, which may not be
just; nor any one, however plausible, which may not be
erroneous.
```

Letter	Tally	Word list
A	7	D emolish
B	4	A cheron
C	7	V owel
D	3	I mmune
E	26	D ebauchery
F	4	
G	1	H ow now, brown cow
H	10	U tter
I	10	M ooch
J	2	E njoyment
K	1	
L	7	N oodle
M	7	A bbot
N	15	T hrow away
O	23	U nity
P	1	R oosevelt
Q	0	A mnesty
R	11	L ithosphere
S	6	
T	12	R eeks
U	5	E ffective
V	4	L oner
W	8	I njection
X	0	G houlish
Y	5	I nmate
Z	0	O ffice
		N ow or never
	179	

Figure 12.1. *Construction of an acrostic puzzle*

COMPLETING THE COMPOSITION

The next-to-last step in composing an acrostic puzzle is associating letters in the acrostic to letters in the quotation. The basic rule is that two letters from one word in the acrostic never appear in the same word in the quotation. (If the quotation has only one *q* and one *u*, your first thought might be to violate this rule. Don't compromise! Redo the acrostic, if need be, with an Arabic word or place name—for example, Aqaba—to separate those letters.)

Three principles augment the basic rule:

1. Avoid "clumping." It's a bad idea to cluster letters from the first quarter of the acrostic in, say, the last quarter of the quotation. It makes the puzzle too easy to solve, and it is tantamount to creating several subpuzzles—just like a crossword puzzle diagram that has nearly isolated regions.
2. Don't assign letters from unusual words in the acrostic list to unusual words in the quotation. It's akin to creating difficult intersections in crossword puzzles.
3. If the quotation has duplicate words (as *life* in the Hume quotation), avoid assigning letters from one word in the acrostic list (as the *f*'s in "effective" in the example) to those words.

Pursue the numbering step methodically. You'll be working with two things at the same time: the quotation as you first copied it and the acrostic you formed from the letters in the quotation. Begin by numbering the letters in the quotation. The first is 1, next is 2, and so on, in order through the complete passage. Write these numbers under the letters in small print.

Next, identify each word in the acrostic by a letter, starting with A. Write these letters to the left of the acrostic words.

Now, if your selection has a single occurrence of some letter (which you can easily determine by checking your letter tallies), find that letter in the acrostic and in the quotation. Copy the identifier at the left of the acrostic word above the letter in the quotation. Copy the number that is underneath the letter in the quotation under the corresponding letter in the acrostic. Your work sheet should look like the example in Figure 12.2.

Notice the singleton *q* in *question* (and in the acrostic word with identifier J). Deal first with any singly occurring letters.

Now find the longest word in the acrostic. Work carefully through that word to assign letters. A reasonable process is to find the first occurrence in the quotation of the first letter in the acrostic word, and assign that one by copying the identifier and number to their respective places. Then jump to the next word in the quotation and begin searching for the second letter in the acrostic word. When you have assigned all the letters in the acrostic word, keep your place in the quotation for searching, and locate the next acrostic word you want to deal with.

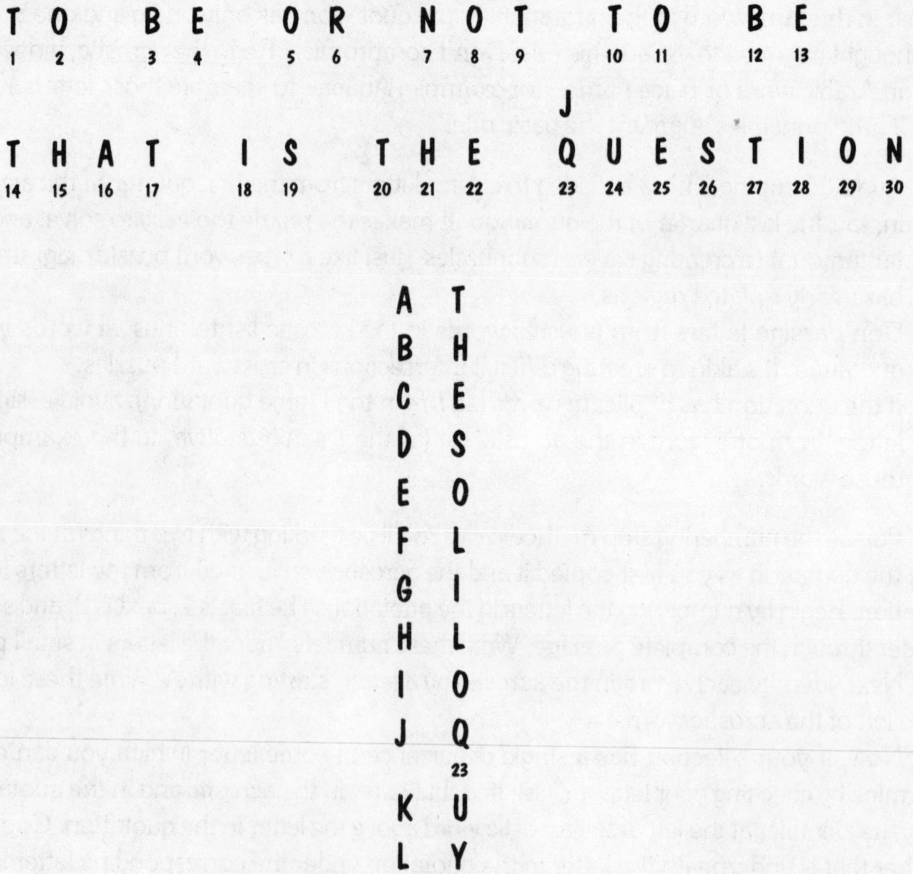

```
T O   B E   O R   N O T   T O   B E
1 2   3 4   5 6   7 8 9   10 11  12 13

                              J
T H A T   I S   T H E   Q U E S T I O N
14 15 16 17  18 19  20 21 22  23 24 25 26 27 28 29 30
```

```
A    T
B    H
C    E
D    S
E    O
F    L
G    I
H    L
I    O
J    Q
         23
K    U
L    Y
```

Figure 12.2. *Assigning letters*

In general, you should assign the letters from the long acrostic words first. Conversely, you should go out of your way to leave at least one unassigned letter in every word of the quotation as long as possible. If you do that, you will have greater freedom toward the end;

that is, you will almost always be able to find a letter you need without violating the rule about two letters in one acrostic word assigned to the same word in the quotation.

It is possible that you might hit a conflict when you get down to the last few words. If so, merely backtrack a few assignments. Be sure to correct your work sheets so that they reflect the final assignments.

DEFINITIONS

Preparing definitions for acrostic puzzles is just like preparing them for crossword puzzles, except that you can be a little wordier. This may open up some possibilities so that you can be a little less direct without being unfair.

Consider MINOR, for instance. An easy, direct clue would be "Under legal age." You are at liberty to incorporate two or more meanings for the same word in one definition. "Less important; type of chord" is fair and also leads to MINOR, yet it is only one semicolon away from being a full-fledged cryptic clue.

When you use a phrase or compound word in the acrostic list, tell the solver so by indicating "2 words" or "hyphenated" after the definition. Publishers normally give the solver this much help, even in difficult puzzles.

HOW LONG

It is easier to compose an acrostic puzzle than a crossword puzzle. We composed the model in this chapter in about forty minutes. It incorporates three phrases, and perhaps it has a shortcoming in that nine words have double letters—although most editors wouldn't notice or care.

With practice, you can compose a good acrostic puzzle in an hour or less.

MARKETING

13

Words pay no debts.
—Shakespeare, *Troilus and Cressida*

In this chapter we discuss the mechanics of getting completed puzzles to market. The steps outlined here may seem tedious compared to the stimulation of composing puzzles, yet attention to detail is an important part of marketing puzzles, because *it's a buyer's market.*

That's it, in a nutshell. Puzzle publishers, whether they produce newsstand magazines, books, newspaper features, or subscription service material, receive more puzzles for consideration than they can use. You can take two steps to insure that your submittals receive due consideration:

1. Send your work to suitable outlets. If you enjoy composing puzzles that have no themes, don't send them to a publication in which every puzzle is thematic. If you tend to write puzzles with a lot of tough words or dry definitions, few markets will be eager to accept your work.

    In short, read puzzle publications to see what they use.

2. Submit puzzles in accordance with guidelines or style sheets supplied by puzzle editors. These guidelines, which vary from editor to editor, standardize the format composers use to submit puzzles. Thus, the editor can concentrate on a puzzle's content without being distracted by typographical items or hard-to-read pages. Editors are human, too, and want to make their jobs as simple as possible.

    Quite a few editors gave us permission to print their style sheets; you'll see them later in this chapter. If you suspect a change (perhaps after a personnel move), you can most easily get a revised style sheet by writing directly to the editor. Be sure to supply a stamped return envelope. (If you want to submit a puzzle to an editor who has not sent you a style sheet, or to a market for which we didn't print one, use our general guidelines as a model.)

GENERAL GUIDELINES FOR CROSSWORD PUZZLES

Squares in the puzzle diagrams you submit should be larger than publication size—say, about a third of an inch on a side. This reduces your writer's cramp and the editor's eyestrain. With squares this size, a 23x23 grid just fits on 8½x11" paper.

You can prepare master grids for conventional puzzles and most cryptic puzzles using ordinary school notebook paper, which usually has three lines per inch. Trace grids of different sizes (15x15, 21x21, and 23x23, for instance) heavily onto sheets of plain white paper. Center each grid for a pleasing look on the page. Type your name, address, and Social Security number in the upper right corner of each page. Make several copies of each master grid at a copying service, and keep them on file.

For conventional crosswords and black-square cryptic puzzles: Don't just draw an **X** through the black squares in your pattern, darken them thoroughly. Use ballpoint pen, soft-tipped pen, or felt-tipped marker. (If you use a marker, which takes some practice, make sure you use a brand whose ink does not bleed through the page to discolor underlying pages.) Check your work at this stage to make sure that you have darkened the correct squares.

For bar-diagram cryptic puzzles, thicken the appropriate bars with ballpoint pen or soft-tipped pen. Take a second look to be sure you got the correct bars.

Number the appropriate squares. Some editors demand that you use a typewriter. To paraphrase Tennyson: Yours not to reason why, yours but to pacify. If you number by hand, use pen, not pencil.

Write the word count of your puzzle on the page. Here's a shortcut you can use to check the count now that the pattern contains numbers. Count the number of squares that begin both Across and Down words. (These squares have a black square or a border both above and to the left.) Add this tally to the number of the last word in the bottom row. The sum is your word count.[*]

Some editors (at *The New York Times,* for instance) want a diagram for their own use—for "test solving." If the editor to whom you want to submit a puzzle wants a solving diagram, either get a xerographic copy of your empty diagram or, if that's inconvenient, prepare a second diagram from scratch.

Complete the composition by filling in the answers in capital letters. Again, some editors want you to use a typewriter. If you're working by hand, print legibly and use pencil

---

[*] Do you see why this is so? Every number is used for at least one answer. You have simply added to the number of the last word the count of times two answers share the same number.

unless the editor's guidelines instruct you otherwise. The editor has the right to change any part of the composition.

Type manuscript pages for definitions and answers. The idea is not to simulate typesetting but to make it convenient for the editor to review clues, answers, and diagrams side-by-side and jot notes or changes. Do not try to put definitions on the same page as the diagram. Start on a new page, and leave ample margins at the top, sides, and bottom. Type your name, at least, at the top of each page. Type definitions and answers double-spaced, and follow the format shown in Figure 13.1. Use one side of the page only. You don't have to start a new page for the Down words.

Tell the editor where to verify any obscure or unusual words, quotations or titles, and less-than-famous names. Do this briefly in parentheses after the word in the answer column, as illustrated in Figure 13.1. Some editors want this notation typed and others want it in pencil. (If you're not sure whether to annotate or not, do it.)

ACROSS

1. Page size   OCTAVO

7. Low-starch bread   GLUTEN   (Am. Herit.)

8. Nebraska city   OMAHA

Figure 13.1. *Format for definitions and answers, including annotation*

The editor's guidelines should indicate how to present certain kinds of definitions. For example, you indicate missing words in fill-in-the-blank definitions by either hyphens or underscores. Some publications insist on periods after the numbers of the definitions, others do not. Some publications help the solver by indicating "2 words" or "phrase" after the definition for a multi-word answer, others do not. The editor will let you know if you use an unacceptable format.

Most crossword puzzles larger than 15x15 carry titles. Some publications confer titles even on 15x15 puzzles. Suggest a title for every themed puzzle you submit, but be sure that title does not use any of the key words in the thematic answers.

Editors refer to crossword puzzles in correspondence (and on check stubs) either by title or by the answer at 1 Across.

GENERAL GUIDELINES FOR ACROSTIC PUZZLES

The guidelines in the previous section apply to acrostic puzzles with some differences.

Individual squares in an acrostic puzzle's diagram should be larger than those in a crossword diagram; they have to hold the identifier as well as the numerals. Squares about one centimeter on a side are a good size. You can buy graph paper with one-centimeter squares in an office-supply store.

A stockpile of master grids may not be of much use. Publishers print acrostic puzzles in different formats—fifteen squares per row, seventeen, eighteen, and so on. So be it. Match your submittal to the format your target publication commonly uses.

As you prepare the diagram, darken one square to represent the space between two words. It is probable that the quotation and dark squares will not exactly fill up the last row of the diagram. Simply darken the leftover squares in that row.

Identify your definitions by letters, not by numerals. The first identifier is A, and they progress in alphabetic order. If your puzzle has more than twenty-six definitions, identify the twenty-seventh by AA or Z1, depending on the style the editor prefers (the twenty-eighth by BB or Z2, and so on).

Represent each letter in a word in the acrostic by three underscores, and type the proper numerals below, just as they appear in a magazine (see Figure 13.2). When a long word requires a second line of type, align the *right* margin, not the left. Or, at least, indent the first answer letter and its underscores on the second line. This keeps the sense of the acrostic clear. (Do the opposite for a telestich puzzle, one that uses the last letters of words instead of the first.)

A. Contribute
    ___ ___ ___ ___ ___ ___
    78   126   1   30   99   88

B. Chiefly (3 wds.)
    ___ ___ ___ ___ ___ ___
    46   9   17   181 156   77

    ___ ___ ___
    209 118   53

Figure 13.2. *Format for acrostic puzzle definitions*

Submit four items as a complete solution to an acrostic puzzle:

1.   Author's name and title of source material, in this form:

>   Author: William Shakespeare
>   Work: *Troilus and Cressida* (Underline the title if you're using a typewriter.)

>   Supply the author's full name and the complete title, even if you have omitted something to reduce the length of the acrostic.

2.   Publisher's name and city, publication date, and page number of the quotation:

>   Doubleday & Co., Inc., NY, 1936, page 838

3.   The quotation itself. If you deliberately skipped an unimportant phrase to reduce the quotation's length, represent the missing part by an ellipsis (three periods).

4.   Your acrostic composition. Type the word list, with identifiers, in two columns:

>   A. Demolish   L. Throw away
>   B. Acheron   M. Unity

All four parts of the solution will fit on a single page, along with your name, address, and social security number.

ENCLOSURES

Enclose a self-addressed envelope stamped with enough postage to cover the return of your puzzle. If you do not, you can never learn that your effort was unacceptable to one editor, and you will never be in a position to submit it to another.

You can also write a short cover letter describing anything important you want to tell the editor about the puzzle—the nature of a concealed theme, perhaps. But don't be chatty just for the sake of being chatty.

SERIAL SUBMISSION

Submit a puzzle to only one editor at a time. Do not send it to another unless and until the first one notifies you of rejection. Some markets, especially newsstand magazines, habitually do not notify puzzle writers at all, except by sending a check. If their backlogs are large, that may in fact not be for a year or more.

Conversely, there's nothing the matter with writing a letter to ask "Whatever happened to . . . ?" if you haven't heard anything for sixty days or more.

REWARDS

When you asked someone what your blind date would be like and you heard the magic words "Great personality," you suspected you were the better looking of the couple. Well, so far as financial compensation is concerned, composing puzzles is really very, very enjoyable. And educational, too.

Actually, you will derive two kinds of satisfaction from composing and selling puzzles. The first is intangible: Seeing your name in print (if credit is given) and knowing that you are providing pleasure to a large number of people.

The second satisfaction is monetary. The payment for a puzzle depends on two things—the size of the puzzle (for a crossword) and the nature of the publication. The fact of the matter is, payment is increasing to reflect fair pay for the work. Payment of $40 is now typical for a 15x15 puzzle, for example, and some markets pay more. Generally, newspaper syndicates and newsstand publications pay the least, collections meant for bookstores pay about the same or a little more, and select markets such as *GAMES*, *The New York Times* and the puzzles-by-mail operations pay the most.

Payment may come before publication, as with the *Washington Post* usually, or several weeks later. Many publishers provide a fringe benefit: a complimentary copy of the book in which your puzzle appears. The *Washington Post* Sunday puzzle appears in a separate magazine section, and you receive a copy of that magazine and the next week's issue with the answer.

By the way, when you offer to sell a puzzle by submitting it to an editor, you warrant that it is original, that it has not been published before, that it does not violate any copyrights, and that its publication will not harm anyone or violate anyone's rights. You sell copyright and all other rights, including reprint rights. Many publishers insist that you sign a contract covering these points.

Whether you sign a contract or not, once an editor accepts your puzzle that market is the only one entitled to profit from any use of that puzzle. For example, Dell publications and Running Press publish omnibus collections of puzzles (perhaps reset in large type) that appeared in earlier books. Times Books reprints puzzles that have previously appeared in *The New York Times*. The publisher has absolute right to decide whether constructors receive any additional payment, even a complimentary copy of a book.

Practically speaking, you have to treat freelance puzzle composing as a hobby that pays for itself with something left over. Most editors make a good living. Some composers, with a great deal of persistence and a lot of time to devote, have their works published regularly, and so they make a fair amount of money. A handful with recognized names, such as Merl Reagle in the conventional crossword field and Emily Cox and Henry Rathvon in the cryptic crossword field, have earned "regular gigs" as sole providers of puzzles for select markets— and at premium reward. As a casual constructor you cannot get rich . . . but you can have a lot of fun trying.

MARKETS

There are three types of puzzle markets. The first is the small but growing custom market, in which puzzles are composed only when commissioned for specific audiences—for example, as personal gifts. Several puzzlemakers are active in this market. To break in, you must spend money up front to reach potential customers through advertising. To make your customers happy you must compose witty, error-free, heavily thematic puzzles using biographic or anecdotal information and present the finished product in a professional, elegant way that will itself be an advertisement. That probably means you must have your own computer with a good printer or you must pay a typesetting service, such as offered by many storefront copier businesses, to produce a good-looking puzzle and answer.

The second market includes special-interest publications such as magazines for hobbyists, magazines promoting geographical regions, and club newsletters. Some of these publications carry puzzles, either regularly or occasionally, but they typically do not have a puzzle editor per se. If you contribute to one of these publications, you must do a thorough job of proofreading your work—particularly the definitions. Investigate publications that do not now have a puzzle feature. If you have confidence in your ability to create enjoyable puzzles and meet regular deadlines, and you are willing to negotiate payment, you can become a regular contributor or "contributing editor" for an exclusive market.

The third, and by far the largest, market includes general-interest publications with a regular puzzle feature (newspapers and the syndicates that supply them), newsstand puzzle magazines, collections sold in bookstores, and the puzzles-by-mail operations. This market is easier to break into than the first two because it needs a lot of material every month. Also, if you want to compose puzzles only casually you will not be under the pressure of a deadline. Publications in this market are prepared to receive puzzles by new composers, and many of the editors will comment on puzzles and otherwise help new composers if they have time.

CURRENT STYLE SHEETS

Several editors were kind enough to give us permission to reprint their guidelines. We removed the payment information, since that is subject to change, but tried to let the editors speak for themselves otherwise. The material is in alphabetical order by market name.

THE CROSSWORDS CLUB

Editor/Mailing address: Mel Rosen; c/o Wordsquare Publishing, Inc.; 123 Elm Street; Old Saybrook, CT 06475

Market: 21x21 grids, no more than 144 words. Puzzles should have normal symmetry and approach the traditional 1/6th rule of no more than 75 black squares.

Themes: Longer entries should have an underlying theme. Traditional topicals, puns, gimmicks, and occasional quotes are fine. Some topics (like flowers, cities, body parts, and animals) have been overworked but new approaches are welcome. Because these puzzles are published in small doses and mailed directly to subscribers, themes must have broad appeal. A crossword that puns titles of rock songs might be acceptable as one puzzle in a whole book; it's not appropriate for this environment. Concerns and foibles of life make good puzzle fodder provided the results are upbeat. Humor is Goodness. One more thing: Themes using the same word in many phrases are less desirable than themes using collections of related ideas.

Thematic consistency and completeness are very important. In a puzzle featuring country names, say, the long entries could involve the names ("On a Slow Boat to China" and "Song of Norway") or their adjectival forms ("An American in Paris" and "Russian dressing"), but must not mix the two. A puzzle featuring days of the week must use all seven. Yes, there's some crossable line: You probably cannot use the names of all the Kentucky Derby winners in one crossword.

Difficulty: On the tough side, but from cleverness, interesting but useful words, and fresh definitions—not obscurities. One way to toughen a puzzle is to use honest ambiguity in the definitions . . . "close" for either "shut" or "near," for instance.

Taboos: Two-letter words; diseases and other medical morbidities; "those" body parts and functions, even if named clinically; ethnic and religious slurs; obscenities; patently made-up phrases ("greet the butcher"); nonesuch letter combinations; strained words ("redrown"); and awkward excerpts from quotations ("arrows of outrageous" from the *Hamlet* soliloquy). And let's retire those Indonesian villages, French socket wrenches, minor 11th-century poets, abbreviations no one knows or uses, and crosswordese fillers and repeaters (including, but not only, these: Edo, eria, evoe, esne, and anoa).

Shun combinations with "a" ("deliver a") unless you can define them as parts of legitimate phrases. Keep foreign, obsolete, and variant forms to an absolute minimum and use brand names only sparingly. Avoid proper names that can be defined only as "Girl's name," names of people who will likely be soon forgotten, and pluralized names that can be clued only in that contrived "and namesakes" form.

Definitions: Fresh, nondictionary clues, including forehead-slappers and quick puns ("Navel blockade?" for LINT), are welcome, provided they agree in number, tense, and part of speech with their answers. Go beyond the primary dictionary definition if possible; bring some new or extra information to the page.

Presentation: A blank "solving grid" is not necessary. Hand-lettered grids are fine. Type definitions double-spaced, with answer words in a column to the right, as in this example:

1	Star Trek doc	BONES	
6	Caraway liqueur	KUMMEL	MW 10C

Do not put definitions on the same page as the composition. Otherwise, you may use either dashes or underscores in fill-in-the-blank definitions, for example, and periods after the clue numbers are optional. The Down words need not start a new page. Put your name, address, and social security number on the diagram page and on the first page of your definitions.

Citations: Please provide source references for unusual answers—including biographical and geographical names and snippets from quotes—after the answer column on the definition sheets (per the example above).

SASE: Supply a return envelope with postage (one stamp outside, and one or two loose stamps inside). It's okay to fold puzzles for mailing.

CROSSWORD PUZZLES OF THE MONTH CLUB

Editor/Mailing address: Henry Hook; c/o Crossword Puzzles of the Month Club; 5311 Fleming Court, Austin TX 78744-1197

Comments: 21x21 grids only. Criteria similar to other premium markets, emphasizing "a minimum of crosswordese and a maximum of fun stuff. Good puns (if that's not an oxymoron) are always welcome."

DELL CHAMPION ANACROSTICS

[Note: "Anacrostic" is Dell Champion's term for "acrostic puzzle."]

Editor/Mailing address: Dell Champion Variety Puzzles; 1540 Broadway; New York, NY 10036

Presentation:

- Use only standard white 8½x11" typewriter paper. Do not use erasable bond, shiny-surfaced computer paper, or oversized paper. Set half-inch margins on all sides for all pages.
- Put your name, address, and social security number on the grid page and first clue page. Put your name on all subsequent pages as well.

Submit:

- One page containing the puzzle grid, and second page *photocopied* from the first, with the quotation filled in—not a retyped version of the first! This is important—you may inadvertently make an error. Black in the grid squares solidly, rather than just x-ing or crosshatching them.
- One set of pages for the clues and matching numbered answer dashes, typed double-spaced.
- An answer page with the *full* name of the author and the title typed in capitals on the first line; next, the quotation in upper- and lower-case; and last, the word list in two columns. Type the quotation exactly as it appears in your source. Put brackets around words in the author's name, title, and quote which you have omitted from the puzzle.
- Use only regular typewriter or computer font—no italics, script fonts, boldface, etc.

Quotation:

- The quotation should be between 150 and 230 letters (about 30 to 45 words) long. If the quotation is particularly good, it may be somewhat shorter or longer. The optimal length is about 200 letters (about 40 words).
- Select quotations that will be of interest to Dell Champion puzzle solvers. Current

books, humorous quotations, fascinating facts about people or places, pointed observations about life, and colorful prose frequently make good anacrostics. Avoid quotations that are trite, overly controversial, or very well-known.

Author's name and source title:

- The author's name and source title together must contain eighteen to twenty-eight letters. Twenty-three to twenty-six letters is optimal; more than twenty-six letters should be avoided if possible.
- You may use the author's full name, initials and last name, or last name only. An author's formal title is normally omitted, unless it's an integral part of his or her name (e.g., Captain Kangaroo, Dr. Seuss). Use the name by which the author is most commonly known (e.g., Mark Twain, not Samuel Clemens).
- You may omit an *initial* article (A, AN, THE) from the title, but it is preferable that the title appear in full. No other words may be omitted from the title.
- The source should be a work actually written by the author, generally a book, but sometimes a short story, essay, poem, etc. Magazine and newspaper articles, or such sources as speeches, interviews, etc., are not acceptable.

Word list:

- There should be eighteen to twenty-eight answers on your word list, each beginning with a corresponding letter of the author's name and title, so that the author's name and title are spelled out when you read down the initial letters of the answers. The author's name must always precede the title.
- If the list has more than twenty-six words, continue after clue Z with AA and BB.
- Important: No word in the quotation may contain more than one letter from the same answer in the word list. In other words, each word in the quotation must be made up of all different clue letters.
- An answer may be a single word or a phrase; a mixture of both is best. Answers should not be overly obscure. Phrases may not be contrived or invented. If an answer does not appear in *Webster's New World Dictionary* or the *Random House Dictionary*, cite the reference or source in which it may be found.
- You may not use abbreviations, prefixes, suffixes, or foreign words and phrases not familiar to a literate speaker of English. Keep plurals, verb forms, adverbs, and comparative forms of adjectives to a minimum.

- Answers must be between four and eighteen letters long; they should average about seven to ten letters each. Avoid four-letter words if possible. The longer your word list, the fewer words of more than ten letters should appear.
- Select words that are interesting to clue. Think of current titles, people or places in the news that won't be listed in a reference book. This will give your puzzle added interest.

Clues:

- Try to make your clues interesting and fresh, but keep them relatively straightforward (i.e., avoid puns and other wordplay). Unusual senses of words and interesting facts make good clues, as do a quotation or two, if clear and not overly long.
- Make a few clues in the puzzle relatively easy to figure out, so that the solver has somewhere to begin.
- If your quotation is short, use easy clues, as it is likely to be used as Anacrostic 1.

Style:

- In typing clues, <u>underline</u>

  a) Book, film, play, and opera titles
  b) Newspapers, magazines, long poems, record albums
  c) Works of art, ships, planes
  d) Foreign words not currently acceptable as English. Check with *Webster's New World Dictionary*, foreign entries are double-daggered or italicized.

- Use quotation marks for

  a) Short poems, short stories
  b) TV or radio shows
  c) Song titles
  d) Comic strips

- Books of the Bible do not appear between quotation marks, nor are they underlined.
- Place a comma inside a closing quotation mark. Place a colon or semicolon outside a closing quotation mark.
- Place explanatory material for a fill-in clue within parentheses following the clue. For example: ___ <u>Streak</u> (1977 film) is correct, and not ___ <u>Streak</u>, 1977 film.
- If the answer is a phrase, indicate the number of words thus: Willa Cather novel: 2 wds. Similarly, show hyphenated answers thus: Sandlot game: hyph.

- When defining a word with two or more definitions successively, separate the definitions with a semicolon.

Grid:

- See "Presentation" above.
- Number each white box consecutively. Follow each number with the letter of the answer on the word list in which the letter of the quotation appears, using capital letters.
- Allot one white box per letter, with black boxes separating words.
- Omit all punctuation except hyphens. Place a hyphen in the quote by itself in an unnumbered white box.

Finally, proofread your work. The most common error is allowing more than one letter from the same answer in the word list to appear in a given word in the quotation. Other common errors include typos, dates, spelling of names, punctuation in titles, accuracy of facts. Do not assume you remember these things correctly. Cite or provide a xerographic copy of your source for anything not readily checkable in standard references, especially if it is very recent. Dell tries constantly to maintain the highest standard of accuracy and quality. Editors cannot help but frown upon contributions that make upholding that standard difficult. But accuracy endears a contributor to our hearts forever.

Include an adequately sized and stamped self-addressed envelope with your submissions.

Happy puzzling!

DELL CHAMPION CROSSWORD PUZZLES

Editor/Mailing address: Dell Champion Puzzles; 1540 Broadway; New York, NY 10036

Grids: We are at present purchasing only crosswords of the sizes 15x15 and 21x21. We occasionally use puzzles of 23x23 or 25x25 for the "As You Like It" puzzle. This feature requires two sets of clues, one easy and one hard. Please consult the editor before constructing such a puzzle.

- In a 15x15, the total number of entries must be 78 or fewer. In a 21x21, the total number of entries must be 146 or fewer.
- The grid must be symmetrical and without an overabundance of black squares.
- All crosswords must be themed.

Themes: Consistency, originality and cleverness are most important in theme choice. Most of the more obvious theme ideas have been used many times before; a brand-new theme or novel twist on an old one are very welcome. Upbeat themes are best, with entries which will be recognizable to a large audience. The top 10 songs on the R&B chart, for example, will not be as widely recognized as best-selling novels, so therefore, not a good theme choice. Punned themes are always welcome, as well as whatever your creative mind can conceive. Timeliness is always a plus.

Generally, the trickier the theme, the harder the rest of the puzzle should be. A puzzle theme suitable for 1- or 2-star status must have non-theme entries of an easier level than those in a 3-, 4-, or 5-star puzzle. In no case is "crosswordese" desirable.

Quotations as a theme: If your theme is a quotation, it must read naturally down the grid and not skip about with parts of the quote out of consecutive order. The quote must be complete. The writer's name should appear somewhere in the grid. Supply proof of the source of your quote; don't use well-known quotes, and remember that humor rules.

Theme entries MUST be the longest in the puzzle and be symmetrically placed in the grid, though shorter theme entries may be included as well. A 15x15 may have three theme entries, but four is better; six is the minimum for 21x21s, but eight is better and ten or twelve is terrific.

Preferred entries: Colorful, interesting, up-to-date words; uncommon words, clued well. Don't elongate a word with plurals or suffixes—stretchers, so to speak—unless absolutely necessary. We do expect solvers of the more difficult puzzles to be challenged regarding their vocabulary, the liberal arts, and their knowledge of current events in politics and the modern world.

Unacceptable entries:

- Two-letter entries
- Contrived phrases, such as "dates boss," "rare peas," and "eats a cookie." Idioms cited in standard dictionaries are fine, but avoid partial phrases, and avoid turning an idiom like "on one's own" into "on his own."
- Trademarks, brand names, company names. They're not absolutely forbidden, but they should be common household words; don't overdo it.
- Words outside the boundaries of good taste (and the editors are rather prim during business hours) as a reflection of our readers' sensibilities. Specifically,

a) scatological references and obscenities
b) serious disease
c) ethnic slurs
d) bad news or disagreeable references

People often solve crosswords to take their minds off a problem; our job isn't to remind them of it.

Entries to avoid:

- References to sex and violence
- Variant spellings, Scottish, Gaelic, dialect, obsolete, archaic
- Obscure abbreviations
- Uncommon foreign words
- Crosswordese; you know what they are. Puzzles loaded with these will likely bring rejection.
- Overused 3- and 4-letter words. These will make your puzzle dull because they're hard to clue in a fresh way. Plan your grid so that these lengths are limited as much as possible.

Clues: Every clue and entry must agree in tense, number, and part of speech. If the entry is an acronym or abbreviation, don't use any part of it in the clue. For example, to clue AMA (American Medical Association), don't use "Doctors' association" or "MDs' group." You may use an abbreviation in the clue to indicate that the answer is an abbreviation, but it isn't a sin to simply tag the clue ": abbr." Note that our style for this is a lowercase "a" in "abbr."

Sacrifice showing off your broad wit and knowledge for the sake of clarity. If your clue is abstruse beyond solving, your reader will feel annoyance and not admiration. Be fair. After saying this, we add that we're always delighted to read a new and fresh clue.

Presentation: Use only white 8½x11" typing paper of the standard kind. Don't use erasable bond, manila paper, or shiny-surfaced computer paper.

Submit grids on separate sheets; a numbered grid for test-solving and another with the numbers and answers filled in. Print the answers by hand in CAPITAL letters as neatly as you can. Black in the black squares completely, rather than just x-ing them out. A clear xerographic copy is acceptable for the answer grid.

Put your name, address, social security number, total word count, and proposed puzzle title on all the grid pages and on the first page of clues. Put your name on all subsequent clue pages, and number the pages.

Using clean typewriter ribbon, and allowing a 1" left-hand margin and a ½" right-hand margin, type the clues double-spaced with the clue answer at the far right. The middle area is needed for editing, so leave plenty of room. Any source information you may want to cite for the editor's convenience can be written in pencil at the far right next to the clue answer, or summarized at the end of the list of clues.

In typing clues, <u>underline</u>

- Book, film, drama, and opera titles
- Newspapers, magazines, long poems, record albums
- Works of art, ships, planes
- Foreign words; check with *Webster's New World Dictionary*; foreign entries are double-daggered or italicized.

Use quote marks (" ") for

- Poems, short stories
- TV shows
- Song titles
- Comic strips

Books of the Bible do not appear between quotes and are not underlined.

Place a comma or period inside a close-quote mark where necessary. Place a colon or semicolon outside a close-quote mark.

Clarify information in a fill-in clue within parentheses following the clue. Example: ___ <u>Streak</u> (1977 film) is preferred, and not ___ <u>Streak</u>, 1977 film.

These are some of the "tags" we use in 1- and 2-star puzzles. They always follow a colon and a space:

: abbr. : Sp. : Fr. : Ger. : 2 wds. : hyph. : prefix : suffix

We never use "colloq." as a tag.

Combining forms are simplified to "prefix" or "suffix."

Proofread all your work: The most common error occurs when a grid change is made as the puzzle is prepared, and the change is forgotten when the clues are typed. Be absolutely sure that all your clues and answer words exactly match the puzzle grid, and that no entries are omitted. Other common errors in presentation include typos, date errors, spelling of names, punctuation in titles. DO NOT assume you remember these things correctly. Check the *New World Dictionary* for words that may be hyphenated, solid, or two words. Verify all facts referred to in the clues. If you believe the source is obscure, cite it or provide a xerographic copy for verification. We do have an extensive library in-house, but current terms may be hard to locate. The better you conform to this guide, the more favorably your puzzles will be looked upon by the editors; they're only human, alas.

Enclosure: Please include an adequately sized and stamped self-addressed envelope with your submissions. Folding your puzzle is okay as long as the envelope won't burst. This request may be dispensed with at the discretion of the editor, or when you're absolutely sure we have your SASEs on hand. That will mean your puzzles have not been returned and you've become part of the team of top-notch constructors we're proud to feature in Dell Champion.

Good luck, and happy puzzling!

GAMES MAGAZINE

Editor/Mailing address: Crossword Editor; *GAMES* Magazine; 19 West 21st Street; New York, NY 10010

General Statement: *GAMES* looks for crossword puzzles with:

- fresh, original themes;
- familiar yet interesting words and phrases;
- clever, entertaining clues.

We welcome queries on novel crossword ideas.

Sizes:

15x15 — word count of 78 or less; all words should be familiar; clues should be easy, designed for beginners.

17x17 — word count of 98 or less; all words should be familiar; clues should be easy to medium in difficulty.

21x21 — word count of 140 or less; clues should be about as difficult as those in *The New York Times*

"The World's Most Ornery Crossword" (25x25) is done by assignment only.

Traditional Rules: All crosswords for *GAMES* should have:

- allover interlock
- open, symmetric pattern
- no unkeyed letters (i.e., letters in only one word)
- a minimum of black squares (preferably under 38 for a 15x15, 50 for a 17x17, and 74 for a 21x21)
- no two-letter words
- no words repeated in the diagram
- no offensive words, and no words suggesting death or disease
- a minimum of abbreviations and cliché words

Payment: Payment is made on publication.

Format:

- Use typewriter paper (8½x11"), one side only, for clues and diagrams.

- Clues: Clues should be typed, double-spaced, in a single column, with answers listed to the right. Follow any answer that involves a hard-to-verify word or fact by a reference. Auxiliary clues (e.g., 2 wds., Abbr., Fr., Prefix) follow a colon. Fill-in-the-blank clues use an underline to represent the missing word. Down clues need not begin a new page.

- Diagrams: Send two grids, one with numbers only and one with both numbers and answers. Black squares should be clearly filled in.

- Sending: Include your name and address on both diagram pages and on the first page of clues. Include a return envelope with postage. Puzzles may be folded for mailing.

L.A. TIMES SYNDICATE SUNDAY PUZZLE

Editor/Mailing Address: James C. Boldt; 6680 Williamson Drive, N.E.; Atlanta, GA 30328

Size and Format: 21x21. Maximum number of words 150. Format as follows:

Name and address in upper left corner (page 1 only)

Page number in upper left corner

```
ACROSS (all caps)
 1 Miss Pitts                    ZASU
 5 Garcia ---, great Spanish poet  LORCA
10 "Twist" dance                 FRUG
   (etc.)
```

- ACROSS and DOWN appear only once, at beginning of each respective set of clues, and are all caps, not underlined.
- Note that blanks in clues are indicated by three (3) hyphens (not underlines).

Quality Level and Philosophy:

- There should be heavy theme orientation and/or strong topicality.
- Puzzles should be reasonably difficult, but with a minimum of obscure, archaic, technical, dialect, and foreign language words. We would like our puzzles to be as challenging as the Sunday *New York Times*, though slightly smaller (we use many of the same constructors).

References: Provide a reference source for any unusual diagram word (generally speaking, any that you have had to check yourself, or derive from specialized knowledge of your own).

Definitions:

- Use fresh, lively definitions, especially for commonly used words, combining a limited degree of ambiguity with a light touch.
- Note the source of any unusual word, especially literary or entertainment names or titles.
- Avoid definitions that are too generalized, such as girl's name, biblical name, poetic word, Italian city.
- *A clue should not have the same number of letters as the solution word.*
- Avoid definitions with a connotation of unpleasantness (sickness, death, drunkenness, disease, etc.). Avoid levity on religious subjects, or anything that might be construed as a religious or political slur.

- Abbreviations in the diagram should be defined wherever possible by at least one abbreviation in the clue (not abbr., e.g., i.e.). On the other hand, abbreviations should not, in most cases, appear in the clues unless the answer is an abbreviation. There are a few exceptions such as WWII, NRA, TNT, JFK, IRA, etc., which have entered the language to the point where periods are not used in them.
- Define foreign language words without the use of :Fr., :Lat., etc.
- Colloquial or slang words in the diagram can be defined by colloquial or slang definitions. The latter should imply a colloquial or a slang solution.
- "Prefix" and "Suffix" should be initial caps preceded by a colon. Do not define multi-word solutions as such (2 words, e.g.).
- Try not to use definitions which duplicate portions of the solution word such as "re," "under," "ation," "ing," etc.
- For words to which an adjective solution is applicable, use

```
23 Word for roses or herring        RED
```

instead of

```
23 Roses or herring                 RED
```

- Where a solution word can be integrated into clue words, such as "corn" in "cornflower" and "cornstalk," use

```
25 Word with flower and stalk       CORN
```

  The component words should be complete words in themselves. Otherwise the definition should be "Prefix for" such as

```
27 Prefix for corn or angle         TRI
```

  Incidentally, this is a preferable way for defining prefixes which might otherwise be giveaways.
- Use of prefixes should be limited to those defined as such in an authoritative reference work.

General Comments:

- Phrases and word combinations should be familiar and natural. When they are colloquial, or derived from titles or quotations, they should be enclosed in quotation marks.

- Trade names: When necessary, only extremely common ones should be used such as Cellophane, Xerox, Kodak, Ford, etc.
- Under no circumstances can the same word appear twice in the diagram. A definition should not be repeated unless this is done intentionally as part of an integrating theme.
- Please submit a blank diagram in addition to the solution diagram.
- With some exceptions we do not use the same constructor more than once or twice a year. A backlog of some 40 or 50 puzzles means that a current submission may not even be edited for several months.

NEWSDAY

Editor/Mailing address: Stanley Newman; P.O. Box 69; Massapequa Park, NY 11762

General statement: The mission of the *Newsday* Crossword: to provide American newspapers with a crossword having broad appeal to all age groups, lively language, and free of unusual and obscure words. The guidelines listed below all stem from this mission.

These guidelines are different from those of other editors. If you are unfamiliar with puzzles edited by Stanley Newman, it is highly recommended that you submit theme ideas and/or entries for approval first.

Things That Must Be Avoided:

- Themes involving repetition of the same word or rhyming words
- Themes involving name wordplay, wordplay where the theme entries are not otherwise related, or wordplay that is not consistently carried out
- Overly exotic themes (two letters in a square, dropped letters, etc.)
- Themes or theme answers that require specialized knowledge to understand or appreciate, such as the names of football coaches or Beach Boys tunes
- References to death, disease, drugs, or sex
- Overly regional references, such as subway-name abbreviations, names of small towns, and brand names that are not nationally known
- Unusual or obscure words in clues or theme answers
- Trite clues for words that can be otherwise defined in a lively, accessible manner

Things to Avoid Whenever Possible (in order of importance):

- *Unusual/obscure answer words.* You should consider a word unusual or obscure if it is unlikely to be seen or heard outside of crossword puzzles. An obscure rock musician or soap-opera actress is as equally taboo as a Eurasian mongoose or Phoenician goddess. *Newsday* Crosswords overall average less than 1 percent obscure words; your puzzle ideally should have NO obscure words. A puzzle will be automatically rejected if obscure words make up more than 2 percent of its answers (two answers in a 15x15, three in a 21x21).

- One-word clues—never use more than 10 percent per puzzle
- Combining forms and variant spellings
- Uncommon forms of common words (REHELPED, INCLUDERS, etc.)
- Common words that can be defined only one common way (SRI, ALAI, etc.)

Things That Must Be Included:

- All puzzles must have an appropriate title and theme (except for Saturday Stumper, see below). The title should not use any keywords that are used in the theme answers.
- References for any answer whose source is not obvious, or an answer that is not easily looked up in a standard reference source
- Always provide a parenthetical subsidiary clue for "fill in the blanks" that are the names of song titles, books, films and the like, unless the work is extremely well known. "___ Rhythm" is OK as is, but add something like "(Clooney tune)" to "Botch-___."

Things to Include Wherever Possible:

- Non-theme clues requiring general knowledge of contemporary culture (names in the news, TV, books, pop music, sports, films, plays, etc.), to be balanced with clues requiring general knowledge of traditional subjects (history, geography, classical music and literature, etc.).
- Common dictionary words defined with contemporary idioms ("Kept out of sight" for HID, "Chow down" for EAT, etc.)
- Lively, evocative non-theme answer words (GLASNOST, CBS NEWS, etc.)

Miscellaneous Guidelines:

- Monday through Friday—Maximum answers: 78. Difficulty level: *GAMES* one-star through three-star. Avoid themes that won't be apparent from the theme clues and title
- Saturday Stumper—Maximum answers: 72. Difficulty level: *GAMES* Ornery "Tough Clues" to *Dell Champion* four-star. Themeless, wide-open pattern, lively answer words and phrases

- Sunday—Maximum answers: 146. Difficulty level: *GAMES* three-star to *Dell Champion* four-star

Puzzles with easier themes should have common answer words and straightforward clues. Puzzles with harder themes (puns, quotes) should have a fair amount of tricky and more difficult clues.

Submissions: Submit puzzles in standard editorial format accompanied by a self-addressed stamped envelope to the Editor. Preferred consideration will be given to puzzles submitted with an IBM-compatible floppy disk containing ASCII files with clues and answer diagrams (contact the Editor for file formats and nomenclature). Macintosh users: use Apple File Exchange utility or outside vendor to convert disk and files to IBM format.

Payment: Payment for daily puzzles will be made by Creators Syndicate upon publication, accompanied by a copy of your puzzle as published.

Payment for Sunday puzzles will be made by the Editor in the month following publication, accompanied by a copy of your puzzle as published.

THE NEW YORK TIMES

Editor/Mailing address: Will Shortz, Puzzle Editor; *The New York Times*; 229 West 43d Street; New York, NY 10036

Crosswords: *The New York Times* looks for intelligent, literate, entertaining and well-crafted crosswords that appeal to the broad range of *Times* solvers.

Themes should be fresh, interesting, narrowly defined and consistently applied throughout the puzzle. If the theme includes a particular kind of pun, for example, then all the puns should be of that kind. Themes and theme entries should be accessible to everyone. (Themeless daily puzzles using wide-open patterns are also welcome.)

Constructions should emphasize lively words and names and fresh phrases. We especially encourage the use of phrases from everyday writing and speech, whether or not they're in the dictionary. For variety, try to include some of the lesser-used letters of the alphabet—J, Q, X, Z, K, W, etc. Brand names are acceptable if they're well-known nationally and you use them in moderation.

The clues in an ideal puzzle provide a well-balanced test of vocabulary and knowledge, ranging from classical subjects like literature, art, classical music, mythology, history, geography, etc., to modern subjects like movies, TV, popular music, sports, and names in the news. Clues should be accurate, colorful, and imaginative. Puns and humor are welcome.

Do not use partial phrases longer than 5 letters (ONE TO A, A STITCH IN, etc.), uninteresting obscurity (a Bulgarian village, a water bug genus, etc.) or uncommon abbreviations or foreign words. Keep crosswordese to a minimum. Difficult words are fine—especially for the harder daily puzzles that get printed late in the week—if the words are interesting bits of knowledge or useful additions to the vocabulary. However, never let two obscure words cross.

Maximum word counts: 78 for a 15x15 (72 for an unthemed 15); 140 for a 21x21; 170 for a 23x23. Maximums may be exceeded slightly, at the editor's discretion, if the theme warrants.

Diagramless Crosswords: Diagramless specifications are: 19x19 grid with twists and turns; a theme; about 80–86 words overall; and a fairly wide-open construction. Shaping the grid to relate to the theme is welcome.

Format: Use regular typing paper (8½x11"). Type clues double-spaced on the left (no periods after the numbers), answer words in a corresponding column on the far right. Give a source for any hard-to-verify word or information. Down clues need not begin on a new page. Include a filled-in answer grid with numbers *and* a blank grid with numbers (for the editor's use). Put your name, address and social security number on the two grid pages, and just your name on all other pages.

Please include a stamped return envelope for reply.

RUNNING PRESS

Editor/Mailing address: Dan and Roz Stark, Crosswords Editors; c/o Running Press; 125 South 22nd Street; Philadelphia, PA 19103-4399

Puzzle Sizes/Maximum Word Counts:

15x15	78 words
17x17	100 words
19x19	124 words
21x21	144 words
23x23	172 words

Word count limits may be relaxed slightly for a really enjoyable theme. Normal symmetry is the rule, but left-right mirror symmetry is worth an occasional outing.

Level of Difficulty: Aim for puzzles that stimulate and refresh (not tire!) the mind and imagination. Remember solvers probably have enough chores in their day, and would prefer their crossword not to be one of them! When they solve a tough corner, let them slap their foreheads, laugh, and think to themselves "Of course!" The word or phrase, once solved, should ring a bell.

Themes: The two main rules for themes are: they must be FUN and the theme entries must be CONSISTENT with each other throughout the puzzle. Puns, word gimmicks, and quotes are all fine. So are the old chestnuts *if* you give them a new twist. Themed 15x15 puzzles should have at least three related entries; 17x17, four; 19x19, five; 21x21, five; and 23x23, six. Unthemed puzzles should be liberally salted with FRESH, LIVELY words and phrases, and should try for a lower word count than the max.

Clues: Like the themes, the clues should be fun to work with. Not every clue can be a champ, but try for ones that are bright, humorous, and evocative of pleasant things. Clues must, of course, be accurate, but stay away from straight definitions from the dictionary. And remember—cleverness, not obscurity, is the goal.

Please Avoid:

- Two-letter words
- Diseases and medical terminology scarier than Band-Aids and splints
- Body parts which would make great-grandma blush
- Anything obscene
- Anything derogatory
- Awkward-looking excerpts from phrases or quotes
- Words and phrases not in common parlance. This includes crosswordese, obscure biographicals and geographicals, variants, archaics, and all but the most familiar foreign words. More than two or three of these bailouts in one puzzle, or any two crossing each other, will cause the puzzle to be returned to its maker. Slang is OK. So are titles of popular movies, books, and songs. Well-known cartoon and comic strip characters are all right, and pop culture items of general interest are fine.

References: The dictionaries we use are:

- *Random House Webster's College Dictionary*

- *Random House Unabridged Dictionary—Second Edition*
- *Merriam-Webster Collegiate Dictionary—Tenth Edition*
- *Merriam-Webster's Third New International (Unabridged)*

Please include verification for entries not found in the above. Crossword-puzzle dictionaries, unfortunately, cannot be used as sources because they have, on occasion, been found to be in error. Especially do not neglect to annotate extremely current entries such as best-sellers, movies, songs, and personalities which have not yet gotten into standard reference works.

Format: Use regular 8½x11" typing paper. Double-space between clues. Type the clues on the left with the answer words in a corresponding column on the far right. A blank "solving grid" is not needed. If your puzzle is themed, give it a title. Put your name, address, social security number, and title (if any) on the grid page and staple all the pages for that puzzle together. Be sure to include a stamped self-addressed envelope for reply.

Payment: Payment is about three months before publication. You also receive a complimentary copy of the book when it appears.

SIMON AND SCHUSTER

Editor/Mailing Address: John M. Samson; Simon and Schuster Building; 1230 Avenue of the Americas; New York, NY 10020

All crossword submissions should include:

a. Numbered answer diagram
b. Numbered clues with answers to the right
c. Theme
d. SASE

Please:

a. Reference all unusual words or definitions
b. Use quotation marks instead of italics
c. Title all crosswords
d. Briefly explain unusual themes

Please refrain from:

a. Disparaging words
b. Disease and medical-related entries
c. Vulgar words
d. Numerous abbreviations
e. Esoterica
f. Two-letter words
g. Nonsymmetrical diagrams

Accepted: All crossword sizes from 15x15 to 21x21

Not accepted: Cryptics or Acrostics

Additional guidelines:

a. Please limit 21x21s to a maximum word count of 148
b. Crosswordese in moderation is acceptable
c. Avoid brand names when possible
d. Themes should be entertaining; avoid technical subjects and repetitive-word themes

TRIBUNE MEDIA SERVICES

Editor/Mailing address: Herb Ettenson; 14460 Strathmore Lane #308; Delray Beach, FL 33446

For the most part, the puzzlement in crossword puzzles should derive from the cleverness with which the constructor selects words, and the ingenuity which he uses in definitions.

The puzzles may be fairly difficult to solve, but their difficulty should not come from the use of obscure words. For example, "fishhook" would be a good word to use because of the uncommon letter combinations, and a clever def would give the solver something to think about. "Arnebia" is not a very good word for a puzzle. Even after it is solved, who cares about adding "a genus of Asiatic herbs" to his vocabulary?

With regard to defs, how about "Stout relative" for "ale"? The idea is not to make the solving of puzzles an exercise for the memory but to challenge the solver's intellect, and give him satisfaction and entertainment.

Specifics: *Do not use unkeyed letters or two-letter words*. Avoid words that may be offensive in any way. If you *must* use some obscure word, see that the words crossing it make it possible for the solver to get that word. If you use a word or a phrase that cannot be found in the usual sources, *give the source.*

Mechanics in general: Send only one diagram with both numbers and words. Print the words *in pencil* in the diagram. Definitions should be typed or printed double-spaced on separate 8½x11" sheets from the diagram. Example:

1	Dogtrot	LOPE
5	Inlet	COVE
9	Chuckled	LAUGHED

Particulars:

Dailies: 15x15. Never exceed 80 words. Fewer are desirable.

Diagramless: Size is optional. Try to stay within the limits of 75–90 words. (17s and 19s are most likely.) The diagram is an essential part of this puzzle. Make it challenging.

Weekend puzzles: 21x21. These may be more difficult. Use some kind of theme. Do not exceed 150 words.

Other remarks: Some of these rules may be waived if the puzzle has characteristics that make it likely to be of great interest. Many puzzles are technically fine, but are unacceptable because they are dull!

Puzzles are processed at least three months prior to their actual date of publication. Keep that in mind when constructing puzzles for particular occasions.

All puzzles accepted and paid for become the property of Tribune Media Services. The company retains the right to permit others to publish the puzzles.

A stamped envelope will ensure manuscript return of manuscripts and/or notice of publication dates.

THE WASHINGTON POST MAGAZINE PUZZLE

Editor/Mailing address: William R. MacKaye; P.O. Box 32003; Washington D.C. 20007

Constructors are paid for an accepted puzzle upon publication, after they sign and return the *Washington Post Magazine Puzzle* contract in which they warrant that their puzzle is original and has not appeared elsewhere. An additional fee is paid to those constructors who include an IBM-compatible 3½" floppy disk of their puzzle prepared in The Crossword

Puzzler format (software marketed by Mel Rosen). If you work on an IBM-compatible computer, it is possible to submit puzzles on disk without using the Rosen program. Write to obtain the technical details if you want them. The *Washington Post Magazine Puzzle* purchases all rights to the puzzle, including the right to resell it to syndicates and to include it in puzzle collections in book form.

Puzzles intended for sale to the *Washington Post Magazine Puzzle* should be constructed and submitted in the light of the following points:

1. Puzzles must be 21 squares wide and 21 squares deep. They must be symmetrical in such a fashion that the lower right area of the puzzle is a mirror of the upper left area. All entries in the puzzle grid must be at least three letters long.

2. Puzzles should include no more than 140 entries. (Occasionally 142 or rarely 144 entries are permitted in puzzles that are otherwise particularly distinguished or unusual.)

3. Submissions should include both a diagram with the answers inked or heavily pencilled in and a blank diagram.

4. On the definitions sheets, each definition should be accompanied by its answer, set out on the right hand side of the page. Keep definitions as short as possible—space for the puzzle is limited. Definitions should be double-spaced. Pages should be numbered and the constructor's name should appear on every sheet.

    Puzzles should be submitted on letter-size paper and sheets should be paper-clipped rather than stapled.

5. Answers that are in any way obscure should be accompanied by a notation of your source—*Merriam-Webster's Second Unabridged, Merriam-Webster's Third Unabridged, Random House, Bartlett's Familiar Quotations, Oxford Dictionary of Quotations, Merriam-Webster's New Geographic Dictionary*, etc.—or a xerographic copy of the relevant page of the source. Our basic sources are *Webster's New World Dictionary of the American Language* and the *Random House Unabridged Dictionary of the English Language, Second Edition,* and we prefer to avoid English words and abbreviations not to be found in one or the other of them. We also prefer to avoid French, Spanish, Italian, and German words not to be found in the small foreign language dictionary listings at the back of the Random House, and alleged Scotticisms wherever they are found. Please be particularly careful to cite generally available sources for titles and quotes from popular songs, which are often difficult to verify. Also be sure to cite sources for all but the best known sports figures. The editor confesses to fatheadedness concerning sport.

6. We frown on puzzlese—ONER is not permitted under *any* circumstances (No such word, constructors, whatever Web III might claim!), and ERN, ERNE, ESNE, ENA, EVOE, ENATE, E LA, TIO, TIA, and their ILK get a generally chilly reception if they turn up in more than the smallest quantity. We do not allow answers or definitions that do not pass the "breakfast table test." References to viscera (e.g., ILEUM), acne, mass murderers (e.g., either end of IDI AMIN), and anything else that one would not want to contemplate along with one's first cup of coffee of the day should not be used. Conversely we celebrate fresh, lively and humorous definitions. Here are two favorites: "Pigeon follower" (TOED) and "Bell boy" (ALEXANDER).

7. Let's say it again: We like humor. Puns, wordplay, definitional ingenuity, and double entendres (of a tasteful variety) are plus points. In a shift from past practice, trade names are now acceptable so long as they are not promotional. Here's one we used lately: "Jag street rival" (BEAMER). Note that in this clue, "street" plays a double role. Jaguars and BMWs are vehicles in the street, and the words "Jag" and "Beamer" are street slang.

8. Definitions like ". . . and namesakes," ". . . and family," and the like are *never* permitted. So, for example, if you want to use the answer EARTHAS, you have to know of at least one other Eartha besides "Singer Kitt." Good luck! I don't. Note: "Never" means NEVER. Please don't exasperate me by sending a clue sheet with a definition in this form even though other markets permit it. In general, avoid forced plurals of words not normally seen in the plural. Occasionally constructional necessity will force you to use a word preceded by an article (A, AN, THE). Such an entry must arise from a bona-fide quote. One constructor tried to pass off AHEEL on me recently by cluing it "Cad descriptive." Fortunately for him, and because I liked his puzzle a lot, I managed to find a line from Byron's *Don Juan*: "She gave ___, and then a lurch to port."

9. Puzzles must have themes that are clued by the name of the puzzle. Theme entries can be a group of words that have some relationship, preferably ingenious, with one another, or portions of a quotation. We have a slight preference for the former over the latter. Generally there should be at least eight theme entries in a puzzle, although if the entries are long you might get away with fewer.

10. Use *no* abbreviations in definitions unless the answer is also an abbreviation. Again, "no" means NO, even though other markets' style may routinely abbreviate such things as names of states. Conversely, signal an abbreviation answer by working an abbreviation into the definition, not by saying "abbrev." Also, prefixes and suffixes should be kept to a minimum.

11. We normally acknowledge receipt of a puzzle shortly after it arrives, but it takes up to four months (and sometimes more) for us to decide whether to buy it. If you haven't heard whether your puzzle is a go or a no-go after four months, do feel free to inquire about a puzzle's status by mail or by telephone. We have never lost a puzzle but we do sometimes mislay them.

12. We appreciate receiving postage stamps to use for returning submissions we decline. Don't bother with providing an envelope—we'll use our own.

13. We are eager to see your work!

PUZZLE MARKET LIST

The alphabetical list of publishers and syndicators that follows covers only the general-publication market mentioned on page 182 and is probably incomplete. New markets appear and established ones disappear. (The *New York Review of Books* began carrying an acrostic puzzle in September 1979. The *National Observer* ceased publication in 1977, after 15 years. *GAMES* ceased publication for some time, then started up again with a new owner.) Omission of an active market from our list does not imply disapproval on our part.

If you don't know the name of a publication's editor, send your work to the attention of the Puzzle Editor. Some editors work for more than one publisher (for instance, a newspaper and a book series). They may instruct you to send contributions to their home addresses instead of the business addresses in our list.

Those markets whose editors provided the style sheets printed earlier in this chapter are represented in the list by one-line entries.

We do not indicate actual payments. Amounts vary, and they are increasing. We encourage you to submit puzzles to many markets (not the same puzzle simultaneously, of course!), to discover which editors like your work, and to decide which publications you want to contribute to on a regular basis.

And we wish you good luck!

> Crosswords Club
>
> Crossword Puzzles of the Month Club
>
> Dell Champion Ancrostics
>
> Dell Champion Crossword Puzzles

[*Note*: the following market, at the same address as Dell Champion, has its own philosophy and editorial staff.]

Dell Puzzle Publications
1540 Broadway
New York, NY 10036

GAMES Magazine

Herald Tribune Publications, Inc.
7002 West Butler Pike
Ambler, PA 19002

L.A. Times Syndicate Sunday Puzzle

Newsday

The New York Times

Running Press

Simon and Schuster

Tribune Media Services

The Washington Post Magazine Puzzle

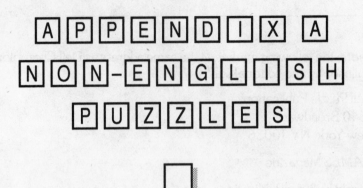

APPENDIX A
NON-ENGLISH
PUZZLES

You may use any language as you choose to indulge in without impropriety.
—W.S. Gilbert, *Iolanthe*

Crossword puzzles are hardly a monopoly of English-speaking solvers. This appendix describes characteristics of crossword puzzles as they appear in some other countries. They are presented alphabetically by language.

Most of the puzzles described here involve conventional definitions, as opposed to cryptic clues. This should not be surprising, since the rampant borrowing that has shaped English has given it a richness, a wealth of synonyms, that no other language approaches. It is precisely that wealth that facilitates the wordplay that is the essence of the cryptic clue.

Diagrams are quite another matter. Perhaps because of patterns of inflection, puzzles in different languages have different types of diagrams.

ARABIC

Arabic crossword diagrams resemble those of black-square cryptic puzzles but are smaller. Horizontal answers are written right-to-left, of course. In Arabic, letters' shapes depend on whether the letters stand alone or join preceding letters, following letters, or both—akin to the difference between printed and cursive Roman letters, but the stand-alone Arabic forms appear only rarely except in schools, alphabet tables in dictionaries . . . and crossword puzzles.

Several kinds of clues appear regularly in Arabic crossword puzzles. One is equivalent to our synonym definition. Another is like our fill-in-the-blank, except that it may read something like "The middle word in the proverb about mothers-in-law," challenging the solver's knowledge of traditional maxims. A third kind exploits a characteristic of the written language: Vowels are merely auxiliary notations connected to their consonants and, as such, are not entered in the grid. Therefore, a clue may read, for example, "The word meaning ___ that would mean ___ if the second vowel were changed to ___."

FINNISH

A Finnish crossword puzzle (*ristikot* or *ristisanatehtävä*) typically uses a German style grid (see below), but more often makes use of pictures and cartoons for definitions and extra entertainment. Black-square and bar grids of Italian, American, and British style also appear in Finnish puzzle magazines. Finnish orthography does not lend itself to the attractive white spaces found in Italian puzzles but does rival those of American puzzles. *GAMES* magazine published a *ristisanatehtävä* puzzle in 1982; when solved, a line of shaded squares spelled out the punch line to a cartoon.

FRENCH

The diagrams of French crossword puzzles (*mots croisés*—literally "crossed words") seem rather undisciplined compared to our own. (See Figure A.1.) They are only somewhat symmetric and need not be square. Unchecked letters appear, but usually no more than one in any one word. Words as short as two letters occur; in fact, up to twenty percent of a puzzle's entries may be that short. Grids are relatively small as a rule—say 9x9 or 9x11— with at least a few of the rows and columns containing only one word.

Rows are usually designated by Roman numerals and columns by Arabic numerals. The definitions for a row or column are strung out, separated by periods or semicolons, after the designation of the row (*horizontalement*) or column (*verticalement*).

Definitions may be conventional or descriptive—that is, composed of a statement about the answer. Consecutive definitions may be related thematically or in form. Puzzles usually lack dominant themes. Descriptive and generic definitions add difficulty. Abbreviations are used rather more frequently than in American puzzles.

Some two-letter answers are not really words at all. The French call these *chevilles* ("ankles" or "plugs"), a term also used to describe filler words that pad poetic meter. Because true definitions are impossible for these nonwords, they are clued solely by cryptic techniques.

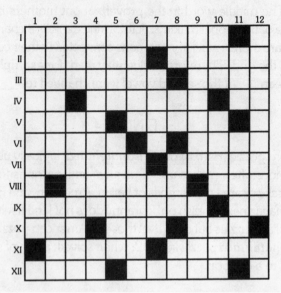

Figure A.1. *A diagram for a French crossword puzzle*

Some Canadian puzzle fans enjoy bilingual crossword puzzles with English definitions for French answers and French definitions for English answers.

GERMAN

Most German crossword puzzles (*Kreuzworträtsel*) are nonthematic. Wherever we would expect to see a black square in the grid, there is the definition of an indicated word that begins nearby. (See Figure A.2 for a small example in English.)

The French started using the style in 1969, the Spanish in the 1970s, and the United States more recently. *GAMES* magazine publishes full-page puzzles of this style under the name "Pencil Pointers." One or two unchecked letters may appear in each word of the solution. The diagram has no symmetry. It is rectangular and often as large as about 10x24.

Variant German-language puzzles have diverse formats. A puzzle *à la USA* is square and symmetric like our modern crosswords but has the unchecked letters we forswore decades ago; definitions are listed as in French puzzles, albeit using only the Arabic numerals;

the grid is presented without black squares, similar to our diagramless puzzles. The *Kreuzwort à la France* is more faithful to the model, but larger. The *Schweden Kreuzwort* is also faithful to the original, with cartoons in square cutouts within the basic rectangle—a Swedish puzzle diagram is otherwise hard to distinguish from a German one. (See the section on Swedish puzzles, below)

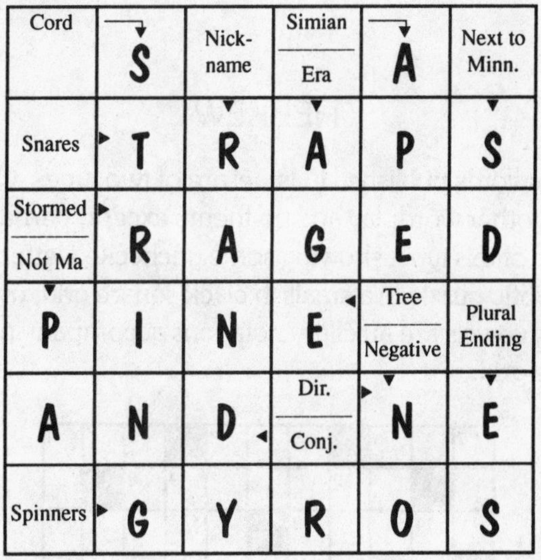

Cord	**S**	Nick-name	Simian / Era	**Ä**	Next to Minn.
Snares	**T**	**R**	**A**	**P**	**S**
Stormed / Not Ma	**R**	**A**	**G**	**E**	**D**
P	**I**	**N**	**E**	Tree / Negative	Plural Ending
A	**N**	**D**	Dir. / Conj.	**N**	**E**
Spinners	**G**	**Y**	**R**	**O**	**S**

Figure A.2. *A diagram for a German-style crossword puzzle*

An appealing form uses the basic German diagram but with numbering like ours. The definitions are unnumbered and are listed separately in random order for the words across (*waagrecht*) or down (*senkrecht*). The diagram is seeded with about ten percent of the solution's letters, none of them the most obvious.

Definitions resemble ours in form. Two-letter words and abbreviations are fairly rare, and some two-letter "words" may be undefined. The three umlauted vowels are entered as two letters, the second an *e*.

Like people here and elsewhere, the Germans buy magazines that contain many types of puzzles, including fill-ins (puzzles with no definitions but with answers listed by length and alphabetically) and novel and more challenging forms. Puzzles occur widely in other publications, even including pornographic magazines.

GREEK

A Greek crossword puzzle (*staurolexo*) is most likely to appear with an Italian-style grid (see Figure A.4), although many others are used as well. A "crossword" or "*mots croisés*" in a Greek puzzle magazine has a French-style grid (see Figure A.1) and, respectively, English or French answers to Greek definitions. An "American" puzzle is what we would call a skeleton or a criss-cross.

HEBREW

Hebrew-language crosswords published in Israel are of two types. One is a straightforward puzzle with no puns or other wordplay and no theme except, perhaps, on holidays. Figure A.3 is a typical diagram of this type, showing some unchecked letters and two-letter words. The other type is a cryptic puzzle in a smallish black-square grid, using wordplay typical of that genre. In Hebrew, vowels are auxiliary notations accompanying consonants; only the consonants go into the grid.

Figure A.3. *A diagram for a Hebrew-language crossword*

ITALIAN

Italian crosswords (*parole incrociate*—again, literally "crossed words") have rectangular diagrams that may have symmetry like ours or none at all. (See Figure A.4.) Unchecked letters exist, but few words have more than one. Puzzles vary in size from about 10x11 to about 21x13. Numbers are placed as they are in our puzzles and the definitions, which are terse and similar to ours in every way, are listed like ours for words across (*orizzontali*) and down (*verticali*).

Novelty puzzles (all forms of which carry the word *cruciverba* in their names) include a diagramless variety, a bar crossword having thickened lines between squares to mark off words, puzzles with unnumbered and unordered definitions for all words, and pairs of puzzles that share the same rectangle and have an irregular border between them that the solver must discover. In this last form, definitions are listed in random order by puzzle and direction and a few letters and black squares are seeded. Puzzles with multiple letters per square, like some published in England, are also found.

Figure A.4. *A diagram for an Italian crossword puzzle*

Long words are quite frequent in Italian puzzles, and some beautiful fields of white—for example, 15x4, 10x5, and 9x8(!)—occur. The even distribution of vowels in Italian words and the absence of a requirement for symmetry seem to make these attractive patterns possible. Conversely, the fact that *e* appears often at the ends of English words and relatively rarely in other positions makes large fields of white rare in English-language crosswords, although some by Jordan Lasher in the 1970s, Merl Reagle, and Eric Albert (who wrote his own crossword-generating program) are remarkable exceptions.

JAPANESE

Most crossword puzzles in Japan rely on the hiragana writing system. (The other writing system, katakana, is used less frequently in general.) Grids are small (8x8 in daily newspapers) because each of the fifty-one hiragana symbols represents a syllable, not an individual letter. Symbols are seeded in some boxes.

As with our own conventional puzzles, clues test vocabulary and knowledge of people, culture, literature, and places.

SPANISH

Spanish crossword puzzles (*crucigramas*) come in many varieties. Diagrams are similar to those used in French, German, British (bar diagrams), or Italian crossword puzzles. Fields of white are smaller in Spanish crossword puzzles than in Italian puzzles; this is probably attributable to the fact that Spanish has fewer predominant word endings than Italian. Definitions (*horizontales* and *verticales*) for most types of Spanish puzzles are identified and listed as they are in French puzzles. Puzzles in Catalan (a Romance language, related to Provençal, that is spoken in the Balearics and eastern Spain) are also popular in certain markets; the first in that language appeared in 1926.

Novelty puzzle forms include diagramless and acrostic puzzles like ours, and various syllable-oriented puzzles.

SWEDISH

Swedish crossword (*Kryss*) puzzles resemble those of Finland, with rectangular cutouts. Like the Finnish puzzles, each cutout contains a photograph or cartoon for which a caption or punch line appears in the solution, either as a single entry or snaking along an indicated path among standard entries. Definitions in the squares that we would blacken make numbers unnecessary. Unchecked letters are used very sparingly, but two-letter words are relatively common. Long words are common, but fields of white are rare.

Definitions are conventional in the type of puzzle described above, but another type of puzzle is also common. The latter type has a smaller diagram like that of a black-square cryptic puzzle and definitions that tend somewhat to the same obliqueness.

SUMMARY

Some crosswords in other languages may seem inferior to ours in some ways, but poverty of vocabulary in languages more insular or more resistant to borrowing may well account for that. On the other side of the ledger, even American and British magazines seem not to have discovered foreign forms, varying only slightly from our own, that might yield solvers and composers great pleasure in decades to come. As in all things, people eventually learn that "different" hardly implies "inferior" and cultural crossbreeding most often works to everyone's advantage.

APPENDIX B
STOCK GRIDS

Take what is given and make it over your way
—Robert Frost

Here are some empty grids for you. Some show up repeatedly, which means many composers find them easy to work with.

Unfilled grids are not protected by copyright, so adapting them to your use poses no legal hurdles.

Each grid in each size meets the traditional rules limiting black squares and total word count. To augment this material, we suggest you copy empty grids you see in the publications you want to sell puzzles to; they obviously meet the guidelines set by those publications' editors.

You can vary the grids by reflecting them about their spines or waists, or by turning them on their sides so rows become columns and vice versa. You can create still more variations by moving or adding individual black squares inside the grids.

15x15 GRIDS

The grids in this section have no more than seventy-eight words and no more than forty black squares.

The following two grids each accommodate three full-width answers. The upper-left and lower-right corners of the first grid join the rest of the puzzle by only one word, so it is mildly weaker than the second.

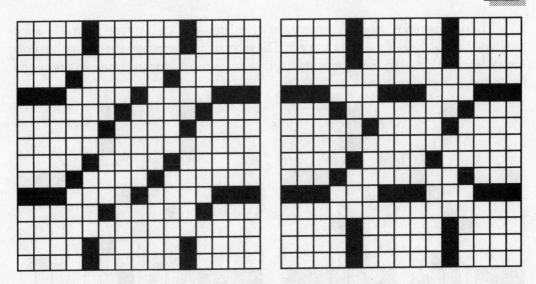

The next two grids each accommodate four nonintersecting ten-letter answers. The first uses a pinwheel arrangement of two across answers and two down answers. The long answers all read across in the second. Removing the two shaded squares in the second grid converts it to hold two fifteen-letter answers and two ten-letter answers.

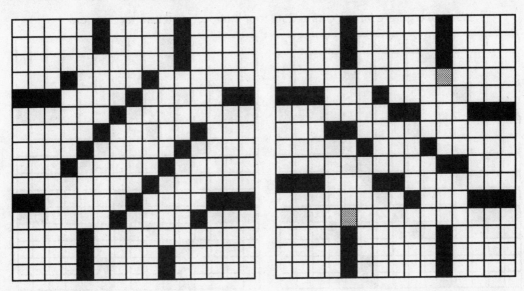

The next two grids also accommodate four nonintersecting ten-letter answers. The first has thirty-six, not thirty-eight, black squares. The second one is appealing because it has only seventy-six words (and no three-letter words), despite having thirty-nine black squares—one more than the other patterns.

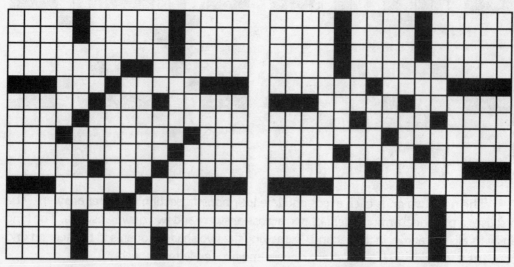

The next two grids each accommodate four intersecting ten-letter answers.

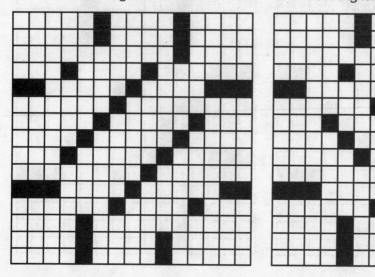

The next two grids have low word counts and are probably better suited for unthemed crosswords. Opening the shaded square in the first grid results in a challenging exercise in puzzle construction.

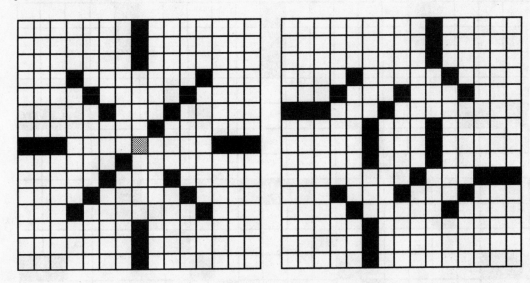

21x21 GRIDS

The grids in this section have no more than 142 words and no more than seventy-six black squares.

The first pattern accommodates ten theme answers of ten or eleven letters with 140 words. Adding cheaters at the shaded squares adapts the pattern by substituting two nine-letter answers for two of the eleven-letter answers.

The following pattern is the same except for relocation of the black squares in the center of the third and nineteenth rows and the center of the third and nineteenth columns; it accommodates eight theme answers: four long ones in a pinwheel arrangement around the outside and four shorter ones in the center.

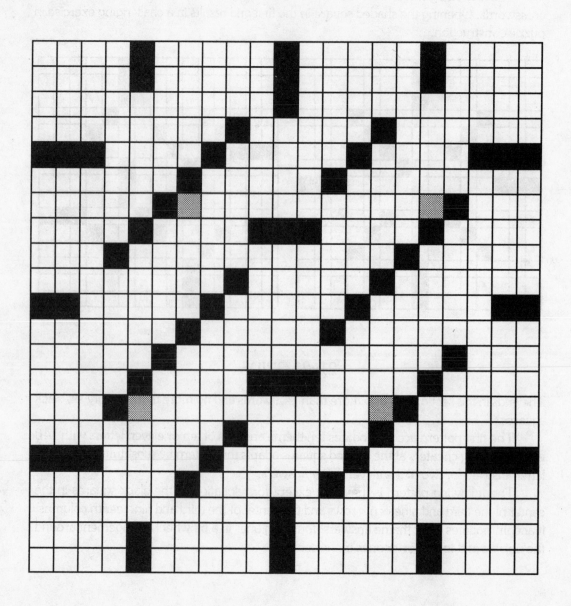

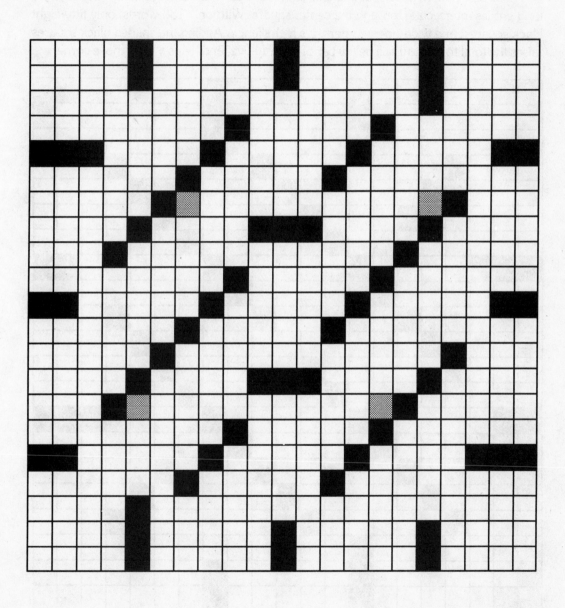

The next pattern holds four thematic entries in a pinwheel arrangement with two more long entries intersecting through the center square. With only 138 words, only fifty-eight black squares, and wide-open corners, it's a challenge. Adding the shaded black squares raises the total to seventy, still below par of seventy-five, and helps a lot in those corners.

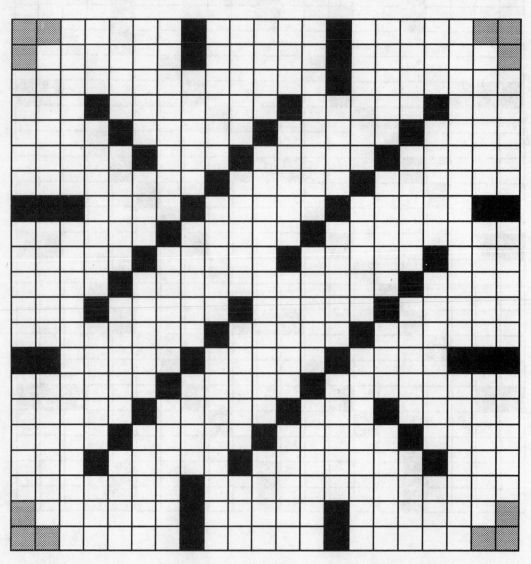

The next pattern accommodates five full-width, nonintersecting entries.

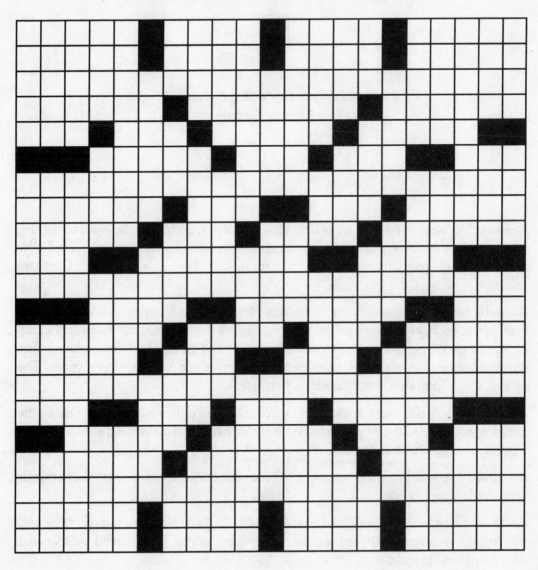

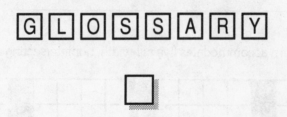

GLOSSARY

Not every chapter needs a cute epigraph
—Rosen and Kurzban

Acrostic   A verse or list of words in which the first letters, taken in order, spell something significant. In an *acrostic puzzle,* the acrostic spells the name of the author and, usually, the name of a book from which a quotation incorporated in the puzzle was taken. Compare *telestich.*

Acrostic puzzle   A puzzle form invented by Mrs. Elizabeth Kingsley and consisting of a quotation or excerpt from some published work, which the solver must discover with the help of definitions; the definitions lead to words made up from the letters in the quotation. The puzzle indicates where in the quotation the letters in the defined words are to be written. The defined words form an *acrostic* or, rarely, a *telestich.*

Afrit's Law   A statement formulated by A.F. Ritchie (Afrit), succinctly expressing the nature of *square-dealing* cryptic clues: While a clue may not mean what it seems to say, it must say exactly what it does mean.

Anagram   A word formed by rearranging the letters of another word or words. In cryptic crosswords, a type of *hint.*

And Lit   Short for *and literally so,* abbreviated *& lit.* A cryptic clue which contains only the "straight" definition when read one way, and only the wordplay when read another way. Also called *read it again.*

Answer   What the solver writes in a conventional crossword puzzle *diagram* to satisfy a *definition,* or in a cryptic puzzle diagram to satisfy a *clue.* In some varieties of cryptic puzzles the solver must apply a *transformation* to change an answer into a *light.*

Bar diagram   A *grid*, usually used for variety cryptic puzzles, in which thickened bars rather than black squares mark the ends of the answers. The grid's border functions similarly.

Black square   A puzzle square, darkened or otherwise differentiated to indicate that no letter is to be entered, marking the start or end of an *answer, light,* or word of a *quotation.* The border of a crossword puzzle (but not of an acrostic puzzle) functions similarly.

Blind corner   A portion of a crossword puzzle's *diagram* connected to the remainder of the puzzle's diagram by no more than one *answer or light.*

Boxquote   A crossword puzzle form devised by Eugene T. Maleska. In this form of puzzle, the solver must discover a quotation running clockwise in a rectangular track in the interior of the diagram. Like the *Stepquote,* the Boxquote solution typically contains the author's name and the title of the source of the quotation.

Charade   A type of *hint* in cryptic crosswords in which the clue writer builds an *answer* by bits and pieces in consecutive order.

Cheater   A *black square* whose absence would not alter a puzzle's *word count* and whose presence simplifies the composer's task.

Circles-in-the-Square   A crossword puzzle form devised by Eugene T. Maleska. In this form of puzzle, the solver must discover a quotation. The letters in the quotation are strewn, in order, through the diagram; the squares in the diagram that contain these letters are indicated by inscribed circles. Like the *Stepquote,* a Circles-in-the-Square solution typically reveals the author's name and the title of the source of the quotation.

Clue   What the *composer* provides to lead the solver to an *answer* in cryptic and humorous puzzles; like *definition* but connoting wordplay in addition to a conventional, although often camouflaged, definition.

Composer   The one who devises a puzzle; also *compiler, constructor, puzzlemaker,* or, in England, *setter.* See also *editor.*

Composition   A puzzle's diagram with its *answers or lights* inserted.

Container   A type of *hint* for a cryptic crossword in which the clue writer perceives an *answer* as one word inside another.

Corner   A rectangular region of a diagram, typically one bounded by the puzzle's border on one side or two sides, and *fingers* on two additional sides.

Crazy Crossword   A *humorous puzzle* composed by Ted Shane or his successors.

Crosswordese   Words most solvers encounter only in puzzles; for example, ESNE ("Anglo-Saxon slave").

Cryptic puzzle   A crossword puzzle whose *answers* emerge through *clues* rather than *definitions.*

Definition   What a *composer* provides to lead the solver to an *answer* in a conventional puzzle; like a *clue*; also, the part of a clue that serves the same purpose.

Definition by class   A *definition* presenting a category of which the *answer* is an example. "Ornamental vine" is a definition by class for IVY.

Definition by description   A *definition* relying on nondictionary information (for example, historical fact or reference to literature or television) to challenge the solver's overall factual knowledge. See *extra-effort cluing* and *tricky clue.*

Definition by example   A *definition* presenting examples of the class named by the answer. "Princetonian or Columbian" is a definition by example for IVY (referring to the Ivy League schools).

Definition by model   A *definition* in which the solver must consider the language and/or format (for example, foreign language or abbreviation) as well as the words' meanings to derive the answer. "*Niño's* mom" is a definition by model for MADRE.

Diagram   A puzzle's squares in which letters are to be entered.

Diagramless puzzle   A crossword puzzle with no *diagram* given, only a list of appropriately numbered *definitions* and the dimensions of its rectangular *grid*. Some publishers provide an empty grid of the correct size as a solving convenience.

Dictionary definition   A definition taken more-or-less straight from the dictionary using either a primary or secondary meaning of a word.

Double entendre   A (so-far unachieved) crossword puzzle having one set of definitions but two equally valid *solutions*; also, a single *clue* exhibiting this property.

Editor   One who receives puzzles from composers and selects and prepares them for publication; unlike most composers, therefore, one for whom puzzles can constitute more than merely a hobby.

Extra-effort cluing   Use of examples, literary and cultural references, mental images, encyclopedic information, and so on, rather than synonyms and dictionary definitions.

Field of white   Rectangle comprising only white squares.

Fill   The smaller words, ordinarily unrelated to the *theme*, that make up the majority of the answers in a conventional crossword puzzle.

Fill-in-the-blank   A *definition* consisting of a phrase in which the *answer* has been omitted. For example, "____ of knowledge" is a fill-in-the-blank definition for TREE. Also called *missing-word definition*.

Finger   Two or more black squares perpendicular to and abutting a border of a *grid*.

Grid   The rectangular arrangement of squares that contains a puzzle's *diagram*.

Hint   That portion of a *clue* that leads to the *answer* by an indirect route involving some type of wordplay.

Homograph   In a *clue*, the use of a word that is spelled just like another, unrelated word. Other words in the clue mislead the solver to the unrelated word, not the word that leads to the answer. Examples of words used in this way are: *sewer* ("one who sews"), *number* ("having less feeling"), *wicked* ("having a wick"), and *flower* ("that which flows"—a river).

Homophone   A type of *hint* in cryptic crosswords in which the clue writer offers a word that sounds like some other word, irrespective of spelling.

Humorous puzzle   An crossword puzzle of ordinary words with imaginative clues. The clues use wit, anagrams, puns, and other types of wordplay, rather than standard *dictionary definitions*. See *Crazy Crossword, Puns and Anagrams,* and *Puns and Twists*.

Ladder   A diagonal arrangement of black squares within a *diagram*; also the (equal-length) *answers* between two such ladders.

Lattice diagram   A *grid*, usually used for cryptic puzzles, in which every other answer letter is an *unch*. The black squares form a lattice pattern.

Letters Latent   A variety of cryptic crossword puzzle in which every clue has an extra letter the solver must ignore, or every answer has an extra letter the solver must remove before writing the corresponding *light*. The extra letters, taken in order, often relate to each other somehow . . . perhaps by spelling something significant.

Light   What the solver must write in a variety cryptic crossword puzzle's *diagram* in satisfaction of a *clue*, after applying a *transformation* to an *answer*.

Linking word   A word or short phrase in a cryptic clue that quietly ties *definition* and *hint* together, much as an equals sign in a mathematical equation.

Missing-word definition   See *fill-in-the-blank*.

Nom de puzzle   A *composer*'s pseudonym.

Number   The integer associated with a *definition, clue, answer, or light*.

Pangrammatic   Having every letter of the alphabet (in the solution of a puzzle).

Partial   Short for *partial phrase*. A short excerpt from a common saying, song lyric, or quotation that is not, itself, a self-contained, grammatically complete entity and that requires a fill-in-the-blank definition. For example, I THEE demands the definition "With this ring ___ wed." Partials are either clever inventions or acts of desperation, depending on your viewpoint. Most editors believe that more than one or two in a composition is not a virtue.

Pattern   A *grid* with *black squares*. A pattern with numbers inserted is a *diagram*.

Pictographic   Having a *diagram* whose outline is suggestive of the puzzle's *theme*; said of a *diagramless puzzle*.

Printer's Devilry   A type of *clue* in variety cryptic crosswords from which the solver must deduce a word. The clue is a sentence that may or may not make good reading on its surface; the solver must insert a word, changing at least one word in the original sentence and respacing (but not rearranging) and repunctuating the remainder of the sentence to make a new, more meaningful, sentence. For example, "Re decal: oft it may help sell your home" plus ORATE produces "Redecorate a loft; it may help sell your home."

Puns and Anagrams   A 15x15 *humorous puzzle* published in *The New York Times*, with *word count* below seventy-three.

Puns and Twists   A 17x13 *humorous puzzle* published in *The New York Times*, with *word count* below seventy-three.

Puzzle   A *composition* and its associated *definitions* or *clues*.

Quotation   What the solver writes in the *diagram* of an *acrostic puzzle*.

Read it again   See *And lit.*

Rebus   A thematic *answer* containing a symbol (that is, something other than an alphabetic character) that the solver must enter into a square.

Relocated theme   A puzzle's *theme* carried out by the *definitions* of the longest answers rather than by the answers themselves.

Selection   In cryptic *clues* and *humorous puzzles*, specification of one or more letters by miniature wordplay. For example, "The first of August" is A.

Signal   That part of a *clue*'s *hint* that indicates a particular form of wordplay.

Skeleton   That portion of a unfinished *composition* formed by tentatively placed thematic *answers*.

Slidequote   A crossword puzzle form devised by Eugene T. Maleska. In this puzzle form, the solution reveals a short quotation in the diagonal running from the upper left-hand corner of the diagram to the lower right-hand corner. Like the *Stepquote*, the Slidequote solution typically contains the author's name and the title of the source of the quotation.

Solution   *Composition* as seen by a solver.

Spine   The central column of a *diagram*, often containing a long answer.

Square-Dealing   Following the precepts of Afrit, Ximenes, and Azed regarding cryptic clues. Every square-dealing clue is grammatically precise as to the constructor's intention and contains a *definition* of the answer, either a second definition or a *hint*, and nothing else. See *Afrit's law.*

Stepquote   A crossword puzzle form devised by Eugene T. Maleska. In this form of puzzle, the solver must discover a quotation. The quotation begins at 1 Across and makes its way through the *diagram* in a stair-step fashion ending in the lower right-hand corner. Typically, the solution also reveals the author's name and title of the source of the quotation.

Style sheet   A statement of an editor's requirements, including maximum *word counts*, formats to follow when submitting puzzles, overall philosophy, pay amount, etc. Also called *guidelines.*

Surface reading   The ordinary sense of a cryptic clue, as though it appeared in plain prose. Also called *surface meaning.*

Telestich   A verse or list of words in which the last letters, taken in order, spell something significant. Compare *acrostic*.

Theme   In a conventional crossword puzzle, the combination of subject matter and design that relates the longest answers to each other. See also *Theme and Variations*.

Theme and Variations   A variety of cryptic crossword puzzle in which a dozen or more answers have no clues. A primary set of unclued answers has a common bond, called the *theme*. Each primary answer has its own set of unclued, related answers, called the *variations*.

Transformation   In some varieties of cryptic puzzles, what the solver must apply to an *answer* to convert it to a *light*. See *Letters Latent* for an example.

Tricky clue   In conventional crosswords, a *definition* using words in a surprising way (often relying on nondictionary information in the manner of *definition by description*) to make the solver think along different lines. For example, "Newspaper source" for TREE.

Unch   An unchecked letter; that is, one appearing in only one *answer*.

Variation   See *Theme and Variations*.

Variety cryptic puzzle   A cryptic crossword puzzle with some sort of added gimmick, which may involve (any combination of) *clues*, *answers*, or *grid*.

Waist   The central row of a *diagram*, often containing a long answer.

Word count   The number of *answers* or *lights* in a crossword puzzle.

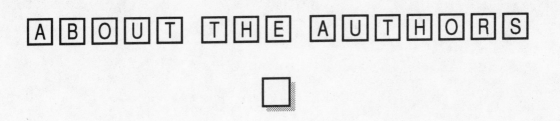

ABOUT THE AUTHORS

Mel Rosen has been selling word puzzles for more than twenty-five years. His work, which includes every type described in this book, has appeared in *The New York Times*, *GAMES*, *The Washington Post*, and the other major markets including collections by Times Books and other publishers. He is one of a handful of people who have won prizes in both puzzle composing contests and puzzle solving tournaments. He retired from IBM after twenty-six years as a computer programmer and analyst, changing his job title to "crossword puzzle editor," in which capacity he now serves at The Crosswords Club. Mel and his wife of more than thirty-five years, Peggy, call Florida home.

Stan Kurzban is also both a prize-winning composer and solver of crossword puzzles. His conventional, humorous, and diagramless puzzles have been published in *The New York Times* and elsewhere. After retirement from IBM, where he worked in systems design and education, he earned a law degree from Pace University's School of Law. He has co-authored a text on computer operating systems and has published many works on computer security. Happily married for over thirty years, Stan and his wife, Nina, live in Chappaqua, New York, with their third child, Amy.